ASPECTS OF MUSIC IN CANADA

Aspects of
MUSIC
in Canada

Edited by
ARNOLD WALTER

University of Toronto Press

SBN 8020 1536 0

61,078

1867 | 1967

"Published on the occasion of the Centennial of Canadian
Confederation and subsidized by the Centennial Commission"

"Ouvrage publié à l'occasion du Centenaire de la Confédération
Canadienne, grâce à une subvention de la Commission du Centenaire"

Foreword

His Excellency The Right Honourable
ROLAND MICHENER, C.C.

MY FAITH in those who have written this book is great and I am
happy, therefore, to write this commendation of their work,
although I may be little qualified to appraise adequately the
fine contributions which it makes to an understanding of
"Music in Canada."

Dr. Arnold Walter and the several authors deserve our
thanks and our encouragement for sharing their specialized
experience and knowledge with those of us who would learn
more about the history, variety and quality of music in Canada,
and about the many people and associations of people who have
given it vitality and growth.

Particularly, I wish to commend the Canadian Music Council
for sponsoring this sequel to their first volume, *Music in Canada*,
published in 1955. It has become necessary because of the
pace of change in the intervening years and the great musical
experiences of Canadians in our Centennial Year. It is symbolic
of the creative vigour and imagination of Canadian musicians

that in little more than a decade there is need for a new statement of Canadian musical achievements.

From the point of view of a man of public affairs in Canada at this particular time in our collective life, music appears as a language which can be understood equally by all Canadians, whatever tongue was spoken by their forbears, or how proficient they are themselves in our two official languages. In so far as our music becomes distinguishably Canadian it will be a common possession in the realm of intellect and emotion. It is, therefore, another brotherly bond to enhance our community of purpose as well as being a fine art to enrich our individual lives.

I hope that many Canadians will read these excellent essays and through them enjoy a greater appreciation of our musical heritage and a greater participation in its evolution. Certainly our economic progress gives us all more leisure time to do so.

April 1968

Preface

THIS IS THE SECOND TIME that the Canadian Music Council has published a collection of essays on music in Canada. The first collection was entitled *Music in Canada* and appeared in 1955; edited by Sir Ernest MacMillan, it contained no fewer than nineteen chapters ranging from Marius Barbeau's notes on folksong to Leslie Bell's appraisal of popular music. The authors reported on the state of music in the country (it had never been done before). They also tried to detect the emergence of a national pattern, of an entity that could justly be called Canadian music: a brave attempt that was only partially successful. In retrospect we understand the fifties better. With all the clarity of hindsight we discern what seeds were sown in those years and how they grew; we know it now, but we could not have known it then.

The pace of our musical development was such that the earlier volume (however valuable when it appeared) has receded into history: it reads like a report on happenings of half a century ago. To bring it up to date—by adding a chapter on "new trends" perhaps—was not to be thought of; a fresh start had to be made.

No doubt there is a need for a new book; the growth of interest in music would alone be sufficient to justify the venture. New information and documentation will be welcomed; but there is more to be done than to narrate, to describe, to illustrate. The acceleration of progress all around us calls for reflection, for an attempt to determine where we are and where we are going—to look ahead, to plan for the future.

The shape of things to come can only be illuminated by the light of past experience. Whatever we discuss will be more sharply delineated if seen against the background of historical events (where folk and aboriginal music play an important part). Composition, performance, whether live or broadcast, and education are the principal threads in the fabric of our musical life. The richer this fabric becomes, the more widely it spreads, the more it depends on organizations of all kinds, be they ladies' committees, departments of education or grant-giving bodies.

Such views led us to begin at the beginning, with historical *praeludia*, and to end with a *postludium* that occupies itself with national organizations serving music. Composition, performance and education hold the centre of the stage.

With seven authors and two languages involved (the essays on composition and performance appear here in translation), this book was long in the making. It had originally been planned as a report on music in Canada on the eve of the Centennial year. Unavoidable delays in publication have made it necessary to take the far-reaching results of that unprecedented event into consideration. At the end of 1967—its *annus mirabilis*—Canada found itself richer by seven art centres and 442 community centres, by 71 museums and art galleries, by 144 libraries; over one hundred compositions had been commissioned and performed. Expo had opened windows to the world, Festival Canada had overcome provincial isolation: music and art had never loomed larger in the life of the nation. Such fundamental changes could not be ignored; it became imperative to revise our study (particularly the chapters on composition and performance) and to obliterate the pre-Centennial flavour that adhered to it from the start.

The essays comprising this book are largely self-contained, although they do overlap at times. That could hardly be avoided. Musical history must deal with composition; reflections on composition need historical perspective. Folk and aboriginal music concern both the historian and the ethnomusicologist. Education and performance are inextricably linked: the National Youth Orchestra, for instance, or Les Jeunesses Musicales are both educational tools as well as performing organizations claiming attention under various headings. One cannot write on patronage, on composition, on performance or on national organizations without referring to the Canada Council. The very fact that certain institutions are mentioned time and again, and in different contexts, merely underlines their importance.

The differences in point of view and emphasis the reader will detect are as unavoidable (and beneficial) as the overlappings. For Andrée Desautels, Canadian composition is a magnificent tree growing out of strong French roots; Helmut Kallmann seems more inclined to compare it to a garden where many plants grow side by side. John Roberts does not discuss the difficulties of Canadian broadcasting—its British and American characteristics, its provincial, regional and national levels, its public and private sectors with all the political controversy pertaining thereto—his chief interest is the documentation of the magnificent record of the CBC, a documentation nowhere else to be found and a record Canadians ought to be proud of. An avalanche of names—of composers, performers, conductors, directors, producers—gives one the feeling of watching a brook turning into a stream, a stream growing into a mighty river of whose size and potency few are aware.

Despite all the differences of opinion (stated or implied), the divers points of view and shifts of emphasis, our book should give a reasonably exact picture of music in Canada at the close of the Centennial year. A picture, not a photograph; not all details are there. And those that are appear in an order that reflects the capacities and convictions of the various authors. They all agree on one point, though: music is one of the brightest feathers in our cap.

The Canadian Music Council wishes to express its gratitude

to the Centennial Commission and the Canada Council, whose grants made the preparation and the publication of this volume possible.

Our thanks are also due to Ezra Schabas for most valuable advice; to Patricia Shand, who acted as research assistant, and to Carroll Burke, who helped with the preparation of the manuscript. Christina Roberts translated the chapters on composition and performers. Veronica Ŝediva prepared the index.

A.W.

University of Toronto
January 1968

Contents

CONTRIBUTORS

ANDRÉE DESAUTELS

Professeur titulaire au Conservatoire de Montréal; collaboratrice, *Larousse de La Musique* Tome II (Paris 1965); commissioner, Man and Music Pavilion, Expo 67

HELMUT KALLMANN

Library supervisor, CBC Toronto; author of *A History of Music in Canada, 1534–1914* (Toronto 1960)

KEITH MACMILLAN

Executive secretary of the Canadian Music Centre

KENNETH PEACOCK

Research fellow of the National Museum of Man, Ottawa; author of *Songs of the Newfoundland Outposts* and various other publications concerning folk music research among Indians and ethnic groups

GILLES POTVIN

Chief, music production of the International Service of the CBC; music critic of *La Presse,* Montreal

JOHN ROBERTS

Supervisor of Music, English Radio Networks, CBC; President, The Canadian Music Council; on the executive of both the International Music Centre and the International Institute of Music, Dance, and Theatre in Vienna

ARNOLD WALTER

Professor of Musicology, University of Toronto; President, The Inter-American Music Council

ASPECTS OF MUSIC IN CANADA

Introduction

ARNOLD WALTER

THERE ARE many aspects to music. The spectrum is wide: it ranges from folk and popular music to fine art music both ancient and modern; from ephemeral tunes lasting a few days to symphonies dominating the repertoire for centuries; from the trivial to the sublime. In the present volume, no attempt is made to cover the whole field. The chapters on composition, performance, broadcasting, education and national organizations deal with what is usually described as serious music—quantitatively only a small portion of the music produced, disseminated and consumed in this country. The reasons for such limitations stem from a set of assumptions regarded as self-evident by musicians of the classical variety, though these reasons are often challenged by persons more sociologically inclined. It is taken for granted that there are higher and lower levels of culture, that the mediocre products of mass society (whatever their quantity) can safely be disregarded, that all that matters is music that forms an integral part of the High Culture of the Age.

Such points of view are certainly defensible, have in fact been defended since the time of Plato. But there is no denying that we are dealing here with a restricted sector of our civilization, that the "High Culture of the Age" affects only a small portion of the population. Aesthetic and sociological arguments invariably clash when problems of subsidies, education or broadcasting come up for discussion; defenders of quality and champions of quantity never see eye to eye. Yet, in the long run, it is the cultural minorities that carry the day. What could have been, in fourth-century Rome, the number of educated persons interested in the works of poets, historians, philosophers, grammarians or dramatists? Five thousand perhaps? Or the number of civilized people in Elizabethan England—seventy thousand as it has been estimated?[1] Culture always has been, always will be, a pyramid with little room at the top.

This, then, is a book about Canada's achievement in the field of fine art music. Surveying this field, we are immediately struck by a tremendous increase in the production and dissemination of music. It is hardly necessary to quote chapter and verse: we have more orchestras than we ever had before, many of them play longer seasons, two at least have attained international standards. Opera is coming into its own; the Canadian Opera Company has been joined by the Théâtre Lyrique du Québec. Three ballet companies must be added to the list, as must the National Youth Orchestra and the full-blown Jeunesses Musicales. Canadian composers are winning recognition at home and abroad, a growing number of our performers are acclaimed the world over. The National Arts Centre will soon open its doors to the public. The Canada Council (aided by local and provincial arts councils) assists and quickens the development.

The picture looks almost too good to be true. Are all of our problems solved? Are there no difficulties yet to be overcome? Alas, there is always another side of the coin. However spellbound we may be by such an array of talent, however dazzled by all the glamour and the enchantment of brilliant perfor- admission: how can one judge the degree of interest in the

1. Edward Shils, "The High Culture of the Age," in *The Arts in Society* (Englewood Cliffs, N.J.: Prentice-Hall Inc., 1964).

mances, we are still haunted by some gnawing questions: do we in fact have the public to sustain a constantly increasing production? Are our audiences capable of understanding the composers, of appreciating the performers, of supporting the tremendous efforts made on their behalf? Are they sufficiently large, sufficiently discerning? Discriminating audiences are obviously the base on which the edifice of culture rests.

It is quite astonishing how difficult it is to find precise answers to these questions. We have, so far, no statistical evidence, at least not from Canadian sources. Various agencies in the United States, however—the Rockefeller Brothers Fund, the Twentieth Century Fund, the American Orchestra League, Broadcasting Music Inc. (B.M.I.), even Congress itself—have set themselves the task of investigating their own spectacular progress in things artistic (they are fond of calling it a cultural explosion). Since we are dealing here with a continent-wide phenomenon, since it is safe to assume that we share many of our problems with our neighbours to the south, we shall not hesitate to use American material; it is, at any rate, the only material at our disposal.

Even the Americans, however, have only recently attempted to find an answer to the all-important problem of audience development. In 1965, the Rockefeller Panel Report on the Performing Arts confessed: "We simply do not know who composes the public for art, nor its exact size, nor the degree of its commitment, nor the factors that have created the interest in the arts that now exist in our sociey. There is, to be sure, evidence both empirical and intuitive to indicate that there has been an appreciable increase in the audience for the arts over the last decade. But against this must be set a strong countervailing impression, equally unprovable statistically, that the arts in general, and the performing arts in particular, do not yet have deep or strong roots in the lives of the majority of our people."[2]

"We simply do not know"—these are the key words. A sad

2. *The Performing Arts: Problems and Prospects* (New York: McGraw-Hill, 1965), p. 184.

performing arts without data on size and composition of the public? To dispel such deplorable ignorance the Twentieth Century Fund commissioned William Baumol and William G. Bowen[3] to undertake a study of the problems common to the theatre, opera, music and dance, a study that would deal with some of the questions left unanswered by the Rockefeller Report. The authors came to startling conclusions. They found that there is a remarkable consistency in the composition of audiences from art form to art form, from city to city and from one performance to another. They also found that the audience is drawn from an extremely narrow segment of the American population consisting of persons who are extraordinarily well educated, whose incomes are very high, who are predominantly in the professions and who are in their late youth or early middle age. This finding, according to Baumol and Bowen:

has important implications for the nature of whatever growth has occurred in audience demands for the arts. Even if there has been a significant rise in the size of audiences in recent years, it has certainly not yet encompassed the general public. If the sociological base of the audience has in fact expanded, it must surely have been incredibly narrow before the boom got under way. The result indicates also . . . that attempts to reach a wider and more representative audience, to interest the less educated or the less affluent, has so far had a limited effect. . . . In these audiences the number of blue collar workers is almost always under 10%; over 50% of the males have completed college; and median incomes are almost always well over $9,000. Obviously, much still remains to be done before the professional performing arts can truly be said to belong to the people.

Having said this, the authors proceed to demonstrate that the income gap (or deficit) with which the performing arts are faced cannot and will not disappear; that this gap is bound to grow by approximately 8 per cent per year which of course leads us to astronomical figures fifty or a hundred years from now. But that is another story. It is today's audience we are worrying about. If Canadian surveys elicited similar results (which is most likely), we should have to accept the fact that our theatre-

3. W. Baumol and W. Bowen, *Performing Arts: The Economic Dilemma* (New York: Twentieth Century Fund, 1966).

going, symphony-conscious, opera-loving, ballet-admiring public amounts to less than half a million people (or 10 per cent of the maximum of five million calculated for the United States). A performing arts audience of that size would certainly be larger than in the past; but if we adjust the figures for price level, population, and income growth, we find to our amazement that we are not much further ahead than we were in 1929.

At first it seems rather difficult to accept such shattering conclusions. The change in our cultural climate, the pace of our artistic development, countless happy memories of stirring performances in Place des Arts, at the O'Keefe Centre or Massey Hall, in the Queen Elizabeth Theatre seem to contradict such findings. Our authors, however, did not say that audiences remained static—they increased in proportion to the overall increase in population, they said: but no more. If a city like Toronto, for instance, had a population of three-quarters of a million 30 years ago and has grown to a metropolis of two million since, if such a city tripled its performing arts audience, the ratio of audience to population would, of course, have remained constant. There may be more halls, more people patronizing them, more performances and splendid activities all round; but the percentage of Canadians taking an interest in the performing arts would be no larger than it was.

It is quite a shock to contemplate these figures. If only 4 per cent of the population over eighteen years of age is affected, what about the remaining 96 per cent? What about the young people under 18? Are they all content with the outpourings of mass culture? If the base of the performing arts is so incredibly narrow, why has it not been broadened by education? Is there a chance of changing a ratio that has remained constant for so long? The questions come tumbling into one's mind: it is hard to adjust to such unfamiliar notions. To find our bearings it might be helpful, and it might also be a fitting prelude to this book, if we drew a realistic map of our musical surroundings.

There was a time when our field was sensibly divided into folk music, popular music and fine art music (often called classical or, worse still, serious music). Folk music belonged to the peasants in the fields, fine art music to the upper strata of society, while popular music (a mixture of the two) entertained the lower classes in the towns. We still operate with these terms without realizing how much the underlying reality has changed. In Europe, where these diverse idioms had long been established and regionally well integrated and from which the classification stems, folk music largely disappeared during the nineteenth century; popular music increased in volume to keep pace with the rapidly expanding urban population; fine art music lost its creative impulse and began to devote itself to the conservation and re-interpretation of the inheritance. Toward the end of that century, it became "classical" in a literal sense, a historical complex creating its own antithesis, the *avant-garde*.

This overall pattern was repeated on the North American continent, though with important modifications. It is obvious that colonization, pioneer life, egalitarian yearnings, transplantation and the subsequent attenuation of European traditions must have inhibited the growth of music. Neither fine art nor popular art could be given "the professional cultivation and patronage, the material plant and equipment that had serviced them in the mother countries. . . . European traditions of music suffered, then, not only the wounds . . . of geographical transplantation but also of three centuries of deprivation of the traditional inter-class and inter-idiom relationships through which the art normally flourished in Europe."[4] When the wounds began to heal—by 1800 or thereabouts—serious music began to be cultivated; but the public ready to absorb it, and to pay for it, was extremely small. North America had learned to live without art, had learned to think of music as a luxury for the idle rich, an item of conspicuous consumption (acquired characteristics that are still being inherited). The development was steady but slow, until it suddenly quickened with the appearance of media that made the music business profitable beyond all dreams and expectations.

Does it still make sense to talk of folk music, popular and fine art music? Folk music depends on a traditional environ-

4. Charles Seeger, *Music and Class Structure in the U.S.*, out of print.

ment. It is now being contaminated and obliterated by the media, which reach the remotest regions. It disappears in the village, becomes a collector's item, turns up in the library and is finally absorbed, on a small scale, into the concert repertory and quite massively into the popular idiom. It can be re-introduced into the mainstream of Canadian life, but it is changed in the process.[5] Folksong by origin, it becomes an art song or a popular song, depending where it is being sung, how and by whom.

That leaves us with two categories—fine art music and popular music. It has been said that our civilization as a whole puts far more emphasis on creativity than on conservation. If true at all, this generalization is certainly not true for music on a higher level. The great repertoire—performed by symphony orchestras, opera companies and soloists all over the world—is everywhere the same and almost a hundred per cent historical. It has aptly been called a music museum containing a collection of significant masterpieces on permanent exhibition. More often than not these pieces lack immediacy; they cry out for explanations, historical reflections, stylistic considerations, critical appraisal. Not that it will always be necessary to set such an intellectual apparatus in motion; but it is easy to see why education is such a decisive factor in the formation of an audience for the performing arts. Contemporary composition forms only a minute part of our concert repertory. It tries very hard to dissociate itself from traditional techniques, but its preoccupation with repudiation and resistance binds it to the very thing from which it tries to escape. Conservation is stronger than creativity. Our music-making (we are still discussing the classical variety) has a historical bias which tends to limit its appeal.

Popular music suffers no such disadvantages. It is all here and now, a-historical, contemporary in every way, ever-present and ubiquitous. Before jazz burst upon the scene in the early twenties, popular music was innocuous enough, a mixture of marches, ballads, waltzes, hymns, vaudeville and light opera

5. See chapter on folk and aboriginal music, p. 62.

selections with some ragtime and blues—a weak entertainment medium; or so it seems in retrospect. Jazz was a different dish. Primitive, aggressive, carnal, alien, evil, it had been called all these things before it was accepted, and soon enough diluted into refined jazz, symphonic jazz, commercial jazz. Then came Rock 'n Roll (a mixture of folk elements and conventional textures) followed by the Beatles, the Weavers, the Hermits, and the Rolling Stones, who became "The champions of the teeny-bopper revolt against adult authority" igniting havoc and hysteria; calling themselves, God help us, "five reflections of to-day's children."[6]

Light music has always existed. It was never quite separated from the more serious kind until our own days, when the a-historical and the historical, the simple and the sophisticated, the transitory and the enduring draw more widely apart every day. Popular music is very different from what it once was. It is an urban product, woven into the patterns of industrial life, destined to bring relief from monotony, to provide amusement without disturbance (though it often ends up by being both monotonous and disturbing without being in the least amusing). It certainly is not just entertainment. That presupposes the will to be entertained. Before anyone touches a dial, puts a dime into a slot machine or a record on a turn-table he is subjected to ubiquitous sounds that are meant to be heard but not to be listened to. "Music by Muzak" is a good example. It reaches sixty million people in America alone. It is said to be helpful in boring and tense situations, to create a feeling of well-being, of euphoria, a sense of belonging. It may also create, in different circumstances perhaps, a sense of privacy and separation.[7]

Clearly music is made to serve as a tranquilizer in an increasingly noisy and irritating industrial civilization. It forms the background of broadcasts, telecasts or films, conditioning the multitudes long before there is any active desire to listen. When that active stage is finally reached, we discover that there is more to pop music than sentimental effusions of the sweet

6. *Time*, April 28, 1967.
7. Kenneth Alsop, "Music by Muzak," in *Encounter*, February 1967.

variety plus jazz in its divers incarnations. We discover a massive influx of the folk element (eroded in the village it turns up in town) that seems a perfect medium for carrying a message. And messages pop up on all sides—protest songs, freedom songs, action songs, as if the seed sown long ago by Hanns Eisler and Pete Seeger had finally come up. All this casts a spell over young people. Our teenagers are members of an adolescent subculture which, sociologists tell us, is an unavoidable by-product of an industrial society. Constituting an "important market," they have clothes and cars and movies of their own, and also records and music of their own—music that is often enough vulgar and cheap but always simple and direct. Since adults have not yet discovered how to break down, or at least to re-shape, adolescent society, the transmission of culture becomes more difficult every day. It is easy to see why youngsters under eighteen stay away from the performing arts (as Baumol and Bowen found to their chagrin).

Ranging all the way from wallpaper music and the subliminal effects of the action songs of a guitar-crazy youth movement, popular music is all around us, ever-present, inescapable. It is probably an understatement to say that pop audiences are twenty times larger than performing arts audiences. Even those who have not the slightest intention of listening to pop music and who are tormented by its unwanted presence, encounter it on all sides. It is true, of course, that concert audiences constitute only a fraction of the public interested in serious music. FM broadcasts and LP records must not be forgotten; they cater to substantial minorities—the same minorities, however, which Baumol and Bowen described: highly intelligent, highly educated people with larger than average incomes; in short high brows, easily outvoted by middle brows and low brows.

Shocked by the Twentieth Century Fund Report, we thought that a realistic map of our musical surroundings would help us to see things as they are. On such a map "great music" would appear as a small island surrounded by a surging sea of popular music covering more than nine-tenths of the territory. For the social historian this is an unavoidable fact and perhaps even a highly satisfactory state of affairs. The cultural monopoly of the upper classes has disappeared; mass education has created a market for mass-culture products which are not meant for a segment of the population but for all the people. Before the Second World War it almost looked as if mass culture would carry the day, as if the "big audience" commercialism was aiming at was becoming a reality. Since then we have discovered that "there is not One Big Audience but rather a number of smaller more specialized audiences that may still be commercially profitable . . . this discovery has in fact resulted in the sale of 'quality' paperbacks and recordings and the growth of art cinema houses, off-Broadway theatres, concert orchestras and art museums and galleries. The mass audience is divisible, we have discovered—and the more it is divided, the better. Even television, the most senseless and routinized expression of Masscult might be improved by this approach."[8] Hollywood has all but lost its adult audiences; radio was chastened by its loss of commercial revenue; there is hope that television will fare no better in years to come.

There is hope, but little assurance. The existence of specialized audiences only proves that commercialism was not wholly victorious. It is still very much with us, still dominating the scene. Given the fantastic proliferation of popular music, given the defection of youth and the fragmentation of education, it is a miracle that the performing arts have not disappeared altogether. It is, then, rather naïve to ask—as we asked ourselves a while ago—why the base of High Culture remained so narrow? Why education had so little effect? What we are witnessing is a battle of opposing forces, a battle between the lords of Kitsch and the champions of Art—between the merchants and the missionaries.

Not so long ago North America was thought of as a cultural void that could easily be filled by European imports. Not so any more; the void (if it ever existed) has disappeared; the indigenous popular arts have taken its place. The entertainment indus-

8. Dwight Macdonald, *Against the American Grain* (New York: Vintage Books Inc., 1965), p. 74.

tries moved in. Music in particular has become the handmaiden of big business and has learned to advertise its products. The merchants have erected a solid front that is difficult to breach. It is no use arguing whether they "give the public what it wants"; it is all too obvious that they cater to the lowest possible denominator, too low for any artistic endeavour.

The "missionaries" try to give the public what it might want if it was more aware. Who are these missionaries? They are the artists themselves, of course, and the members of auxiliary organizations such as symphony boards, grant-giving bodies, government agencies (the CBC, the National Film Board) and finally the entire educational apparatus. Educators may not think in terms of beauty alone. They may favour the arts as antidotes to social evils (the frightening results of alienating methods of production, for instance, or the yawning emptiness of leisure time). Still, they are valuable allies.

Unfortunately, the missionaries have not been too successful so far. We mentioned earlier the adolescent subculture persisting in colleges and universities. Young people generally seem to feel that the culture of the West, which the schools try to pass on, is not relevant to them. That attitude is a new and dangerous phenomenon, indicating that older ways of thinking and feeling are fast disappearing. Why is this happening right now? What is the basic objection to the existing culture? We might find one possible answer by comparing the two aspects of our civilization which C. P. Snow has called the two cultures. The essence of the humanities as we practice them today is not literature as it has so often been said; it is history. Ours is an Alexandrinian age characterized by museums, art galleries, libraries, archives and a virtually changeless repertory. We are tirelessly collecting, cataloguing, and annotating the treasures of the past, without ever having the courage to call them gothic or barbaric in order to free our hands—as the Greeks once did and the men of the Renaissance.

Our scientists have that courage. They have an anti-historical bias. If you ask one of them, in the manner of Herbert Spencer, what knowledge is most worth having he will speak of the prodigious advances made in the physical and life sciences; he will praise mathematics, mention technology, communications and finally the social sciences without paying much attention to literature or the arts which, he would say, "adorn" life. The point is that all he thinks worth knowing is new, advancing, rapidly progressing, pregnant of the future and virtually unconnected with the past.[9]

Humanistic culture, on the other hand, has a strong traditional flavour, being static and conservative by comparison with its scientific counterpart. That may be its essence, its glory if you will, but it has little attraction for young people reared in a technological age. It does not help to tell them that Einstein played the violin and believed in God; they shy away from both.

Humanistic and scientific approaches to education have been attacked and defended since the time of J. S. Mill, Thomas Huxley and Matthew Arnold. Here, however, we are not dealing with a new chapter to the old debate between educators; what we *are* deeply concerned with is the non-involvement on the part of the students. Resisting the humanities, they resist the arts also—though not completely. There is a historic and an aesthetic aspect to the arts as they are embedded into the humanities; it is the first that is falling into disfavour. Art without epoch, art as a timeless phenomenon is holding its own; but the world of philologists, textual critics, bibliographers, biographers, literary historians, and their counterparts in music and the visual arts, looks a bit grey.

It would be interesting to speculate on the changes the teaching of the humanities will have to undergo in order to survive; but it would take us too far afield. The point we wished to make was simply that the schools are willing but rather weak allies.

It is anybody's guess what will happen to the two cultures, whether they will merge or draw further apart; but it seems that the utopian imagination far outpaces reality. For some time

9. Sir John Cockcroft: "A Transatlantic View," in *The Knowledge Most Worth Having*, ed. Wayne C. Booth (Chicago: University of Chicago Press, 1967).

now it has been predicted that public concerts and opera performances will disappear altogether, that film and television will take their place. (We know of artists who have stopped playing in public because of that conviction.) Similarly, there is a growing feeling that our instruments will soon be obsolete, that composers working directly on tape will do without performers. These are entirely reasonable observations, it could very well happen. The point is that it has not happened yet, although filmed concerts, television opera, and electronic music have been with us for years. It is quite astonishing that opera, for instance, is still with us, that it has outlived its aristocratic past and its adventures with the nineteenth-century bourgeoisie proving itself eminently adaptable and stronger than the media. Film can do better in almost every respect except one: it has no living, breathing, singing actors—but that is of course the central phenomenon in opera and its greatest glory. The co-existence of live opera, film opera and television opera, cheek by jowl, so to speak, is the opposite of merging and melting.

So far we have considered a variety of topics that seem only tangentially related to our main theme: the increase in "production" (i.e., in composition and performance); the stunted growth of audiences; the rise of popular music; the power of commercialism; the need for assistance for the arts, particularly through education; the troubles of a humanistic education here and now; C. P. Snow and all that—they were all brought in to relate music to the larger historical scene, to show it in the context of a fast-changing society. Music is often thought of as something growing naturally and gracefully, like flowers in a secluded garden; but it is not like that. Music, like everything else, is buffetted by the winds of change, it is subject to all sorts of social pressures and is dependent on governments, on the business community, on media executives and educators at all levels. Canadian music must also be seen as a constituent part of a continent-wide musical civilization in which similarities often outweigh the differences.

It was only recently that Canadian patterns of patronage changed for the better. In the past the point was invariably made that the majority should not be taxed for what concerned only a minority (and a small one at that). If richer, better educated, or more sophisticated people preferred artistic entertainment they should pay for it themselves. The concept of culture did not enter the picture. This straightforward, no-nonsense attitude governed grant-giving and subsidizing during the first half of this century: patronage was pluralistic. (To a certain extent it still is.) The necessary funds were collected by symphony boards, opera guilds, ladies' committees or women's auxiliaries who organized raffles and rummage sales, teas and balls and musicales to help the good cause. But the contributions, coming from individuals, foundations or corporations were never large enough to enable the managers of performing arts organizations to plan ahead. They were forced to limp from year to year, from deficit to deficit.

Even now, in the sixties, foundation grants for the performing arts are insignificant. (One remembers with chagrin that a few years ago the Ford Foundation alone—in the United States of course—made more than $80 million available for American symphony orchestras.) Canadian corporations are not too generous either. No more than one per cent of corporate net profits before taxes goes to charitable donations. Only one per cent of all our companies (and there are 200,000 of them) accounts for the money coming in; which means that ninety-nine per cent do not contribute at all. Donations from individuals are rather modest, too. Fifty per cent of the tax-exempt dollars serve religious purposes, twenty per cent education, twenty-five per cent health and welfare; that leaves four per cent for civic and cultural enterprises and an estimated one per cent for the arts. In 1963 (these are the last figures available) 350 million dollars were claimed in standard deductions (three-quarters of all taxpayers took standard deductions) of which perhaps 40 per cent were real gifts while sixty per cent, or 210 million dollars, remained unused.[10]

10. The figures are taken from Arthur Maybee, "Private Philanthropy and Canadian Cultural Programs—Changing Patterns and Problems," in *Music in Canada, Its Resources and Needs* (Toronto: Canadian Music Council, 1967).

Yes, subsidies *are* forthcoming for the performing arts—a fraction of one per cent of corporate profit, one per cent of individual donations. The private sector has little to boast about. It certainly was not responsible for the rapid development of the performing arts we noted with pride. That came about as a result of thoroughly un-American activities, i.e., the granting of government subsidies.

In 1956 the Greater Montreal Arts Council came into being, a few months later the Canada Council. The intervening years have seen the establishment of three provincial arts councils— in Quebec, Ontario and Saskatchewan; municipal, provincial and federal agencies have become patrons of the arts.

Of course, state patronage is nothing new in itself. It would be easy to cite figures from Switzerland, Austria or Holland, from Italy, Denmark, Hungary, Poland, to say nothing of France, Germany or the Soviet Union; Frederick Dorian's "Commitment to Culture" quotes chapter and verse.[11] The point is that Britain, Canada and the United States had long been disinclined to follow continental examples. By 1945 they were the only countries of the West to leave the arts to the tender mercies of the private sector. Their attitude began to change when the Arts Council of Great Britain came into being. Its establishment emboldened the Massey Commission to recommend the endowment of an analogous institution to be called the Canada Council. The Americans were late in the game; but when they entered it they did so with characteristic exuberance and incredible speed. Nine years ago New York was the only State in the Union to have an arts council; there are now forty-nine state arts councils, four territorial and over 250 community arts councils. At the top is a national Council on the arts. So far it has only modest funds at its disposal, but they will undoubtedly soon be increased.

Canada's development was less tempestuous perhaps but remarkable nevertheless. On the municipal level, Montreal has set an example that presents a challenge to every city in the

11. See Frederick Dorian, *Commitment to Culture* (Pittsburgh: University of Pittsburgh Press, 1964).

land. The Greater Montreal Arts Council derives its funds from a special city tax and uses them to assist the performing arts— choral and instrumental music, opera, ballet, drama, a summer festival, a film festival: altogether a magnificent achievement.[12] On the second level of government it is the Province of Ontario's Council of the Arts that gives effective leadership. "Through its programs and grants," says John P. Robarts, Prime Minister of Ontario, "the Ontario Arts Council is stimulating our citizens to contribute to the cultural well-being of their fellowmen and, most important, to realize their own latent potential. A natural revolution has taken place in North America. We have emerged from the simpler, external challenges which faced the frontier society to the infinitely more complex problems and demands of a highly industrialized technocracy. The time has come when it is imperative to give serious attention to President Adams' view of the ultimate goal of our struggle to build this society." Noble words—and a welcome affirmation of the responsibility of government to assist in the struggle.[13]

The federal agency assisting the arts is, of course, the Canada Council. Twelve of the existing twenty-three orchestras, the Canadian Opera Company, the Vancouver and Edmonton opera associations, the Canadian Music Centre, the League of Composers, the National Youth Orchestra, Les Jeunesses Musicales du Canada—they all (and many more) profited from the enlightened patronage of the Council. During the first nine years of its existence it spent $11,350,000 on arts organizations of all kinds with four and a half million going to music.[14] Without the help of the Canada Council it would have been utterly impossible for the Montreal Symphony Orchestra to increase its budget by 640 per cent in nine years, for the Toronto Symphony Orchestra to reach an increase of 85 per cent over the

12. Leon Lortie, "Montreal as a Cultural Centre," in *Music in Canada, Its Resources and Needs* (Toronto: Canadian Music Council, 1967).
13. The Province of Ontario Council of the Arts, *Second Report 1965–66*.
14. See Peter M. Dwyer, "The Canada Council and Music," in *Music in Canada, Its Resources and Needs* (Toronto: Canadian Music Council, 1967).

same period, for the Canadian Opera Company to augment its budget by 430 per cent. The Council's activities are not, of course, limited to music; theatre, ballet, literature, even the social sciences are equally within its province. Nor is the Council content to give grants to worthy recipients and leave it at that. Its officers are aware of the planning necessary to integrate the diffused and un-co-ordinated efforts in education and performance.

Eleven years ago, when the Canada Council Act was undergoing debate in the House of Commons, a great deal of resistance was encountered; many a member felt that culture was not a government concern. In 1965 the government announced an additional grant of ten million dollars to the Council: contrary to expectation, there was no dissent in the House. The Council's work was praised by practically everyone. Opposition to government subsidies had vanished, and "the first paragraph of a national philosophy toward the arts had been written. Members of Parliament and, indirectly, Canadians had accepted the responsibility for developing a national culture."[15]

Development was quickened when the federal government provided no less than 91 million dollars for Centennial celebrations. The activities sponsored were varied, ranging from the historical roadshow of the centennial train and military tattoos to Festival Canada and Expo 67. As to music: a great many compositions were commissioned, the works were all performed, the performances involved soloists, orchestras, ballet and opera companies in turn. For one year at least the whole process of music-making was forced into high gear. Festival Canada on Tour (distinct from Festival Canada at Home) visited 210 communities, gave 690 performances, sold over 650,000 tickets and reached an average audience capacity of 76 per cent. Such unprecedented events left their marks on composition and performance; they also opened the eyes of the public. A great many people realized for the first time that the arts can be an asset to the country, that they are by no means monopolies of aristocratic societies or totalitarian regimes—

15. *Seminar '66,* Canadian Conference of the Arts (Toronto 1966).

that democratic governments are duty-bound to encourage and to protect them. It is one of the happiest results of the Centennial that government responsibility for the arts is now widely accepted.

Accelerated progress is not all gain, however. It creates troubles too, particularly when it grinds to a halt. The Centennial had been planned as a one-time thing but when it came to an end people did not want to extinguish the centennial flame (a symbolic gesture), did not want to lose the impetus of a glorious and successful year. Can we maintain the 1967 level of artistic production? Can we continue with Festival Canada on Tour? These and similar questions occupied the Canadian Conference of the Arts at a 1967 meeting in St. Adèle. Everyone present was aware of diminishing resources but few were prepared to cut the coat according to the cloth.

If composition and performance progress rapidly while audiences are not increased we are in trouble too. And it can happen very easily because building audiences is a slow process, slower still than professional music education. It has been quite impossible, so far, to regulate the speed of progress in the various fields; we can only point to the problem without offering any solutions.

The Centennial Commission is fading out of the picture, but the federal government's involvement in the arts remains and acts as a centripetal force in a sometimes centrifugal milieu: for the United States—so stimulating, so dangerously friendly—influences Canadian music to a very great extent.

For European observers Canadian music has a distinctly American flavour though the Americans themselves would be the first ones to recognize the difference. Media and management, the (relative) size and composition of the performing arts audience, the rising tide of popular music, patterns of patronage and educational procedures are similar, even identical in some cases; the facts of geography and contiguity exert themselves. There are distinctive traits, however, that ought to be emphasized. Kenneth Peacock's chapter on folk and aboriginal music mentions Eskimo songs, folksongs from old Quebec, songs of Newfoundland outposts, songs of the Doukhobors and a great many others that exist nowhere else. The earliest strands woven into the tapestry of our musical history were the solemn *Te Deums* intoned by priests and missionaries, songs of *coureurs de bois*, of voyageurs and habitants. Canadian broadcasting is certainly *sui generis*. Even contemporary composition, for all the imitative furor of its practitioners, guards a delightfully provincial flavour. "Ni européens au sens de l'Europe, ni américains au sens des Etats Unis, mais européens d'ici, américains particuliers, les Canadiens s'enrichissent de certaines singularités ethniques qui se portent garantes de leur originalité."[16]

Composition, performance, broadcasting and education are the most important segments of a country's musical life; taking them one by one, we find Canadians hard at work to put their house in order. There are segments, however, in which we are overshadowed by the United States. Our orchestras (as Keith MacMillan points out) have no organization of their own, they belong to the American Symphony Orchestra League; our musicians' associations, or unions, are affiliated with the American Federation of Labour; a host of music teachers are members of the Music Educators National Conference of the United States. Reviews in the *New York Times* carry more weight than those in our own metropolitan papers, though it is pleasant to acknowledge that their music columns are a great deal better than they used to be. Not so long ago they found their place in the "entertainment" section; the disappearance of that hateful label—in some papers at least—is a good omen.

It is too early perhaps to wish for learned journals comparable to the *Musical Quarterly*, *Notes* or *Ethnomusicology*. Our public is neither large nor learned enough to sustain such ventures. The music journals we do have are more restricted in scope, serve special purposes, and are often house organs of

16. Andrée Desautels, "Les Trois Ages de la Musique au Canada," in *Larousse de la Musique*, Tome II (Paris, 1965), p. 314.

specific organizations. *Musicanada* calls itself a newsletter of the Canadian Music Centre.[17] *Vie Musicale* (edited by Wilfrid Pelletier) is published by the Ministère des Affaires Culturelles of Quebec, "elle se voudra un reflet vivant et dynamique de toutes les sphères de la réalité musicale du Québec actuel."[18] *The Canadian Composer* (bilingual) owes its existence to CAPAC. *Le Journal des Jeunesses Musicales*[19] enhances the work of the sponsoring organization. *The Amateur Musician* (also bilingual) presents the views of CAMMAC. The Canadian Music Educators' Association, the Ontario and the Alberta Music Educators' Associations issue small journals of their own, but the giant *MENC Journal* still reigns supreme over the continent. *Opera in Canada* deserves special mention. Under the editorship of Ruby Mercer, it is, both editorially and pictorially, an unusually attractive magazine documenting and aiding operatic development throughout the country.

From 1956 to 1962 there existed a musical quarterly far wider in scope and more comprehensive than any of those mentioned above: the *Canadian Music Journal*, edited by Geoffrey Payzant and published by the Canadian Music Council. The reasons for its disappearance were rising costs and falling circulation, occupational diseases affecting many a cultural publication. There is a well-founded hope that the *Journal* will soon be resurrected. A rapidly expanding musical life calls for documentation and criticism, for evaluation of the increased output of book publishers, music publishers and record makers, and for an appraisal of national achievements. Six volumes of the old *Journal* testify to the fact that it attempted all those things —prematurely, perhaps, but valiantly. Its greatest asset was a group of writers encouraged (in some cases discovered) by the editor, all working for a common cause. Among the regular contributors were John Beckwith, Leslie Bell, Marvin Duchow, Chester Duncan, Peter Garvie, Graham George, Helmut Kall-

17. French and English editions.
18. Jean-Noël Tremblay, *Vie Musicale*, 5/6, 1967.
19. French and English editions.

mann, Udo Kasemets, Sir Ernest MacMillan, Geoffrey Payzant, Murray Schaefer, Ken Winters and Arnold Walter.

Although music publishing is a thriving business in the United States, Canadian music publishers find it difficult to compete with the powerful American firms. Hemmed in by a small market, they are distributors rather than publishers. Some of them have nevertheless managed to print a considerable number of scores by Canadian composers. BMI Canada Ltd. is by far the most active of the firms in question, but Boosey & Hawkes, Leeds, The Oxford University Press, G. Ricordi and Co., Gordon V. Thompson Ltd. and The Waterloo Music Co. must also be mentioned.

When it comes to books on music, our record is not impressive. Helmut Kallmann's *History of Music in Canada 1534–1914*[20] heads the list. Of the biographical essays available, Eugène Lapierre's *Calixa Lavallée* is the only one worth its salt. The thirty-four capsule biographies of Canadian composers prepared and distributed by the International Service of the CBC are a welcome reference tool.[21] The output is meagre— quite necessarily so. Musicological research started in Toronto in the late fifties, the study of ethnomusicology (also in Toronto) dates from 1966; the impact of both disciplines has yet to be felt. The first musicological treatise written by a Canadian, Warren Kirkendale's *Fuge und Fugato in der Kammermusik des Rokoko und der Klassik*,[22] was published, curiously enough, in Germany; one would have wished that the work had not escaped the notice of Canadian university presses.

Turning to folk music and music education, one encounters a much livelier scene. Kenneth Peacock[23] reports on folk music research (much of it centred in the Musée de l'homme of the National Museum) and subsequent publications. For music

20. Helmut Kallmann, *A History of Music in Canada 1534–1914* (Toronto: University of Toronto Press, 1960).
21. International Service of the CBC (Montreal 1964).
22. Warren Kirkendale, *Fuge und Fugato in der Kammermusik des Rokoko und der Klassik* (Tutzing: Hans Schneider, 1966).
23. See chapter on folk and aboriginal music, p. 62.

educators this is an age of anxiety, an age of analysis, an age of conferences whose reports are repositories of a great deal of research. The reports of the Canadian Music Council conferences of 1965, 1966 and 1967 belong to that category, as do those of the Canadian Association of University Schools of Music (1965, 1966), Ezra Schabas' report on Community Orchestras in Ontario (1966), and a host of others.[24]

A field of research in which Canada excels is that of electronic music. The term covers two distinct operations: the discovery of new sound sources, and the use composers can make of electronically derived tone material. Theoretically at least the scientist (or inventor) provides the apparatus, the composer manipulates it to execute his design. But in practice it often happens that scientists try their hand on composition while composers acquire enough scientific background to enable them to suggest modifications of the electronic equipment at their disposal.

The movement started in the early fifties in Paris and Cologne with Pierre Schaeffer, Herbert Eimert and Karlheinz Stockhausen. The man who transplanted it to Canada was Hugh LeCaine who directs the electronic music division of the National Research Council. The leading role of the NRC in this area is recognized all over the continent. LeCaine's inventions —particularly the Multi-track Tape Recorder and the Serial Sound Structure Generator—are coveted by every studio in existence; Canadian studios are all dependent on his encouragement, help and advice. There are four Canadian electronic music studios in operation—at the University of Toronto (directed by Gustav Ciamaga); at McGill University (directed by Istvan Anhalt); at Simon Fraser University (directed by Murray Schaefer) and Otto Joachim's private studio in Montreal. The University of British Columbia and the Conservatoire de Musique are planning to institute electronic music divisions in the very near future.

The most important research centre by far is Dr. LeCaine's laboratory in the National Research Council; although research

24. See chapter on the growth of music education, p. 247.

conducted in the Toronto studio (the oldest and best equipped in the country) is producing valuable results too. The late Myron Schaeffer wrote numerous papers on studio techniques; Paul Pedersen investigated the Mel scale, dealt with problems of musical perception; James Gabura and Gustav Ciamaga developed a sound production programme employing hybrid computers; Lowell Cross compiled a valuable *Bibliography of Electronic Music.*[25] Of course, research is only one of the functions of the Toronto studio. Another is teaching on the graduate level, still another composition: Louis Applebaum, Harry Freedman, Harry Somers, Pierre Mercure, Norman McLaren (to name but a few) were all attracted to the centre; Andrée Desautels reports on some of their works in the domain of "musique expérimentale."[26]

As we noted earlier, the proximity of the United States is a powerful stimulant. Yet there is no need for Canadians to regard themselves as junior partners in a Continental system. It is true—in research and criticism, in publications and library resources, that the Americans are far ahead of us. Their music education, however, is every bit as disorganized as ours, in spite of all the fanfares in *fortissimo.* The performing arts in the United States have grown by leaps and bounds; so has the entertainment industry, a doubtful blessing. Canadian broadcasting is certainly better. And, when it comes to composition (the heart of the matter), we find the Americans struggling for identity, dependent on European models, endlessly repeating yesterday's *avant-garde*—no better off than we are ourselves, perhaps even less so.

Nonetheless, the magnet to the south is there. Canadian schools, performing and grant-giving organizations, have a problem on their hands: how to integrate their actions to keep Canadian talent in Canada. Some say that it is not worth trying to solve the problem; fortunately, there are others who have no desire to join that strange chorus solemnly intoning the lament for a nation.

25. Lowell Cross, *Bibliography of Electronic Music* (Toronto: University of Toronto Press, 1967).   26. See p. 90.

Historical Background

HELMUT KALLMANN

On Sunday, October 3, 1535, Jacques Cartier, the French discoverer of Canada, paid a visit to the Indian village of Hochelaga, a palisade settlement of some 3,000 Iroquois on the site of present-day Montreal. He and his men received a most hearty welcome. Overawed by the strange attire and manner of the visitors, the Indians presented their sick for healing. Thereupon Cartier recited from the Gospel of St. John, and rings, knives and other presents were given to the Indians. "The Captain next ordered the trumpets and other musical instruments to be sounded, whereat the Indians were much delighted. We then took leave of them and proceeded to set out upon our return."[1] Thus the recorded musical history of Canada begins at the climax of the first ceremonial meeting between European and Indian in Canada.

General Note: A dozen years of research since the earlier edition of *Music in Canada* have provided some corrections of factual information, some additional quotations and a reassessment of conclusions. Since the subject matter of the chapter is history, preservation of large sections of the original text is unavoidable.

1. H. P. Biggar, ed., *The Voyages of Jacques Cartier* (Ottawa: Public Archives of Canada, 1924), p. 166.

There had been music in North America for several thousand years before Cartier's arrival. Indian and Eskimo music, like that of the white settler, is not confined to the geographical boundaries of Canada but forms part of a larger cultural area. Less than one-fifth of all Eskimos live in Canada. But unlike European music, that of the aborigines has left no written documents and only the recently developed methods of ethnomusicology may, in retrospect, add a chronological-historical element to it. By the comparison of scales, instruments, texts and social functions of songs, it may become possible to discern a family-tree pattern among the many tribal sub-cultures. Research in the music of Canada's first human inhabitants is described by Kenneth Peacock in a separate chapter of this book.

To trace the musical history of modern Canada we need go back no further than the time of the early French explorers, for aboriginal art has made little impact on the musical life of the white majority. European works like Rameau's *Les Indes Galantes* or Grétry's *Le Huron* bear no genuine relationship to Indian music. While Léo-Pol Morin, John Weinzweig, and other twentieth-century Canadian composers have utilized aboriginal melodies and rhythms, and while recordings and printed collections of such music may soon become available in larger numbers, only Indian and Eskimo musicians themselves, trained along both native and Western lines, will be able to infuse the heritage of their forefathers into the mainstream of our musical history.

But are we justified in talking of musical "history" at all if we consider that composition—developing more slowly than either literature or painting—became only in the first half of the twentieth century an integral part of our cultural life? We are justified in using the term if we can free ourselves from the approach that equates music history with the history of composition. Indeed, the development of composers and of styles can be understood properly only in the context of musical life as a whole, with its educational system, its technical apparatus and its social aspects. Seen from this point of view, Canada is a veritable treasure house for historical study. Our growth from colony to nation has been accompanied by an amazing variety of values placed upon music and of musical practices, from the plain-chant and folk song of New France to the symphony orchestras and operas of today.

In another sense, however, the term history applies less satisfactorily to our musical record. The history of a given country implies elements of cohesion, continuity and self-awareness. Modern Canada has grown not from one colony, one geographical region or one ethnic stock, but from a variety of colonies and races, all with their own independent story of early settlement. The inhabitants of the lower St. Lawrence Valley, the fishermen of the Atlantic regions, the fortune-seekers of the gold rush era in the West, the Doukhobors and Mennonites of the Prairies all opened up new country; they all had their own musical traditions. Geographical distances and language barriers reinforced their ignorance of one another and discouraged the exchange of artists and the pooling of musical resources, except on a regional scale. This isolation has begun to break down only in recent decades, largely as a result of the establishment of radio networks. Thus for a long time musical history meant the sum total of many regional and local histories.

The source of musical inspiration for each of these regions usually did not lie in the local capital but in Europe or in the United States. It is natural that in all settlements music began with the transplantation of European traditions and their modification or attenuation in a new environment. But whereas in many rural areas of eastern Canada this initial process was followed by a sealing off from the mother country and the preservation of the song heritage in a very pure form for several centuries, in the towns and cities transplantation became a permanent pattern. Each new generation of Canadians received a stronger impact from European models than from the Canadian musicians of the older generation. New musical trends were introduced by successive waves of immigrants, who have always made up a large proportion of our music teachers, performers and composers. Often disappointed by the sparseness of musical culture in Canada, they have been surprised and delighted by the wealth of natural talent. Musical pioneers would, immediately on arrival, gather receptive people around them and, by teaching, organizing and performing, begin to re-create the musical atmosphere of their homelands. The folk songs of the early immigrants, the music of the concert hall and most of the musicians themselves were imported from abroad.

Under pioneer conditions, the means were lacking by which local Canadian traditions might be established and fused into a cohesive nation-wide culture. It was difficult to print music, to give advanced instruction to talented students and to provide professional outlets. And yet, the "history of music in Canada" began to change into "Canadian musical history," slowly at first, but gaining momentum about the middle of the nineteenth century, at the same time as did the political birth of the nation. This new element showed itself in the values attached to musical experiences that would be commonplace in Europe. When the first explorers and missionaries set foot on the new shores, their *Te Deums* or *Ave Marias* rang with an intense feeling of gratitude for having survived dangerous months of sea voyage, and when they set out on uncharted and endless forest lands, inhabited by savage people, the *Veni Creator Spiritus* would be meaningful beyond the routine chanting of a French parish priest. Later the pioneer settlers who would travel across many miles of snowy expanse to hear a famous artist or join in a musical competition festival, revealed a hunger for music and conviviality conceivable only in colonial surroundings. When William Lyon Mackenzie saw the grand romantic opera *The Devil's Bridge* performed in Toronto (then York) in 1826—it was his first visit to the theatre in seven years—his pleasure must have been out of proportion to the quality of the music or the performance.

A local element asserted itself not only in the new values placed on musical experiences but also in changes in folk song texts and the interchange of dances between people of varied origins. Thomas Moore's *Canadian Boat Song* (1804)—inspired by the tune of *Dans mon chemin j'ai rencontré*—and the Arctic explorer George Back's collection of *Canadian Airs* (1823) introduced the concept of Canadian Music to Europe. Theodore Molt's setting of Isidore Bédard's poem *Sol canadien, terre chérie* (words 1829) and *The Canada Union Waltz*, composed by "A Canadian Lady" and published in England (1841), are among the earliest examples of music in the service of Canadian patriotism. These were the modest beginnings of a specifically Canadian music history: its mature stage was entered much later, toward the middle of the twentieth century, with the growth of creative expression, of educational autonomy and of nation-wide organizations.

Permanent French settlements date from the early seventeenth century—the time of Samuel de Champlain's explorations. Port-Royal, the short-lived colony in what is now Nova Scotia, is remembered for its "Ordre de Bon Temps," an attempt to banish loneliness by entertainment. Here Marc Lescarbot, a young lawyer from Paris, wrote a masque, *The Theatre of Neptune*, which called for incidental music and was performed on barges "upon the waves of the harbour." The first historian of Canada, Lescarbot took an interest in music and noted down in 1612 Indian music which he heard outside the wigwam of the Micmac chief Membertou. Through Lescarbot we also learn that Baron de Poutrincourt, the commander of Port-Royal, composed some of the music regularly used in divine service.

Early historical incidents like these have a charm of their own, even though they may have little significance as typical examples of musical conditions in their time. The French missionaries found music not only a source of spiritual strength in carrying out their dangerous assignments but a helpful means in their efforts to befriend and to convert the Indians. "Sa Majesté désire," wrote Mother Marie de l'Incarnation in 1650, "qu'on francise ainsi peu à peu tous les sauvages, afin d'en faire un peuple poli. L'on commence par les enfants."[2] Typical

2. Letter written by Marie de l'Incarnation, #85, September 27, 1650, quoted in E. M. Faillon, *Histoire de la colonie française en Canada* (Montreal, 1866), III, p. 271.

of the missionaries' musical activities is a report by Father Louys André who tells us how in 1670 he set out from Sault Ste Marie on an assignment to an island in Lake Huron. After his arrival he conceived the plan of composing some spiritual canticles. "No sooner," he writes, "had I begun to have these sung in the Chapel, accompanied by a sweet-toned flute . . . than they all came in crowds, both adults and children; so that, to avoid confusion, I let only the girls enter the Chapel, while the others remained without, and thus we sang in two choruses, those without responding to those within."[3] Father André's account illustrates the Indians' great musical aptitude and the fascination that the music of the Church held for them.

The use of instruments to attract the natives was as characteristic as the composition or adaptation of liturgical tunes, the words of which were often translated into native dialects. In 1676, Father Jean Enjalran exclaimed: "The nuns of France do not sing more agreeably than some savage women here; and as a class, all the savages have much aptitude and inclination for singing the hymns of the Church, which have been rendered into their language."[4] It is quite possible that missionaries to be sent to Canada were chosen for their musical as well as other talents. Certainly music played an important part in their successes, limited though they were. The chants taught to the Indians by missionaries three hundred years ago have made a permanent impression on certain Indian tribes of eastern Canada. On the occasion of a visit to Lorette in 1749, the Swedish botanist Peter Kalm observed: "The divine service is as regularly attended here as in any other Roman Catholic church, and it is a pleasure to hear the vocal skill and pleasant voices of the Indians, especially of the women, when singing all sorts of hymns in their own language."[5]

Almost from the time of its foundation in 1608, music was a

3. *Jesuit Relations and Allied Documents, 1610–1791*, R. G. Thwaites, ed. (Cleveland, 1896–1901), LV, p. 147.
4. *Ibid.*, LX, p. 145.
5. Adolph B. Benson, ed., *Peter Kalm's Travels in North America* (the English version of 1770, New York, 1937), II, p. 462.

part of daily life in Quebec, the centre of missionary and trading activity. The priests' reports to their superiors in France, the famous *Jesuit Relations*, enable us to trace musical life in some detail: how in 1635, when the French population of Canada was less than one hundred, Father LeJeune (1591–1664) began to instruct French and Indian boys in the elements of Gregorian chant and musical notation; how Ursuline Sisters began to teach music to girls a few years later; how every musical boy, clergyman and "gentleman" was asked to sing or play during divine service; and how the number of flutes and viols increased. Quebec had eight hundred French inhabitants when Mgr Laval returned from Paris in September, 1663, with a fine organ, which was probably first played in the following year. It may not have been the first organ in Quebec, but, even so, it antedates the first known organ in the United States by about thirty years. In Montreal, which was founded in 1642, an organ was installed at the beginning of the eighteenth century. From that time also dates the oldest preserved composition in Canada, the liturgical *Prose de la Fête de la Sainte Famille*—a plain-chant surviving in a number of unsigned copies and attributed to the second priest born in Canada, Abbé Charles-Amador Martin (1648–1711). Once thought to have been written in the 1670s, the music is more likely to date from the turn of the century.

Examination of these and many other documents of church music in New France reveals that even under the most primitive conditions of colonization music is a complex affair: vocal and instrumental performance, education and even composition are all represented. But closer study, like that undertaken by Dr. William Amtmann of Ottawa, may also reveal the beginnings of a negative pattern—the pattern of inadequate patronage—that runs through our musical history like a red thread. While Bishop Laval imported some thirty sculptors, carvers and other master craftsmen to establish a school of arts and crafts at St. Joachim, he does not seem to have established a school for training church musicians. Dr. Amtmann found that omission, rather than the hardships of pioneer life, retarded the musical life of New France. There is little doubt that music might have been encouraged more systematically.[6]

Church music was the first European music introduced to Canada because the first settlers were priests and explorers, rarely farmers. The one thousand soldiers who arrived in the mid-1660s included two drummers and one fife player in each regiment, hardly an enrichment of musical life. The situation was soon to change when Jean Talon, the energetic Intendant of New France, brought to Canada a great number of farmers and fishermen from northwestern France. The French-Canadian population increased from 2,500 in 1663 to 6,700 in 1675. After this time, population grew by natural increase rather than immigration.

These immigrants brought to Canada one of our most valuable possessions: the folk songs of French Canada. It has been estimated that of the seven to ten thousand songs that have been collected in the Province of Quebec in recent decades, no less than nine-tenths are derived from the songs brought to Canada before 1673. The very mention of folk song in Canada sounds odd to many who think of Canada chiefly in terms of its great industrial development. The fact remains that Canada has been not only a great preserver, but also, to a limited extent, a producer of folk song.

We cannot, however, draw a complete picture of music in early Canada without stressing the enormous importance of singing and dancing in the lives of the *habitant* and *coureur de bois*, and later, of the *voyageur* and the settlers of Nova Scotia, Newfoundland, and New Brunswick. Song was the faithful companion of work in the fields, at the spinning-wheel during long winter evenings, of travel through endless stretches of bush and lakes. Song preserved the memory of the ancestral home, enlivened social gatherings and added cheer to dreaded days of cold, want, and solitude. The French Canadians in particular were passionately fond of singing, dancing and fiddling. The music of no other class of people has been given so many

6. See Dr. Amtmann's review of *A History of Music in Canada 1534–1914, The Canadian Music Journal* (Autumn 1961).

glowing reports than that of the *voyageurs*, the men whose canoes were the sole means of transportation between the settled regions along the St. Lawrence River and the western and northern wilds. The glorious period of *voyageur* song was the late eighteenth and early nineteenth centuries. With the coming of the railway and steamship, the *voyageur* disappeared and with him many of his typically Canadian songs. Of the numerous eye-witness accounts, we shall quote one, by John Mactaggart in 1829:

They are good at composing easy, extemporaneous songs, somewhat smutty, but never intolerant. Many of their *canoe-songs* are exquisite; more particularly the *air* they give them. . . . We must be in a canoe with a dozen hearty paddlers, the lake pure, the weather fine, and the rapids past, before their influence can be powerfully felt. Music and song I have revelled in all my days, and must own, that the *chanson de voyageur* has delighted me above all others, excepting those of Scotland.[7]

Until the early nineteenth century, folk song was the predominant music in all parts of Canada. However, with the growth of urban society, the importation of printed concert and popular music began, and consequently the gulf between the music of the city and that of the country was widened. Although Ernest Gagnon's collection (1865) made the world familiar with a hundred-odd Canadian folk songs, it was not until early in the twentieth century that scholars like Marius Barbeau, E.-Z. Massicotte, and Helen Creighton opened our eyes to the vastness of our treasure.

The struggle for control of Canada between England and France, begun in the early seventeenth century, ended in 1760 when the British became masters of all of Canada that had been explored up to that time: the country east of the Great Lakes and a few outposts in the west and north.

The first few decades under the new regime witnessed a rapid rise in the cultivation of secular art music. Under the French, art music, though not unknown, had led a very precarious exis-

7. John Mactaggart, *Three Years in Canada* (London, 1829), I, pp. 254–5.

tence. Maisonneuve, the founder of Montreal, knew how to play the lute and Jolliet, the explorer of the Mississippi, was skilled at the keyboard. Jacques Raudot, Intendant of New France from 1705 to 1711, "aimait beaucoup la jeunesse et lui procurait chez lui d'honnêtes plaisirs. Son divertissement était un concert mêlé de voix et d'instruments. Comme il était obligeant, il voulut nous faire entendre cette symphonie, et plusieurs fois il envoya ses musiciens chanter des motets dans notre église. On ne chantait presque chez lui que des airs à la louange du Roi, ou des noëls, dans la saison."[8] In the several winters before the fall of Quebec, the upper ranks of society engaged in a never-ending round of receptions, masquerades, dances and music (usually referred to as "les violons"), much to the annoyance of Marquis de Montcalm, the military commander. Once or twice, Montcalm's journal refers to a concert, such as that in December, 1757: "L'intendant a rassemblé, à l'occasion du concert exécuté par des officiers et des dames, nombreuse compagnie. Il y a eu d'aussi bonne musique qu'il soit possible d'en exécuter dans un pays où le goût des arts ne peut avoir gagné."[9] It is important to remember, though, that the people engaged in this convivial music-making were usually temporary residents rather than settlers.

The most significant stimulus secular music received under the new British regime was provided by the regimental bands stationed in garrison towns such as Halifax, Quebec, Montreal, and Niagara. These bands were large in comparison with the drum and fife bands of earlier days. Among the four thousand Hesse and Brunswick troops serving in Canada in 1777, there were no fewer than one hundred and two musicians, usually fifteen in each regiment. In times of peace the officers serving in Canada had plenty of time to indulge in hobbies—horses, dances, music and theatre, perhaps in that order—and, in alliance with the well-educated Loyalists from New England and

8. Mère Juchereau de Saint-Ignace, *Histoire de l'Hôtel-Dieu de Québec*, 1751, p. 463.

9. Abbé H.-R. Casgrain, ed., *Journal du Marquis de Montcalm, 1756-1759* (Quebec, 1895), p. 325 (Vol. VII of *Collection des Manuscrits du Maréchal de Lévis*).

such artistic French immigrants as Joseph Quesnel and Louis Dulongpré, they brought the performing arts to a modest flourishing, certainly remarkable for its day. For once in our musical history, the patronage problem seems to have been solved: the will to support music and the artistic resources matched one another.

In addition to performing at military functions, regimental bands became a true community force, reaching a wide and warmly appreciative public. Almost daily a band could be heard: at a gathering of high society, at a garden party, on a public square or, reinforced by amateur performers, in a subscription concert. An Englishman visiting Quebec in 1785 remarked that "the music of the two bands and the company of so many officers must be a very great inducement for preferring this place to any other,"[10] and a decade later another traveller observed that "Every evening during summer, when the weather is fine, one of the regiments of the garrison parades in the open place before the chateau, and the band plays for an hour or two, at which time the place becomes the resort of numbers of the most genteel people of the town, and has a very gay appearance."[11]

During many a winter Canadian towns—none of which had yet reached the ten thousand population mark—would be enlivened by subscription or benefit concerts of "vocal and instrumental music," followed by dances. Coffee houses and taverns were among the makeshift scenes for these performances, although Quebec boasted a concert hall, at least in name, as early as 1764. Yet, these improvised auditoria must have been comfortable enough to attract audiences for hours on end: Mrs. Mechtler's benefit concert in Halifax in 1791 featured no less than four symphonies (or overtures) by (J.C.?) Bach, Vanhal and Stamitz as well as two concertos and four vocal numbers. A series of weekly subscription concerts in Quebec late the fol-

10. Douglas S. Robertson, ed., *An Englishman in America, 1785, Being the Diary of Joseph Hadfield* (Toronto, 1933), p. 150.
11. Isaac Weld, Jr., *Travels through the States of North America, and the Provinces of Upper and Lower Canada, during the Years 1795, 1796, and 1797* (London, 1799), pp. 201–2.

lowing year included symphonies by Pleyel, Gyrowetz and Haydn, concertos by Avison and Corelli, overtures by Handel and, perhaps most remarkable, a Mozart piano concerto, as well as a variety of chamber music. Has new music ever reached Canada more quickly than it did in the late eighteenth century?

Opera, that is to say French and English light opera of the period, was occasionally provided by foreign troupes of actors and singers. The newspapers inspected to date allow us to estimate that by 1810 there had been about one hundred operatic performances in Canada. One production, at least, was a local amateur effort in Montreal, to be repeated fifteen years later in Quebec. Staged by Dulongpré, a music and dancing teacher best known as a portrait painter, *Colas et Colinette* (1790) was written and composed by Joseph Quesnel (1749–1809), a French ship's officer who had settled in Canada in 1779. He found leisure to write poetry and plays, composing his own music for the latter. The music of *Colas* belongs to the "comédie mêlée d'ariettes," a genre cultivated by Grétry and other French composers of the period. Though only the vocal and second violin parts are extant, Godfrey Ridout was able to restore the orchestral accompaniment for a revival in 1963 which proved a musically rewarding experience.

While the existence of an operatic composer in eighteenth-century Montreal was something of a freak in our history, composition itself was not unknown. The Abbé Charles Ecuyer (1758–1820) of Répentigny and Yamachiche wrote church music, including a *Sanctus* (reconstructed and published in 1877), and, on New Year's Eve 1776, the first anniversary of the repulsion of American rebel invaders from Quebec, a specially written Ode, was sung in that town, with "arias, ariettas, recitatives and choirs."[12]

The nineteenth century, with a rising merchant class and its twin attitudes of commercialism and puritanism, failed to maintain the artistic level that had been established in the closing

12. *Vertrauliche Briefe aus Kanada und Neu England vom Jahre 1777 und 1778*. Aus Herrn Professor Schlözers Briefwechsel, Heft XXIII und XXIV (Göttingen, 1779), p. 22.

years of the eighteenth. British regimental bands remained the backbone of instrumental music in Canada until their replacement after Confederation by Canadian units. Sometimes bands were interchanged between various parts of the Empire, and thus Canadians had an opportunity to hear some of the finest British bands. (Many of these were brought to Canada as a special attraction of the Canadian National Exhibition, held annually in Toronto since 1879.) The personnel in earlier years included a number of musicians of non-British origin, especially German bandmasters. Many of the musicians, upon retirement or discharge, stayed in Canada as performers, teachers, instrument-makers or music dealers.

Beginning with the 1820s, civilian bands were formed in many towns. Some were established on a family or neighbourhood basis, others were attached to the local fire-brigade or volunteer militia. Some played just for their own amusement, whereas semi-professional "name" bands offered their services to taverns, weddings, lake-steamers and the like.

In Quebec, one of the earliest bands was organized by a German bandmaster, Jean-Chrysostome Brauneis (1785–1832), in 1831 and was revived by a native Canadian, Charles Sauvageau (1809–1846), in 1836 under the proud title "Musique Canadienne." Its history in these turbulent and rebellious years was closely linked with French-Canadian struggles for a greater share in Canadian government. This band was made up of three clarinets, piccolo, bassoon, three horns, trumpet, trombone, serpent and percussion.

The first local band in Upper Canada to achieve fame belonged not to a city, but to a little village south of Lake Simcoe. The residents of Hope (now Sharon), the "Children of Peace," were a splinter group of the Quakers. In reaction to the severity of the latter they evolved a quaint and colourful cult of their own of which the Temple at Sharon is an extant reminder. Following the initiative of their leader, David Willson, a self-made theologian, music became a prominent feature of their community. About 1820 a choir and a band were formed. Their first organ, of the same time, is supposed to have been the earliest built in Upper Canada. It has one hundred and thirty-three pipes and two barrels of ten sacred tunes each. Its sounds still charm visitors to the Temple Museum. The example of Sharon proves that musical excellence owes more to inspired leadership than to the external setting. A more recent case in point is the famed Anglo-Canadian Concert Band of Huntsville, Ontario (1919–1924), recruited largely from among the workers of a local tannery and led by the renowned cornetist Herbert Lincoln Clarke. The mediocrity of so many other musical enterprises is too often explained in terms of our youth as a nation, the thinly spread population and the preoccupations of pioneer life. These are half-truths: the real blame often attaches to a lack of public support and skilled leadership.

After Confederation many Canadian military bands were established, often with musicians from the departing British bands as instructors. The first notable Canadian bandmaster was Joseph Vézina of Quebec (1849–1924), the founder and leader of several bands and a prolific composer for this medium. In any Canadian town one could now find a bandstand and on summer evenings concerts would be given regularly—a custom which is only a memory in many of our cities today.

What the bands did for instrumental performance, church music did for singing. For generations of Canadians, musical experience has been rooted in the church service. Generalization must stop here, for there was a startling variety of attitudes towards music. This is revealed not only by comparison of the numerous denominations but of different members of the same congregation. The Roman Catholic and Church of England cathedrals provided the most elaborate music; many churches were equipped with fine organs and most of the early publications of music in Canada were intended for use by the clergy and choirs of these denominations. At the opposite extreme stood those who felt that music, and instrumental music in particular, had no place in divine worship. A Quaker who visited the Children of Peace in 1821 and heard their organ felt "that the Almighty was not to be worshipped by the workmanship of man's hands, so left the meeting."[13] And a Toronto Presbyterian left his congregation after twenty-four years of membership, declaring in a printed *Memorial* (1859) "That I cannot conscientiously continue to attend upon the public worship of God in a Church where a musical instrument is used in praising God, whether as an accompaniment or otherwise...."[14] The offender was a meek melodeon, used in sustaining and reinforcing the choir, which had recently diminished in size.

In between these extremes were other sects who frowned upon secular music-making but gave full musical expression to their religious feelings. A Primitive Methodist recalled that in her youth in the 1830s "novel reading was a sin, and a fiddle was a terribly wicked thing. It was the devil's instrument to snare the young into dance; but a bass viol was not in the same category because consecrated to the service of God. Father never allowed us to sing songs, he considered them wicked. . . ."[15] The same writer also remembered the visit of a minister to one of the missions in 1856: ". . . the congregational singing he never heard excelled. Their voices were musical, and so many could sing well and in perfect time. They had no instrument, but they could take all the parts of a tune. They had some Old Country music with fugues, and they could all modulate their voices, or sweep in a volume that carried all the congregation in one burst of song."[16]

In addition to the old country influence in church music there was a strong American element. Singing masters would travel from town to town, organizing "singing schools" in which the rudiments of notation and choral singing would be taught. Hymn collections and books of the rudiments of sacred singing

13. Leslie R. Gray, ed., *"Phoebe Roberts' Diary,"* Ontario Historical Society Papers & Records, "Ontario History," XLII, 1, 1950, p. 20.

14. *The Organ Question: Statements by Dr. Ritchie, and Dr. Porteous, . . . in the Proceedings of the Presbytery of Glasgow, 1807–8 . . . to which is annexed, A Memorial to the Presbytery of Toronto . . . on the same subject* (Toronto, 1859) Appendix, pp. 76–80.

15. Mrs. R. P. Hopper, *Old-time Primitive Methodism in Canada (1829–1884)*, (Toronto, 1894), p. 77.

16. *Ibid.*, p. 213.

with a Boston or Philadelphia imprint are displayed in several of our regional museums.

In 1841 responsible government united Lower and Upper Canada and, with Confederation in 1867, the Dominion of Canada was born. Coincident with these steps of political maturing, was the development of trade and industry and the increase of population, the characteristic features of urban musical life. Out of the resources of bands and church choirs, musical societies were formed, musicians of professional stature and instrument-builders were attracted to Canada, world-famous artists found it profitable to include our cities in their tours, publishers set up shop, and, a little later, conservatories and musical periodicals appeared. Last but not least, gifted young Canadians took up music as a career, specializing in teaching and performance and engaging in composition as an occasional activity. The true era of musical pioneering had begun.

The pioneer musician had to be versatile, enterprising, and idealistic. In August of 1849 Henry Schallehn advertised in the Toronto *Globe* as a piano and guitar teacher. A year later we find him acting as singing master at Upper Canada College and as concert master of the Philharmonic Society, performing a solo violin piece by Paganini. As though this were not versatile enough, a Torontonian, writing some years later, remembered Schallehn as a "clever clarionet player and bandmaster of the 71st regiment."[17]

The story of Edward Thomas Day, who had served as band-master in India for seven years and settled in the town of Elora, Upper Canada, illustrates what is meant by enterprise.

From the stirring life of a Regimental Band Master to a solitary home in the backwoods of Canada, and from the tropical climate of India to the cold of a Canadian winter! For a few years he was kept busy on his farm, until, with the assistance of his sons, they had some comfort in their home. Then he concluded that . . . he must have some music mixed with [farming], so he became the bandmaster of the first Elora band, which was organized in the fall of 1848. He also undertook the leadership of the second band in Guelph . . . and later

17. *Music in Toronto (Toronto Mail,* December 21, 1878).

was leader of a band in Berlin [now Kitchener] and another in Owen Sound. Although the distance from his home to Elora and return was ten miles, and to Guelph and back was thirty-six miles, he always walked to these places to attend every band practice; and at another time he tramped to Dundas and back that he might write down the music of a song that he had been told some one there could sing for him correctly.[18]

It was idealism, perseverance, and honest salesmanship that distinguished the genuine pioneer musician from the charlatan who was willing to cater to the vanities of the newly rich. The growth of Canadian cities coincided with the spread of mass-produced entertainment on a low level of taste. Considering the lack of facilities for musical training and of opportunities to hear good music, common alike to native Canadians and to many of the poorer immigrants from Europe, it is not surprising that superficiality reigned over musical taste.[19] In the early decades of the nineteenth century those who owned pianos and indulged in domestic music-making, usually members of the privileged or educated classes, cultivated their hobby with sincerity. But, in the opinion of the contemporary Ottawa musician Gustave Smith, by 1882 the chase for dollars and luxuries had corrupted the custom of spontaneous music-making among friends, and among musicians "nous avons peu d'artistes—en profession, mais nous comptons, en revanche, beaucoup de professeurs sans profession."[20] Music now became chiefly an "accomplishment" of young ladies who played the piano and delighted their suitors with waltzes, polkas and assorted salon pieces, pretty and sentimental. The various *chansonniers* published in French Canada represent a curious mixture of "national airs," comic parlour songs and operatic tunes. Upright pianos and parlour organs appeared now in every middle-class home, but serious practising was shunned, and an artistic ca-

18. John R. Connon, *Elora* (Elora, 1930), p. 100.
19. There is a striking parallel in the degradation of architectural taste that characterized much of Canadian building after the middle of the nineteenth century.
20. Gustave Smith, *Du mouvement musical en Canada* (*L'Album Musical*, Montreal, mai 1882), p. 23.

reer, like any other pursuit not aimed at the acquisition of wealth and social position, was regarded with suspicion. The musician was apt to be classed with the Bohemian and the morally loose person. The attitude of those most able by wealth or position to patronize the arts culminated in the view that if music cannot stand on its own feet financially, it does not deserve to exist. The critic who in 1868 complained about the "very indifferent taste evinced for *good music* by the higher social and better educated classes of this city" has often been re-echoed since.[21] It is this type of attitude that has contributed to the impression that Canada is a country without a musical past. That impression ignores the intensely musical atmosphere of the pre-industrial age and the many achievements of early musical societies.

It is against this background that we have to measure the accomplishments of pioneer musicians and music-lovers who strove to raise the level of taste and knowledge by teaching, performing, and organizing musical societies. Their reward was not glamour and fame, but the quiet glory of awakening people to the beauty of music, people who had never before heard an orchestra or a chorus. In spite of Gustave Smith's negative appraisal, there existed an idealistic minority, and music did find its wealthy patrons. Calixa Lavallée and Guillaume Couture as music students both found sponsors—a butcher and a priest; Toronto's Massey Music Hall (1894, now Massey Hall) is another outstanding reminder of private munificence.

All pioneer work was concentrated in the musical societies and the instrumental or, more often, choral groups. To trace in detail the varying fortunes—enthusiastic beginnings, shipwrecks, reorganizations and so on—of every philharmonic society from Halifax to Victoria would require a volume in itself. Yet even though musical life ran along independent local and provincial lines, musical conditions were strikingly similar everywhere. It will suffice to give the dates of some of the

21. *Evening Telegraph*, Feb. 5, 1868, on a "Grand Concert of the Montreal Amateur Musical Union." Seen in the F. H. Torrington scrapbooks, on file in the Toronto Public Library.

earliest societies and to trace the achievements of a few of the most famous ones.

Possibly the earliest of all was the Philharmonic Society of Halifax, which presented an oratorio at St. Paul's Church in 1769 but does not appear to have been a permanent organization. One of its successors, an Amateur Glee Club organized in 1837, was noteworthy as an early musical organization of working men. In 1770, the year of Beethoven's birth, a series of "Gentlemen's Subscription Concerts" took place in Quebec. In Toronto an Amateur Musical Society began to rehearse glees, and piano and flute music in 1835, and the first large musical event in Hamilton was their Philharmonic Society's performance of the *Creation* in 1858, with a chorus of ninety and an orchestra of twenty-five. Over two thousand miles to the west, in Victoria, the oldest town on the Pacific coast, we find in 1859 a Philharmonic Society and a few years later a German *Singverein*.

About the time of Confederation, musical societies, at first unstable and short-lived, hindered by intrigues, change of personnel or a fickle public, became much stronger and many flourished for decades. Choirs of two or three hundred voices, drawing many of their singers from church choirs, became very popular. It was far more difficult to train orchestras and keep them together. As a rule, therefore, these were assembled for each individual concert from among regimental musicians and other professional and amateur performers. Some players might be borrowed from neighbouring towns, but, even so, certain instruments would often be lacking and the balance would be unsatisfactory.

This type of concert depended largely on the resources available. For some concerts, almost anybody willing to stand on a podium and face an audience might be invited to participate. There would be a colourful succession of amateurs and professionals, singers and instrumentalists, whose selections would be interspersed with a few orchestral numbers. Such performances can still be heard at some church or small-town concerts. The programmes were often a hodge-podge of operatic fantasias, national songs, and showy instrumental pieces. As early as the 1850s and increasingly in later years, many concerts did, however, contain a large amount of serious music: overtures, symphonic movements or entire symphonies; oratorio and operatic selections by Handel, Haydn, Mozart, Beethoven, Rossini, Weber and Mendelssohn. Radical composers, from Berlioz to Debussy, were rarely heard. Altogether, concert life could be compared to that of provincial towns in England or France.

In the twenty-two years of its existence, the Montreal Philharmonic Society (1877–99) gave close to ninety concerts, devoted chiefly to oratorios, masses, and other large-scale choral works. Many of the soloists were guest artists from the United States or Europe. The conductor during most of the Society's existence was a native Montrealer, Guillaume Couture (1851–1915); his memory is still alive in that city. He graduated from the Paris Conservatoire with high honours and was considered a musician of profound craftsmanship and discipline. As examples of the Philharmonic's enterprise, we mention performances of Mendelssohn's *Elijah* (1884), Mozart's *Requiem* (1888), Beethoven's Ninth Symphony (1897), and concert performances in the 1890s of *The Flying Dutchman* and *Tannhäuser*.

It is significant that the Society and its conductor for the first few years, P. R. McLagan, had English names; Anglo-Canadians have always been natural organizers. Yet dependence of musical life on organized activity has been a weakness as well as a strength. Musical societies often achieved spectacular successes, but once they collapsed, all musical activity collapsed with them. Among the French Canadians music was far more taken for granted: if you had a healthy voice, a violin or a piano, you did not need organized activity.

In Quebec City, owing to foundations laid in the early years of the century, chamber music enjoyed popularity. The Septuor Haydn (1871–1903) under Arthur Lavigne (1845–1925) gave hundreds of concerts in Quebec and throughout the province. It consisted of string quintet, flute, and piano. It seems to have been the general practice in Canada that chamber ensembles were essentially miniature orchestras, more frequently playing orchestral works in arrangements rather than genuine chamber music. Indeed, it was Lavigne's ambition to create an orchestra in Quebec, and his dream came true in 1903, as the Société Symphonique de Québec took the place of the Septuor Haydn.

In English Canada, the centre of population and culture had begun to shift from the Maritimes to Ontario. The Toronto Philharmonic Society (1846–57, intermittently; 1872–94) was in many ways similar to its sister group in Montreal, but it never ventured into opera. Its programmes included many Canadian first performances, including those of the Mendelssohn oratorios. The climax of the Society's history came with the great festival of 1886. Typical of the time, it was a concentrated effort involving over a thousand singers and a large orchestra. From 1873 on, the conductor of the Philharmonic Society was Frederick Herbert Torrington (1837–1917), a musician of English birth who had come to Canada as a young man and was one of the first to play Bach fugues on a Canadian church organ. Torrington continued to play a notable part in the musical life of Toronto until well after the turn of the century.

An important stimulus for the improvement of performance standards was given by the occasional visits of world-famous artists. The invention of the steamship and the railway made these visits easier, but the chief factor was the proximity of the United States with its larger population. Those who performed before Canadian audiences between 1840 and 1880 included John Braham, Ole Bull, Jenny Lind, Henri Vieuxtemps, Sigismund Thalberg, Hans von Bülow, Louis Gottschalk and others. The Germanians, a German-American orchestra, celebrated some of their first triumphs in Quebec, Montreal (where they gave no less than nine concerts), Kingston, and Toronto in their tour of 1850. Their repertoire was an excellent one. Later in the nineteenth and early twentieth centuries many American orchestras paid visits to Canada, often to support a Canadian choir.

Visiting companies also provided the bulk of operatic entertainment, and, from Confederation until World War One, operas were heard more frequently than in the succeeding fifty years (apart from broadcasts). Performances with Canadian talent were rare. The first act of *Lucrezia Borgia* had been presented with piano accompaniment in Toronto in 1853, but Ontario directed its prime efforts towards oratorio. An early instance of the cultivation of opera in the province of Quebec is the 1846 production of Rousseau's *Le Devin du Village* in Quebec City, and local productions of *Si j'étais roi*, *La Dame Blanche* and other operas date back to the 1860s. Opera classes established in Halifax in the 1890s led to performances of *Martha, Faust* and *Der Freischütz*. It is astonishing that some of Wagner's operas were introduced to Canada before those of Mozart. Even *Parsifal* was performed by a visiting company in 1905.

The light musical stage, from minstrel shows to Gilbert and Sullivan, was amply represented by travelling and amateur groups all over Canada. *The Mikado*, for instance, was performed in Halifax only two years after its world première.

The reader may well ask who, if any, were the composers writing music in the days when Paul Kane and Cornelius Krieghoff, Thomas Haliburton, and Louis Fréchette won early laurels for Canadian painting and literature. In devoting ample space to nineteenth-century concert life, we merely reflect the fact that the performer was considered far more important than the composer. It is significant that the first musicians of world fame to impress Canadians were performers, not composers. The public was addicted to that star-worship which puts all the emphasis on virtuosity. This often led to unjust neglect of the native artist, particularly the composer. To be exact, we should speak not of composers but rather of musicians who earned their living as teachers, performers or in the service of the church, and who composed in their leisure hours. The environment certainly did not stimulate composition. A wealth of printed masterworks from Europe was available for those who craved good music. Guest artists and immigrant musicians did not take the trouble to find out the local composer. Audiences, relying on foreign judgment in most musical matters, were too timid to appraise the composer independently. Chances of performance and publication were small and the composer had little hope of gaining more than local reputation. Thus, until the early years of the twentieth century, composition was largely restricted to everyday functions of dancing, marching or teaching, and nearly all composers wrote music for the service of their church.

For nearly half a century after the death of Joseph Quesnel, composition appears to have been limited to a sporadic march, patriotic song or anthem. Only Stephen Codman (1792?–1852?), English-born organist of the Anglican Cathedral in Quebec, has left evidence of skilled craftsmanship. While *A la claire fontaine* was considered the quasi-national song of French Canada, Sabatier's *Le Drapeau de Carillon*, Lavigueur's *La Huronne* and Labelle's *O Canada, mon pays, mes amours* became very popular about the middle of the century. One of the earliest works with local colour to be published in Upper Canada was Clarke's *The Lays of the Maple Leaf, or Songs of Canada* (1853), a cycle of seven songs and glees. On an even larger scale were Sabatier's *Cantate* for the visit of the Prince of Wales in 1860 and Labelle's cantata *La Confédération*.

With Confederation there was a need for a national hymn. Many national songs were written (and still are), but only two won wide and lasting favour: *The Maple Leaf Forever* (1867) by the Toronto school principal Alexander Muir, restricted in its appeal to Anglo-Canadians, and Calixa Lavallée's *O Canada* which was first performed on June 24, 1880. Today we remember Lavallée (1842–91) chiefly for this single composition. We forget that it was not *O Canada* that made him famous. The reverse is true: it was due to his great reputation as composer, conductor and pianist that Lavallée was asked to write a national song. The story of his short life has been told by Eugène Lapierre in a book which has had several French editions and which is long overdue in an English adaptation, with the incorporation of newly discovered material. It was a life full of adventure and struggle, disappointment at home and reward abroad. Few other musicians have been so consciously Canadian; few have sacrificed so much for their country. Yet Lavallée did not succeed in inducing the authorities to help establish a national opera and a national conservatory, which he considered our greatest needs. Throughout his life he had spent various periods in the United States, as accompanist and opera conductor, and there he finally went into exile in the very year when the famous song was born. His greatest reward was his election as President of the Music Teachers' National Association (United States) in 1886.

As a composer Lavallée revealed his talent early. Even in 1873, before completing his studies in Paris, he was hailed as "Canada's national musician." His works include almost every type of music: light operas, symphonies, chamber compositions, music for band and piano, and songs. Most of the larger works were written outside Canada. The *Bridal Rose Overture* is still performed occasionally, and the piano piece *Papillon* had at least ten different publishers. From the few surviving works one may conclude that Lavallée was little influenced by the radicals of his time. Rather, his strength lay in facility of invention and melodic fluency. The greatest tribute to Lavallée was paid by Augustus Stephen Vogt, himself one of Canada's foremost musicians. Vogt, who as a music student had met Lavallée in Boston in the 1880s, is quoted as saying: ". . . he impressed me as a man of extraordinary ability—not merely as a clever executant of the piano, and not merely as an adroit deviser of pretty melodies and sensuous harmonies, but as a genuinely creative artist, a pure musical genius."[22]

Besides Lavallée, a number of French-Canadian musicians of his generation took a serious interest in composition. Born between 1844 and 1864 were Romain-Octave Pelletier, Joseph Vézina, Guillaume Couture, Ernest Lavigne, Alexis Contant and Achille Fortier. With the exception of Vézina's band music and operettas, Lavigne's songs and Contant's chamber music, the output of these composers centres on church music. Among

22. J. D. Logan, "Canadian Creative Composers," *Canadian Magazine*, September, 1913.

Anglo-Canadians, Angelo M. Read, William Reed and Wesley Octavius Forsyth, a friend of Cyril Scott's, were the first with impressive lists of compositions.

Many other composers were immigrants. Antoine Dessane and Gustave Smith were church musicians trained at the Paris Conservatoire, while the Belgian violinist François Jehin-Prume, probably the first virtuoso of international recognition to settle in Canada, wrote chiefly for his own performance. A great number of British musicians, brought up in the tradition of cathedral music, wielded an enormous influence as organists and choirmasters as well as teachers and conductors. Some of those who settled in various parts of Canada between 1880 and World War I are Charles A. E. Harriss, Albert Ham, William Hewlett, Herbert Sanders, Alfred Whitehead and Healey Willan. On the other hand, a few Canadians sought their fortunes abroad. Best known among these are Clarence Lucas, Nathaniel Dett, Gena Branscombe, one of our first women composers, the songwriter Geoffrey O'Hara and, at a later date, Colin McPhee, the expert in Balinese music.

Most of the native composers named studied abroad, usually in Paris or Leipzig, rarely in England. In Europe they became imbued with the music of Wagner, Franck or Gounod, but on returning to Canada, there was little impetus to write serious works and less hope of material reward. Above all there was no broad public with cultural interests, so essential for the artist's encouragement. Thus many a good talent was condemned to stagnation.

And yet a surprisingly large number of cantatas, masses, oratorios and operettas were produced, some even published. Contant's oratorio *Caïn* (1905), Couture's *Jean le Précurseur* (1914) and Harriss' opera *Torquil* (1896) are outstanding examples. Composition culminated in the choral work with orchestral or organ accompaniment—Ernest MacMillan's *England* (1918) is one of the finest as well as one of the last works representative of this period—but there is no evidence of symphonies or concertos by resident composers having been performed in Canada before World War I.

Access to this music, largely forgotten for decades, has fortunately become easier in recent years. The National Library in Ottawa has a large collection of copyright deposits of Canadian publications, the Toronto Public Library and Laval University have collections of more regional interest. (However, publishers were more prone to print "successes" like R. S. Ambrose's *One Sweetly Solemn Thought*, Edwin Gledhill's parlour songs or H. H. Godfrey's mass-produced patriotic songs, than the more serious type of music.) A number of broadcasts and recordings have also made it possible to judge the style of our turn-of-the-century composers.

In general the music of both native and immigrant composers reflected either French or English influences (the latter under the spell of German romanticism). The craftsmanship and the idealism of the composers compels admiration, but one does not often come across originality or what would then be modernism. There was little relationship between composition and the folk song of Canada, and few composers used folk song material.[23] In short, the nineteenth century did not produce a distinct school of composers in Canada. Music which lacks an intimate relationship with its human and geographical environment is often derivative and sterile.

With the increase of performance and composition came a need for musical education, for music printing, for instrument manufacture and for the exchange of news through music journals.

From the days of Father LeJeune in Quebec until the early nineteenth century, educational facilities remained primitive. Instruments were scarce, music had to be taken down by hand from the teacher's copy and, above all, good teachers were rare. As early as 1800 newspapers included advertisements by music teachers, but these men rarely stayed in one place for a long time, and teaching rarely was more than a sideline with them.

23. Those French-Canadian songs which remained popular even in the cities, were often strung together in medleys or "rapsodies canadiennes." Not only Canadian composers, for example Vézina (Mosaïque, 1880), but also Europeans like Paul Gilson and Sir Alexander Mackenzie wrote such works.

The first man to exercise influence through teaching and writing of musical textbooks was Theodore F. Molt (c. 1796–1856), a German immigrant to Quebec who visited Beethoven, Czerny and Moscheles on a brief return trip to Europe. Another musician of German descent, J. C. Brauneis (1814–1871), introduced the *études* of Cramer and Czerny, whereas Paul Letondal (1831–1894), a French immigrant, spread the pianistic methods of Kalkbrenner. The fruitful presence of these and many other German, French and, later, Belgian music teachers in French Canada, just as the presence of music teachers from an even greater variety of countries in twentieth-century Toronto and Montreal, is one of the most convincing arguments against cultural separatism.

Early in the nineteenth century, music also appeared on the curriculum of several "higher ladies' academies" and boys' colleges. In 1846 the first musical baccalaureate was conferred on James P. Clarke by the University of Toronto. It was several decades, however, before regular examinations for degrees in music were held by Trinity College, Toronto, and other universities. By the outbreak of World War I, about fifty doctorates in music had been granted by Canadian universities. There were no faculties of music; instruction was given through affiliated conservatories and the universities supervised the examinations.

Most music teaching was private and of very uneven quality. The unwary layman found it difficult to distinguish the quack, often operating under an assumed "professor" title, from the genuine artist. The teacher, in turn, found few serious students, for taking music lessons had more to do with one's social status than one's musical talent.

Among the conservatories, too, it was—and still is—hard to single out the authentic music school from the two or three teacher establishments inflated by a grandiose name. The genuine educational institutions which still exist include the Quebec Académie de Musique (founded 1868), an examination and award board, the Toronto (now Royal) Conservatory

(1886), the Halifax (now Maritime) Conservatory (1887) and the McGill Conservatorium (1904) in Montreal.

In elementary and secondary schools systematic music instruction was rare and too often depended on the presence of a qualified teacher and a sympathetic school board.

The first music published in Canada was for church use. In 1800 and the following two years, three bulky volumes appeared in Quebec, entitled *Le Graduel [Processionel, Vespéral] Romain*. They contained Roman Catholic liturgical music in four-line Gregorian notation. From then on, textbooks of musical rudiments and collections of hymns and sacred songs appeared from time to time. Music-lovers would also keep manuscript books in which they copied their favourite songs, hymns or dances. The bulk of music, however, was imported from Boston, London or Paris—collections of sacred or national songs, parlour ballads, dance music of all kinds and melodeon instruction manuals. It can be stated with certainty that, contrary to the impression given by recent folk song publications, by the middle of the nineteenth century far more music was circulated by means of print than by oral transmission: the tunes from *The Bohemian Girl* or *La Traviata* had a larger public than did folk music.

Some of the earliest printed compositions appeared as appendices to literary journals, for instance in the *Literary Garland* (1839) or *l'Album littéraire et musical de la Revue Canadienne* (1846). The extent to which sheet-music publishing depends upon the size of the local market is dramatically illustrated by a recent bibliography which lists 10,000 American publications for the period 1801–1825 alone, whereas in Canada separate sheet-music publishing made its appearance only in the mid-1840s. During the nineteenth century A. & S. Nordheimer, with headquarters in Toronto, was the leading firm in the field. A. J. Boucher of Montreal, founded in 1861, is the oldest existing music dealer in Canada, though no longer active as a publisher. Sheet-music publishing assumed respectable proportions towards the end of the century with a yearly average output of some one hundred and fifty items. Though one must regret that publishers paid more attention to utilitarian than to artistic music, it must be admitted that few other household articles provide a better insight into Victorian Canadian society.

Concert reviews became frequent in newspapers and journals about 1850 and the first periodicals to refer to music in their titles were *Le Ménestrel, Journal littéraire et musical* (Quebec, 1844–45) and *L'Artiste* (Montreal, 1860). They were followed by many other short-lived publications, such as the Toronto *Musical Journal* of 1887 and 1888, the first in the English language. Short-livedness, whether for financial or other reasons, has become a chronic ailment of our music journals, defeating even the scholarly and comprehensive *Canadian Music Journal* (1956–62), although at least three flourished for long periods, *Le Passe-Temps* (1895–1948), the *Canadian Music Trades Journal* (1900–32) and *Musical Canada* (1906–33).

Instrument building developed into a lively industry. Perhaps the cost and danger of shipping big instruments across the ocean—to early Manitoba settlements via Hudson Bay and to Victoria via Cape Horn—as well as the abundance of wood in Canada, contributed to the establishment of piano and organ factories.

The pioneer work of the second half of the nineteenth century culminated in a genuine flourishing of music in the opening years of the twentieth. Orchestras, formerly organized primarily as adjuncts to choral societies, now assumed a large degree of independence. Professional, semi-professional, and amateur orchestras were founded in most of the large cities. In solo appearances the amateur gave way to the professional, and many world-famous artists appeared in the cities every season. On the other hand, an astonishing number of amateurs participated in choral singing. Every town from coast to coast had choirs of all possible sizes, for church and concert music, singing *a cappella* or with accompaniment. Toronto claimed to be "the choral capital of North America." This prestige was based on at least five large choral organizations that flourished in the early years of the century: the National Chorus (Albert Ham), the Oratorio Society (Edward Broome), the Schubert Choir (H. M. Fletcher), the Orpheus Society (Dalton Baker) and the Mendelssohn Choir (Augustus Stephen Vogt). The latter was founded, oddly enough, in the very year, 1894, when a thirty-year-old group by the same name in Montreal (Joseph Gould), with an excellent reputation, was disbanded. It is the only one of the choirs just mentioned which survives in Toronto, having been reorganized by its founder on a grander scale in 1900, after a three-year lapse. The variety of tone colour and the discipline of Vogt's choir were likened to those of an orchestra. The Toronto Mendelssohn Choir was the first Canadian ensemble to gain an international reputation.

If Anglo-Canada was a land of choral music, French Canada inclined toward opera. A large musical venture there, crowning decades of pioneer work, was the Montreal Opera Company under Albert Clerk-Jeannotte, which presented opera in various Canadian cities and in Rochester, New York, from 1910 to 1913. It relied heavily on foreign talent. The first season (thirteen operas in seventy-three performances) ended without financial loss in spite of an expenditure of $80,000. Eventually, however, the lack of an adequate hall or theatre in Montreal—remedied only with the opening of La Grande Salle (now Salle Wilfrid Pelletier) in 1963—rendered the Company's continuation financially impossible.

The Canadian west, opened up rapidly after the completion of the transcontinental railway in 1886, found characteristic musical expression in the competition festival, first held in Edmonton in 1908, and in Saskatchewan, Manitoba and British Columbia in the following year. The isolation of many prairie settlements stimulated amateur effort and the annual trip to the festival became an occasion to visit a city and meet old acquaintances.

All in all, Canada had definitely become music-conscious. A British musician, J. Mackenzie-Rogan, wrote after his tour of 1903: "I had no idea until then of the fine taste for music prevailing in the Dominion. I remember it all even now with glowing pride and pleasure. . . ."[24] Canadians themselves also took stock of achievement. This is reflected in the numerous surveys which appeared in reference books. An attempt by J. D. Logan to write our musical history was not carried through, but B. K. Sandwell edited a large volume entirely devoted to the record of music in Montreal from 1895 to 1907. In the field of composition, pride of achievement was evident in the first recital entirely devoted to Canadian music, given in Montreal in 1903.

When war broke out in 1914, choirs and orchestras were seriously depleted and many musical enterprises collapsed. The Toronto Symphony Orchestra, for instance, which had given fine service for almost ten years under Frank Welsman, was disbanded in 1918, and Toronto lacked an orchestra until 1923.

The post-war period was one of fundamental changes. The most obvious ones resulted from technological advance. Mass communication through phonograph, record, radio and, later, television caused a great shift in emphasis in our musical habits. Radio carried music for the first time to distant regions where the appearance of outstanding concert artists was out of the question. For a time at least, amateur participation in musical organizations and music-making at home declined. On the other hand, records and radio introduced to Canadians standards of performance hitherto known to only a limited number —standards which spurred our own musicians to greater efforts. The shift in popularity from vocal to instrumental music may also be partly accounted for by these technological changes. In any case, it is characteristic that the Canadian group with the widest international fame in this period was an instrumental ensemble, the Hart House Quartet of Toronto, which made numerous North American and two European tours.

The former centres of musical life—bands, churches, theatre orchestras and choirs—lost much of their relative importance. The new musical leaders are orchestra conductors, composers,

24. J. Mackenzie-Rogan, *Fifty Years of Army Music* (London, 1926), p. 152.

radio and television producers, concert agents, school and union officials, most of whom have less direct contact with the amateur than had the old leaders.

Hand in hand with professional specialization went the secularization of music. The organist-choirmaster has become less and less the undisputed leader of music in his community. Formerly the musical experience of many Canadians originated in the church service; now it roots largely in the secular music of the radio and other mass distribution media.

The second and third decades of the century also brought into full play the musical talents and traditions of Canadians of other than British or French origin, an obvious consequence of the great influx of immigrants before World War I. Before this time a good many Belgian, German and Italian musicians had settled in Canada as fully-trained professionals; their ranks were now swelled by artists from nearly every European country. But music also began to flourish on the community level among these various immigrant groups. On the whole, the religious and folk traditions of our ethnic minorities have remained quite unassimilated. They are rallying points for preserving old country memories and a cultural identity. The outsider has only a faint idea of the vitality and intensity of the string ensembles, church choirs and folk dance groups of the Ukrainian, Estonian, Icelandic Canadians and many others. He cannot help being aware, however, of the great encouragement these immigrants give to the musically talented among their children. Today our symphony orchestras could not exist without their players of Italian, Jewish and Ukrainian origin.

At the same time, many Canadian artists helped to enrich the musical life of other countries. Fortunately many of these kept up ties with their homeland or returned here in their later years. One thinks of Edward Johnson and Wilfrid Pelletier, both of whom were associated with the New York Metropolitan Opera House, of singers like Pauline Donalda and Raoul Jobin and the violinist Kathleen Parlow.

The twentieth-century trends just described have intensified considerably in the two decades after 1945. The long-playing record has helped the consumption of music to reach enormous proportions; post-war immigration has emphasized the cosmopolitan aspect of the profession. Thirty years ago nearly all music departments of our English-speaking universities were controlled by British musicians. Now they are administered by musicians of a great many different origins. Our two leading symphony orchestras are led by a German and a Czechoslovakian conductor.

Mid-century developments have departed in many ways from previous patterns. This becomes obvious by a consideration of the interrelated themes which we have followed throughout earlier periods: the cohesion of musical activities, the need for patronage and the growth of Canadian identity.

One of the strong points of the years between the two world wars was the presence in Canada of many musicians, native and immigrant, of great musical erudition and general culture, albeit generally quite conservative in musical taste. To recall a few names means to omit others of equal importance: Ellen Ballon, Mona Bates, Claude Champagne, Douglas Clarke, the Cherniavskys, Harry Dean, Jean-Baptiste Dubois, Herbert Fricker, Henri Gagnon, Alberto Guerrero, the Hambourgs, Luigi von Kunits, Jean de Rimanoczy, Hugh Ross, Leo Smith, Reginald Stewart, J. D. A. Tripp and Healey Willan. To these must be added the names of our two elder musical statesmen: Sir Ernest MacMillan, formerly conductor of the Toronto Symphony Orchestra and the Mendelssohn Choir, principal of the Toronto Conservatory and dean of the faculty of music of the University of Toronto and until recently chairman of the Canadian Music Council, and Wilfrid Pelletier, first conductor of Les Concerts Symphoniques of Montreal, director of the Province of Quebec Conservatoire de Musique et d'art dramatique and more recently head of the music department in the Quebec Ministry for Cultural Affairs. To this generation of musicians of international stature many of our orchestras, choirs and university music faculties owe their foundation and their excellence; many of our best known younger artists and composers are their pupils.

The present purpose is not to present a roll of honour, nor even to trace influences from one generation to another, but to note a characteristic difference between two generations. One cannot help observing that, men like MacMillan and Pelletier excepted, the concern of these older musicians ended with their specific professional job well done: a student well trained, a choir well rehearsed. Whether it was a matter of lacking vision or lacking power, few thought in terms of national development as such. The few existing country-wide or regional organizations, such as those of the organists, music teachers and bandmasters were largely concerned with professional interests and standards. Now this isolation of effort has largely broken down; the new type of musician is group-conscious and more intimately concerned with Canadian affairs. The mere fact that we now have organizations in nearly every sphere of musical activity, from composers to librarians, from university administrations to folklore specialists, is of profound consequence. There is discussion between city and city, between province and province; there is also a sharing of artistic experiences, through tours of artists and ensembles and through the nation-wide networks of the CBC.

It is largely through such group effort, such thinking in terms of the musical needs of the country as a whole, that we have moved far to improve the element of patronage and public support. We are fortunate to live in a period of economic prosperity: the musicians of the 1920s and 1930s had to operate on shoestring budgets, there was no money for building concert halls, and opera performances were a rare luxury. Today cultural life has become a public concern, subsidies, scholarships and commissions are forthcoming more frequently, and the resulting benefits are plainly visible.

The growth of a Canadian musical identity was fostered in the 1920s by the re-discovery of folk song. Through the medium of folk song and handicraft festivals and through songbooks, Canadians were made aware of the variety and wealth of their heritage. Our composers were not slow to take an interest in this movement and many of the best of the period arranged or harmonized French or Indian songs: Hector Gratton, Alfred Laliberté, Sir Ernest MacMillan, Leo Roy, Healey Willan and others. Among those using folk music as inspiration for extended compositions Claude Champagne was the foremost figure. Musical nationalism did not develop into a school of composition; nevertheless, many composers of the period did speculate on the possibility of a typically Canadian music in terms of melodic idiom and local flavour. This is true especially of French Canada.

Today relatively few composers are preoccupied with folk music as a basis of a distinct Canadian style of composition. Their orientation is necessarily international, for in view of the widened opportunities of studying abroad and of analyzing contemporary music at home by means of scores and recordings, withdrawal into a nationalistic enclave has become nearly impossible. All major trends of composition are represented in Canada, and many composers have more in common with like-minded colleagues in Europe or the United States than with their fellows teaching at the same conservatory.

Similar developments are taking place in other aspects of musical life. The point of time at which we have reached a fair measure of musical self-sufficiency coincides with the breakdown of cultural barriers between nations. Our inventory includes facilities for professional study and musicological research, we have electronic music laboratories, professional opera and many of the other institutions characterizing musically mature nations. At the same time we experience developments identical with such nations: the enlargement of the concert repertoire (in terms of its span of centuries as well as nations), the growth of summer music festivals and camps, the cultivation of ancient instruments, the experimentation with educational systems such as those of Orff and Kodaly, to mention but a few examples.

Canada has become an active contributor to the mainstream of western musical culture. Does this integration threaten us with a permanent loss of individuality? This need not be feared as long as we continue to cultivate and exploit more fully our artistic resources. Individuality will be a natural result of the process. We should—and we do—explore and make known our regional folklore, revive the best of early Canadian compositions, or search for teaching methods suitable for our specific needs. At the same time we should not neglect to study and make use of techniques and experiences from other countries. Our composers have found inspiration in Canadian scenery, literature and folk song; they have also learned from many a foreign model. What matters is that the last few decades have produced some twenty orchestral works which have had perhaps as many performances each: the beginning of a Canadian repertoire. The character of the best of these works and the personalities of the best composers will ultimately determine the individual characteristics of Canadian music.

Folk and Aboriginal Music

KENNETH PEACOCK

ONE EVENING back in 1960 I heard an aspiring young Canadian folk singer in one of Toronto's newly-opened coffee houses. I enjoyed her singing very much but was somewhat disappointed to learn that her repertoire included only American folk songs and variants, no Canadian. Being a rather militant Canadian myself, I asked her afterwards about this strange oversight and received her astonished (and astonishing) reply: "Are there any Canadian folk songs?" I told her that there are indeed many Canadian folk songs—thousands of them—and immediately supplied her with a list of sources. Since that time she has added dozens of excellent Canadian folk songs to her repertoire and performs them ardently wherever she sings.

I mention this isolated incident not so much to point out a typical Canadian attitude but to indicate how much this attitude has changed, even in the past seven years. The few pioneer professional folk singers of the past generation are now being joined by a growing army of young folk singers whose orientation is becoming more and more Canadian. But my main purpose in mentioning this incident is to emphasize the appalling lack of communication which exists among academic, creative, professional, and traditional musicians interested in Canadian folk music. The folk music field in Canada is so vast and varied that no one person can possibly encompass its boundaries. Quite aside from the above-mentioned problem of providing young professionals with good traditional music, there is the monumental task of conducting basic folk music researches among possibly 100 cultures scattered over an area of nearly 3,700,000 square miles. If we are to do a proper job, the folk music of all these cultures should be collected, documented, archived, transcribed, analyzed, compared, and published in a variety of formats acceptable to both the academic community and the layman.

I am certain this ideal will never be achieved because folk music has a habit of changing even while it is being collected and analyzed. The Eskimo music recorded by Jenness on Edison cylinders in 1914, for example, has either disappeared or has been modified by acculturative processes. All we can really say about a recorded traditional folk song is: "This is the way it was sung by a particular singer in a specific place at a precise moment in time." Folk songs can thus be "frozen" on a sound track or on the printed page and studied at leisure by ethnomusicologists in future generations. They can also give researchers in other disciplines—ethnology, literature, linguistics, history, anthropology, etc.—valuable insights into those cultures which are being assimilated into the general Canadian environment. Possibly most important of all, regional traditional folk songs (which might otherwise have been lost) can be reintroduced into the mainstream of Canadian life via the electronic media so that the re-creative process of oral tradition can be continued on this new level of communication.

But all this is speculation about the future. My main purpose in this essay will be to outline the state of folk music and folk music research in Canada here and now. The essay will be partly historical and partly based on the contemporary folk music research conducted by my colleagues and myself. My research experience among more than twenty-five cultures in Canada might seem to have given me a special sort of insight into Canadian folk music. Quite the contrary. The more I learn about our folk music resources the more I realize how little we actually know. All I can really do is to describe those features of our traditional music which have so far been revealed by research. The remainder still lies hidden beneath the surface and is largely unknown.

Although I began this essay with references to professional folk singers and the "new folk music," I am afraid there will be no space to continue these subjects. I shall deal exclusively with folk music collected from informants living in traditional environments or born and raised in traditional environments. For all practical purposes a traditional environment is one which has experienced a minimum of influence from all the mass communication instruments and techniques of the new technology. Fishing and agrarian communities are good examples of traditional environments. Since Indians and Eskimos live in the culturally most isolated environments I shall discuss their music first.

ABORIGINAL MUSIC

It may stretch the connotations of the word "research" somewhat, but I cannot resist mentioning the four Micmac songs noted in Port-Royal and transcribed into the tonic *sol-fa* system by the French lawyer Marc Lescarbot, who published them in 1609 in his *History of New France*. They were again published in 1635 in Sagard's *Histoire du Canada et Voyages*. Almost three hundred years elapse before the 1898 appearance of the Ontario Archaeological Report which contained thirteen Seneca songs with explanatory notes. The songs were sung by Chief Kanishandan of the Grand River Reserve and were prepared for publication by Alexander Cringan.

It was not until 1910, however, that systematic research on Indian music was begun in earnest by Edward Sapir for the new Anthropological Division of the National Museum of Canada in Ottawa. In 1911 Marius Barbeau, together with a number of other researchers, took over the work of expanding the collection. During the next thirty-five years they recorded approximately three thousand songs on Edison wax cylinders among thirty-one Indian tribes of the Northwest Coast, the Eastern Woodlands, and the Plains. This constitutes the largest early collection of Indian music made in North America. Over fourteen hundred cylinders have since been transferred to magnetic tape, but the bulk of the material remains untranscribed.

The most significant publication to emerge from this collection is Marius Barbeau's "Tsimshian Songs," including seventy-five musical transcriptions and analyses published as part of the larger book *The Tsimshian: Their Arts and Music.* The songs were selected from a collection of two hundred and fifty-one items recorded by Barbeau on the Skeena and Nass Rivers in northern British Columbia from 1920 to 1929, and of four recorded by James Teit in the Yukon in 1915. Barbeau writes:

The custom of the Tsimsyan and their neighbours of singing to words rather than to meaningless syllables, as other Indians frequently do, opens up wide vistas of historical and literary interest. Their songs are valuable for their texts no less than for their melodies. They belong to a world rather apart in America, a world that is reminiscent of Asia and the Pacific. The continued study of our large museum collections of songs from the Northwest Coast will undoubtedly lead to comparisons with similar materials from eastern Asia. It is likely that the genetic relations already hinted at on other grounds between the tribes on both sides of the Bering Sea will meet with further confirmation.

For those who want to follow up these Asian influences further I refer them to Barbeau's interesting but somewhat inconclusive paper, "Asiatic Survivals in Indian Songs," in the *Musical Quarterly* (XX, 1, January, 1934).

So little is known about the music of either the Northwest Coast or Siberian peoples that it is impossible to say at present whether the influence is actual or merely hoped-for. Certainly the seventy-five Tsimshian songs published in Barbeau's monograph offer a fascinating variety of modes and scales. Over a third of them are pentatonic, a few are "modal" (Phrygian, Dorian, Aeolian), some are diatonic or "chromatic." Mme Marguerite Béclard d'Harcourt, who was responsible for the musical analyses, found sixteen songs so complex that it was impossible to classify them. There is a marked difference between songs recorded on the coast and in the mountains. Coastal songs are narrow in compass, sung in a deep, throaty style, and are concerned mostly with rituals and ceremonies. Those in the mountains are more lyrical and are characterized by their high compass and pronounced voice vibrato similar in effect to Plains Indian singing. Future musicological researches on the interrelations among Indian tribes in Canada and their ancestors in Asia will rely heavily on "Tsimshian Songs," a pioneering work on the subject.

Other published material based on the National Museum's wax cylinder collection of Indian songs includes Margaret Sargent McTaggart's "Seven Songs from Lorette," musical transcriptions and analyses of Huron songs recorded by Marius Barbeau early in his career in the village of Lorette, fifteen miles north of Quebec city. The paper was published in the *Journal of American Folklore* (LXIII, 1950). Mrs. McTaggart worked for the National Museum in 1948 and 1949 and began the huge task of transcribing the wax cylinder collection. The eighty-eight Huron-Wyandot and many Iroquois songs she transcribed remain unpublished.

Europeans also showed an early interest in Canadian Indian music. In 1885 a group of Bella Coola Indians from the West Coast visited Germany and sang for the famous psychologist and musicologist Carl Stumpf. "Bella Coola Melodies," together with detailed annotations, was published in 1886 in the journal *Vierteljahrschrift fuer Musikwissenschaft*. Stumpf stressed the importance of investigating the music of relatively simple cultures as a contribution to the history of music, psychology, and aesthetics. Such studies, he stated, would also contribute to anthropological research by offering new indications of relationships and cultural ties between migratory peoples who have lost contact with one another.

Another important German study was "Phonographierte Indianermelodien aus British Columbia" published in 1906 in the *Boas Anniversary Volume*. In this paper Otto Abraham and E. M. von Hornbostel gave transcriptions and analyses of forty-four Thomson River Indian melodies. This was a model study which applied for the first time exact tonometric measurements to the vocal music of "primitives." The measurements seem to indicate that intonation features in exotic music which deviated from modern European standards of "pure" intonation were not due to a crude technique of singing but to consistent tendencies based on certain musical principles inherent in particular cultures. Thus the thesis of "cultural relativity" expounded by the anthropologists of the period was for the first time applied to the field of music.

The vastly superior sound quality of electronic disc and tape recordings heralded a new era in research on aboriginal music in Canada. In 1941 the National Film Board sent Laura Boulton on a cross-Canada tour to make disc recordings of folk music in various ethnic communities, including Indian and Eskimo. Her collection is stored in the sound archives of the Film Board, and copies of some of the material have been made for the folk music archives of the National Museum. Private collectors have also been busy. Ida Halpern's disc and tape recordings constitute the largest and most significant collection of West Coast Indian music made on modern electronic equipment. Kwakuitl and Nootka songs form the bulk of her collection of two hundred and fifty items, which have been catalogued by Margaret McTaggart for the National Museum and are being prepared for publication. With the assistance of Mrs. McTaggart, Dr. Halpern prepared a selection of twenty-eight songs that was released by Folkways Records in 1967 (*Indian Music of the Pacific Northwest Coast*). The booklet accompanying the album contains musical transcriptions and analyses as well as other ethnological data. Another collection of Kwuakiutl music comprising more than one hundred and fifty songs was recorded by the late anthropologist Franz Boas and transcribed, in 1934, by Mieczyslav Kolinski; the material has not yet been published.

Iroquois ritual dances and songs are being meticulously researched by Gertrude Kurath who has developed a set of choreographic symbols to indicate the dance steps and patterns. Musical transcriptions and analyses accompany the choreographic symbols. Her publications include *Iroquois Music and Dance*, *The Iroquois Eagle Dance* (American Bureau of Ethnology), and a Folkways record, *Songs and Dances of the Great Lakes Indians*. Her National Museum publications include *Dogrib Indian Music and Dance* (from the collection of Nancy Lurie) and an exhaustive musical and choreographic study entitled *Dance and Song Rituals of the Six Nations Reserve*.

As usual, the institution most active in Indian music research since the advent of the tape recorder has been the National Museum of Canada. The 532 items I recorded in 1953–54 among various Plains tribes and the Kootenay Indians of British Columbia is the largest single collection in the National Museum's Indian tape archives. For some reason these tribes had been largely overlooked by earlier collectors using Edison wax cylinder equipment. An extensive variety of material was recorded—social dance-songs of various types, secret-society songs, animal and artifact totem songs, war songs, love songs, Cree macaronic songs (in English), the Blackfoot Tobacco Dance ritual, stick-game songs, "personal" songs, souvenir songs, medicine-pipe songs, sun dance songs of various types, and excerpts from an actual two-day Cree sun dance. Selections from this collection have been issued by Folkways Records as *Indian Music of the Canadian Plains*.

Plains Indian songs reveal two quite distinct styles of singing, depending upon whether the songs are ritualistic or social. Ritual songs usually are musically archaic, narrow in range, metrically vague, and rather monotonous to a musically sophisticated ear. Social dance-songs are quite different. The drum beat (duple or triple) is steady, and the compass of the voice fantastically wide. The celebrated high C of operatic tenors is only middle register for some Cree and Blackfoot singers. The dramatic effect is further enhanced by a pronounced voice vibrato, especially on the high tones. It has been suggested that this is an attempt to imitate the howling of the prairie coyote. Be that as it may, the social dance-songs of the Plains Indians are the most dramatic and vocally-acrobatic aboriginal music surviving in Canada today. The scales and modes upon which they are based seem perfectly accessible to the Western-oriented musical ear. The intervals are simple and stable and possess none of the tonal ambiguities researchers have found in other aboriginal cultures. The music of the Kootenay Indians is another matter. Some of their songs are similar to Plains music (they were formerly a Plains tribe who moved into the mountains), but there is an alien musical element which makes some of their songs quite distinctive. I remember particularly a lullaby which had some of the strangest tonal and interval relationships I had ever encountered. Whether this alien element is an archaic survival from the old culture or the result of a later cultural contact remains to be established. This is the sort of ethnomusicological research which remains to be done in Canada on our various aboriginal musical cultures.

The remainder of the National Museum's Indian tape collection consists of music from a variety of tribes, the Iroquois being the most important. The entire Indian tape archive consists of 1,672 items, most of them untranscribed.

Research on Eskimo music has suffered because of the relative inaccessibility of the Arctic and its brutal climatic conditions. Recordings of Eskimo music have usually been made in conjunction with other research, almost as an afterthought. No expedition has so far been sent to the Arctic for the sole purpose of conducting ethnomusicological research, although the National Museum plans to do this in the near future.

The most significant publication on Eskimo music to date is the 1925 book *Songs of the Copper Eskimos*, volume XIV of the *Report of the Canadian Arctic Expedition, 1913–18*. The songs were recorded on Edison cylinders by D. Jenness between 1914 and 1916, either at Bernard Harbour in Dolphin and

Union Strait or at Eskimo settlements in the immediate vicinity. Bernard Harbour was the headquarters of the Southern Party. The songs were recorded from every age group of both sexes. There seemed to be a great preponderance of dance-songs in this area, though Jenness also recorded a few weather and healing incantations. He writes that "there are no work-songs in this region, no chants for the trail or caribou-hunt; no game-songs, although these are fairly common among Eskimos in other places; and practically no rigmaroles or children's chants. Every notable incident, every important experience or emotion in the daily life is recorded in a dance-song . . . ."

The dance-songs recorded from the Copper Eskimos may be divided into two types according to the dances they accompanied, *pisiks* or *atons*. Jenness relied on Eskimo assistants for their classification, and difficulties of communication probably account for the confusion later encountered in elucidating the structural characteristics of each type. Jenness found "that the atons, as a rule, were less formal than the pisiks: that is to say, they were not so palpably built up on the principle of verse, refrain and connective." However, Helen Roberts, who did the musical transcriptions and analyses, could find no differences in the musical structures of the *pisik* and *aton* dance-songs. This is yet another example of the difficulties encountered by ethnologists and musicologists when they seek to transcribe the oral literature and music of exotic cultures into codified structures comprehensible to the analytically-oriented Western mind. In any event, the *pisiks* and *atons* are quite distinguishable as dance forms. The *pisik* is performed by the solo dancer who plays the drum himself, while the rest of the people sing. In the *aton* the drum is played by a member of the audience while the dancer sings and acts out the adventures he experienced during the summer hunt.

With regard to the music itself, Helen Roberts states that the songs are cast either in the major or minor modes or occasionally in a combination of both. Her transcriptions record minute pitch fluctuations by means of special pitch modifying symbols. Whether these pitch fluctuations are actually inherent in the music or are the result of using primitive Edison recording equipment in the sub-zero Arctic of 1914 is beyond conjecture at this time. Certainly her designation of the melodies as simple "major" and "minor" should be accepted only after comparative studies have been made with Eskimo songs recorded on more sophisticated equipment. This may well be impossible considering the immense changes which have taken place in the culture of the Eskimos in the past fifty years. As things stand now, we at least have this early record of one hundred and thirty-seven meticulously transcribed songs, the largest collection of Eskimo music ever published in Canada.

The Eskimo songs in the most recent tape archives of the National Museum cover a much wider variety of material than the music investigated by Jenness and Roberts in *Songs of the Copper Eskimos*. The tapes were recorded by Asen Balikci and Father Rousselière in Pelly Bay, Povungnituk and Iglulik. In addition to traditional material like drum-dances, lullabies, hunting songs, "personal" songs, children's game-songs, animal songs, incantations, and toponymical songs, there are acculturative items like fiddle and jew's-harp tunes. A traditional genre I found particularly interesting are the improvised "throat games" (*kataktatok*) recorded in Povungnituk. These are not actually songs but aspirated and glottal sounds combined in complex rhythms by women performing in pairs when their husbands are away on the hunt. The unique sounds and rhythmic patterns produced are impossible to describe in words or to render into music notation. But these *kataktatok* are only a small portion of the wealth of Eskimo material which lies virtually unexamined in our archives of one hundred and sixteen tapes. In 1963 I prepared some of the material for release by Folkways Records, but so far the record has not appeared.

FRENCH FOLK MUSIC

Early collections of French folk music in Canada include the 1823 publication *Canadian Airs*, collected by Captain Sir George Back during the Arctic expeditions under Captain Sir

John Franklin. In 1830 Edward Ermatinger collected the music and words of ten voyageur songs of the Northwest which are preserved in the manuscript archives of both the National Museum and the Public Archives in Ottawa. The most significant publication of the nineteenth century, however, was Ernest Gagnon's *Chansons populaires du Canada*, a pioneering collection of one hundred folk songs that appeared in 1865. Musicians of the period assumed that Gagnon's collection, small as it was, had virtually exhausted the supply of authentic French folk songs and that the encroachments of "modern" society had dried up the sources of local tradition.

It was not until fifty years later that Marius Barbeau disproved this assumption. Beginning in 1915, Barbeau and his colleagues travelled about French Canada armed with notebooks and Edison machines and found a truly staggering amount of material. Local traditions were as much alive as ever. During a period of fifteen years, over 6,700 French folk songs and variants were noted. These recordings and manuscripts, together with later additions, are housed in the folklore archives of the National Museum where research on French-Canadian folklore and folk music has continued under the leadership of Carmen Roy, director of the Museum's Folklore Division. Dr. Roy's personal tape collection alone runs to some 2,500 folk songs. Musical transcriptions of many of these songs appear in her National Museum publications *Littérature orale en Gaspé* and *Saint-Pierre et Miquelon: une mission folklorique aux îles*. The National Museum's total archive of French folk song—wax cylinders, manuscripts, tapes—now consists of more than 16,000 items. Of these, 2,684 have been transcribed into music notation.

But research on French folk music in Canada has not been limited to the National Museum. Luc Lacourcière, a protégé of Marius Barbeau, has taken over the directorship of les Archives de Folklore at Laval University and, with the assistance of several colleagues, has built it into an institution of international reputation. Like the National Museum, Laval is pursuing French folk music research on all levels—collection, transcription, classification, analysis, and publication. One of the most useful publications to date is Conrad Laforte's immense *Le catalogue de la chanson folklorique française*. Unfortunately, the statistical information I requested on the folk music archives at Laval did not arrive in time for inclusion in this study. All I can say is that the collections are vast, well-documented, and housed under the most modern conditions.

Many English-speaking Canadians will be surprised to learn that a sizeable collection of French folk songs has been made in northern Ontario. Since 1948 Father Germain Lemieux and his students have built an archive of 2,500 French folk songs, collected mostly in the Sudbury area. Originally sponsored by the Société historique du Nouvel-Ontario, Father Lemieux's researches are now carried on under the auspices of the recently formed Institut de Folklore de l'Université de Sudbury, a miniature version of the Archives de Folklore at Laval. Father Lemieux is also planning to investigate the folk music of other ethnic groups living in the area.

It can be seen from the above statistics that French folk music is by far the most intensively researched body of traditional music in Canada. Research has been conducted in all the Atlantic provinces as well as in Quebec and Ontario. The sheer magnitude of the collections and publications precludes any illuminating examination in a short essay, especially by someone like myself whose only first-hand knowledge of French folk song comes from limited research in the Acadian communities of the west coast of Newfoundland. I shall therefore refer to the writings of Marius Barbeau, the dean of French-Canadian folklorists. Instead of using his large and scholarly 1962 book, *Le Rossignol y Chante*, I shall quote from his earlier National Museum publication, *Folk-Songs of Old Quebec*, which appeared in both French and English editions. Speaking of the early recordings he made, Barbeau writes:

Tabulating the first collection of records and comparing them with those of provincial France made it clear that perhaps nineteen out of twenty Quebec songs were fairly ancient; they had come overseas with the seventeenth century immigrants. . . . To this ancient patrimony new songs were added by rustic song-makers. These form purely the Canadian repertory, perhaps only ten per cent of the whole. All the others have come from France more or less in their present state. Some of them were composed during the last three centuries and brought into Canada in the form of broadsheets and books of canticles . . . the bulk of the repertory [was brought by] the early immigrants of New France between 1608 and 1673.

Thus we find three classes of songs: the genuine folksongs of old France, those introduced since 1680 and mostly composed or transmitted by way of writing, and lastly, the true songs of French Canada....

In the past three hundred years, the ancient French tunes in Canada have undergone marked changes. They do not always resemble their French equivalents. Parallels, indeed, are the rare exception, particularly in the old songs; this is partly due to the paucity of French records for comparison....

Because of this melodic fluidity, the tunes in our repertory are more Canadian than the words; their local colour is pronounced, yet they retain a medieval flavour. . . . Singing in the remote districts of Quebec, like Charlevoix and Gaspé, is more archaic than elsewhere, as a result of prolonged isolation and ingrained conservatism. . . .

The true folk-songs arrived in Canada before 1680 with the early settlers from the provinces of Normandy and the Loire river. These songs far exceed all others, and they are incomparably the best. Their style is pure and crisp, their themes clear-cut and tersely developed. Their prosody differs widely from that of the *troubadours* and from literary French. . . . Here is decidedly not the work of untutored peasants, nor a growth due to chance, but the creation of poets whose consummate art had inherited an ample stock of metric patterns and a wealth of ancient lore common to many European races....

The old repertory of folk-songs is quite varied. It does not consist, like that of the Mediterranean border, of lyric songs exclusively, nor of narratives and ballads, like that of Scandinavia. But it is mixed, both types being represented.

The ballads and narratives of the North Sea belong to Normandy and northern France. . . . The lyric songs thrived in southern France and on the Loire river. . . . This contrast between northern and southern France assumed particular significance when it was found that the eastern districts of Quebec had far more ballads and *complaintes* (come-all-ye's) than those of Montreal to the southwest. Quebec proper is predominantly Norman, whereas Montreal owes more to the Loire river.

Much collecting and research has been done since Barbeau wrote these words, and the broad areas he outlined in his early research have been filled with a multitude of detail, both by himself and other researchers in Canada and from France. Song texts and their thematic classification have been the subject of much research, especially at Laval. However, similar musicological studies on the melodies themselves lags far behind, a failing common to all areas of folk music research in Canada.

ENGLISH FOLK MUSIC

The first serious research on English folk music in Canada was done by Roy Mackenzie in Nova Scotia. As a graduate of Harvard University in English and an accomplished musician, Mackenzie was unusually well equipped to pursue folk music researches on both the literary and musical level. However, his main contribution turned out to be literary. In 1909 he and his wife began collecting in the Tatamagouche and River John area where he was born. He told the story of these and later researches in *The Quest of the Ballad*, a book which has since become a classic in its field. In 1928 Harvard University Press published his *Ballads and Sea Songs of Nova Scotia*, which contained one hundred and sixty-two texts and forty-two melodies. Until his retirement in 1952 he taught English at the University of Washington in Missouri and published no further books on his folk music researches before his death in 1957.

Fortunately the work of collecting Nova Scotia folk songs was continued by another pioneer researcher, Helen Creighton. From 1928 to 1942 she financed her own field trips, confining her activities to areas within easy commuting distance of her native Dartmouth. In fact, just about all the material published in her first two books, *Songs and Ballads of Nova Scotia* and *Traditional Songs from Nova Scotia*, was discovered within a thirty-mile radius of Halifax. In 1943–44 and again in 1948, the Library of Congress in the United States supplied her with funds and disc recording equipment to collect Nova Scotia folk songs for its archives. Since 1947 her work has been sponsored by the National Museum and has taken her to New Brunswick and Prince Edward Island as well as Nova Scotia. Her Museum tape archive of English folk song (aside from Gaelic, French, and other songs) consists of 2,027 items.

Between 1957 and 1961 I made 1,250 musical transcriptions from her collection, 1,040 of them in English. Dr. Creighton asked me to grade these songs according to their musical interest, and 170 of the best were published in *Maritime Folk Songs* in 1961. From a purely musical viewpoint, this is probably the finest collection of English folk songs ever published in Canada. The traditional singers represented sing in a variety of styles; sometimes simple, sometimes highly ornate. Most of the melodies chosen were modal, with the Dorian and Mixolydian modes predominating. Other modes are also represented and occasionally combined or chromatically altered to produce tonal and intervalic relationships of the highest interest. As with the aboriginal and French material, however, serious musicological investigation of our English folk music remains to be done.

In many respects Newfoundland is the most valuable laboratory left in Canada for the study of English folk music and folklore. As "England's oldest colony," Newfoundland has preserved a body of archaic survivals and created a host of flourishing local traditions that are unique in North America.

The folk music resources of the island were first investigated in the 1920s by Elizabeth Greenleaf and Grace Mansfield, two American girls from Vassar who published the results of their survey in *Ballads and Sea Songs from Newfoundland*. In 1929–30 Maud Karpeles came from England and collected one hundred and ninety-four English folk songs and variants in manuscript. A photostatic copy of this collection rests in the manuscript archives of the National Museum, and it is soon to be published by Faber and Faber in London. In 1934 thirty songs from her collection were provided with piano accompaniments by Vaughan Williams and others and published by the Oxford University Press as *Folk Songs from Newfoundland*.

In the meantime a local amateur collector, Gerald S. Doyle, had begun collecting Newfoundland songs of local origin, which he published in three booklets in 1927, 1940, and 1955 under the title *The Old-Time Songs and Poetry of Newfoundland*.

Large scale and systematic research on Newfoundland folk music was not undertaken until 1950 when the National Museum sent Margaret Sargent McTaggart to make a preliminary survey in the St. John's area. In 1951 I took over the research and in the next decade travelled to all parts of the island during six summer seasons. The results of my survey were published in 1965 by the National Museum in three large volumes entitled *Songs of the Newfoundland Outports*. This comprehensive survey, the largest of its type ever published in Canada, contains four hundred and eleven different songs and nearly one thousand variant melodies and texts (including forty-two French songs and a few Gaelic). It was designed primarily as a source and reference book for musicologists, professional musicians, students of traditional verse, and historians. Such a book attempts, in effect, to make a private archive available to the greatest number of people, who otherwise would have to spend much time and effort searching the archive individually. Whether or not this is a viable method for publishing folk music materials in Canada remains to be seen. Smaller collections of "polished gems" have the advantage of lower cost and can illuminate specific areas of a musical culture much better. But only a comprehensive collection in all its variety can give a panoramic view of the total folk music scene in a particular area or culture. It is my hope that in Canada we shall be able to continue publishing folk music materials in both formats. The National Museum has not forgotten Labrador in its survey of English-Canadian folk music. The one hundred and thirty-eight songs reproduced in Mac-Edward Leach's *Folk Ballads and Songs of the Lower Labrador Coast* provide valuable material for comparative studies of variants collected elsewhere in North America.

Folk music research in New Brunswick has taken a rather unique turn. Instead of tramping about remote areas with a tape recorder in the classical manner, Louise Manny has reversed things and invites traditional singers from the districts surrounding Newcastle to sing on her weekly radio programme of traditional folk singing which has been running since 1948. Thus, in what is generally considered to be one of Canada's more "backward" areas, an electronic medium is being used to stimulate oral transmission of folk songs. The singers themselves apparently love it. They vie with one another to get the most complete versions of ballads and songs, and all Dr. Manny has to do is turn on her tape recorder or monitor the radio programme. So far she has collected four hundred songs, mostly from the Miramichi area, and is preparing many of them for publication. Interest in traditional folk music has been further heightened by the Miramichi Folk Festival, an annual three-day get-together of traditional singers from the area which Dr. Manny started in 1958. In 1966 a special Children's Festival was added. The Miramichi Folk Festival is unique in Canada and, in recent years, has attracted visitors from all over the continent.

As Canada's most industrialized province Ontario would not seem to be a likely area to conduct researches on traditional folk music. England's Maud Karpeles had noted a few English folk songs in Peterborough in 1929, but it was not until 1956 that Edith Fowke began to reveal Ontario's unsuspected wealth of traditional English folk song. Working mostly in southeastern Ontario, Mrs. Fowke has since amassed a huge body of material that ranks with the finest English collections in North America. Compared with Nova Scotia and Newfoundland, Ontario has not preserved a great number of Child ballads and other early survivals. Mrs. Fowke has so far noted twenty-two Child ballads. On the other hand, the Ontario collection contains an unusually rich selection of British broadsides and American and Canadian ballads. Mrs. Fowke has also recorded songs of other types, many of which have not been reported elsewhere. Musically speaking, the Ontario collection offers much that is of interest; but by and large, it does not match the East Coast collections in this respect. The percentage of modal and pure pentatonic survivals is lower, and the highly ornate style of singing practised by several traditional singers in the Atlantic provinces does not seem to have survived in Ontario. This is probably the result of the preponderance in Ontario of broadsides and other more recent songs and ballads that are nearly always cast in the later diatonic modes.

Long known as a popularizer of folk songs through her numerous radio broadcasts and song books, Edith Fowke has acquired over the years a truly encyclopedic knowledge of English folk song texts in publications, manuscripts, and on discs. This knowledge has served her well in her latest and best book, *Traditional Singers and Songs from Ontario,* a collection of sixty-two exhaustively researched song texts with musical transcriptions by Peggy Seeger.

As we move further west we find our knowledge of English folk song becoming increasingly vague. Barbara Cass-Beggs and Richard Johnston have done some collecting in Saskatchewan, but so far their findings have been inconclusive. Mrs. Cass-Beggs reports that "there were few Child ballads, more of the British broadsides and quite a few American ballads." In British Columbia, Philip Thomas has collected in the Interior and on the Gulf Islands. He has uncovered some folk music of local origin, but the material, as I heard it in 1962, did not have the musical or literary interest of the eastern collections. This is corroborated by the British Columbia survey conducted in 1966–67 by Fern Pickering and Ken Peterson for the National Museum. Of course, any of the western provinces may suddenly blossom forth as a prime area for English folk music research, as Ontario did in the 1950s, but I think this is highly unlikely considering the dearth of good material so far collected. However, the results of the latest Pickering-Peterson survey may cause me to modify my somewhat pessimistic appraisal of the English situation in the West. I hope so.

ETHNIC FOLK MUSIC

Although all traditional music in Canada is "ethnic," I am using this term only in reference to language and racial groups other than Indian, Eskimo, French, and English. These include all the peoples who emigrated from Europe and Asia during and since the nineteenth century. The one exception are the Gaelic-speaking Scots who arrived earlier and whose ethnic folk music was the first to be investigated.

Cape Breton is the centre of Gaelic culture in Canada, and one hundred and twenty-three of the one hundred and forty-eight Gaelic songs in the tape archives of the National Museum were recorded there. Edith Fowke and George Proctor have also recorded Gaelic songs in Ontario, and I have a few from Newfoundland. In 1964 the National Museum published Helen Creighton's *Gaelic Songs in Nova Scotia* with Gaelic texts and English translations by Calum MacLeod and musical transcriptions by myself and others. Of all the types of Gaelic songs found in Cape Breton those used at so-called "milling frolics" are the best known. Several people, grouped around a sturdy table, alternately knead and pound a length of wet wool homespun to the accompaniment of a milling song. The table, in effect, becomes a huge drum. A leader sings the verses of the song, and everyone joins in the refrain. These "wild Celtic airs," sung to the slow, steady boom of the table-drum, generate a musical excitement that belies the dour and reserved qualities we sometimes attribute to the Scot.

Little was known about the *traditional* folk music of our smaller ethnic communities until 1962 when I began making surveys in central and western Canada for the National Museum. I emphasize the word *traditional* because the "folk music" performed by the choirs and instrumental groups of various ethnic communities at festivals, banquets, and so on is really a type of concert folk music analogous to the "new folk music" our English and French professional folksingers perform in coffee houses and on radio and television. Again, what I was searching for among the smaller ethnic groups was authentic traditional folk music performed by informants living or born in traditional environments. As a consequence, the first researches were conducted in the agrarian communities of central and western Canada, where various ethnic communities have been established for several generations. During my preliminary survey of 1962 I made sample recordings of folk music among sixteen ethnic communities—Chinese, Croatian, Doukhobor, Dutch, Finnish, Hungarian, Hutterite, Icelandic, Japanese, Lithuanian, Mennonite, Negro, Norwegian, Polish, Sikh, and Ukrainian. The results were overwhelming. Here was a completely new frontier for the study of folk music materials in Canada. As was suspected beforehand, the Slavic communities, especially Doukhobor and Ukrainian, had preserved their traditional music to a greater degree than any of the others.

In 1963 and 1964 the bulk of my research was conducted in more than twenty Doukhobor communities scattered across western Canada from the Manitoba-Saskatchewan border to British Columbia. Nearly five hundred religious and secular folk songs of various types were recorded. Pending detailed literary and musicological research on this large collection, I have prepared an introductory outline entitled *Songs of the Doukhobors* published by the National Museum in 1968. The book contains fourteen choral transcriptions of religious songs and thirteen secular folk songs sung in solo, duet, and trio form. Texts are in Russian and in English translation. Since no publications have been issued by Soviet Russia on Doukhobor folk music, this is the first time their singing will have been transcribed into music notation. This statement is not strictly accurate, for I have included five Doukhobor songs in my *Twenty Ethnic Songs from Western Canada*, which the National Museum published in 1966. (The book also contains folk songs of Mennonite, German, Hungarian, Ukrainian and Czech origin.)

The choral and part-singing of the Doukhobors is confined strictly within the limits of oral tradition. They have no written music and no choral directors. I must admit that when I first heard their complex choral singing I was constantly on the alert for evidences of surreptitious musical arrangements and ghost conductors. None ever appeared. Their musical culture is completely oral. Of course, such sophisticated choral and part-singing does not arise spontaneously. Preliminary research indicates the influence of Russian Orthodox Church music at various periods since proto-Doukhobor sects began to break away from the mother Church in the fifteenth century. Then there is the influence of Bazilewski, a Church father who, almost two hundred years ago, defected to the Doukhobors at the Tavria colony and helped them preserve the ancient forms of singing which they still practised. Even so, to have projected these ancient musical forms via oral tradition into the alien environment of Canada in the mid-twentieth century is an astounding cultural feat.

But the Doukhobors have not been content merely to preserve the musical heirlooms of the past. Since coming to Canada at the turn of the century they have composed a large body of contemporary hymns, all in the old Russian style. They have also borrowed hymns from non-Russian sects like the Mennonites and Baptists, but sing them in Russian in their own inimitable style. Still, this seems to me the weakest part of their repertoire, both from a musical and a literary viewpoint. The purely Russian repertoire is far superior. Recreational material includes a sizeable body of secular folk song drawn from Russian folk tradition—ballads, lyric songs, and lullabies.

The earliest body of traditional music and literature surviving in Doukhobor tradition are the so-called "psalms" which, while based occasionally on Biblical materials, have no relationship to the Psalms of the Bible. They were composed mostly by the Doukhobors themselves or were inherited from proto-Doukhobor fundamentalist sects at an early period. Psalm-singing is practised in its most authentic form only by Doukhobor elders. The unison melody is embellished with primitive contrapuntal devices, but occasionally the structure bursts forth into a "daring" major or minor triad. Both music and texts are unmetrical. Staggered breathing is used quite unconsciously to produce a continuous flow of sound. The words and syllables of the text are stretched over fantastically long melodic time spans. In one psalm it takes about eleven minutes to sing just five words. Nowadays, only the first few words of a psalm are sung and the remainder is recited by a member of the congregation.

Early, transitional, and contemporary Doukhobor hymns (a genre distinct from the psalms) have symmetrical texts and melodies. There is no staggered breathing. The musical structures are primarily harmonic, though gifted members of the congregation provide contrapuntal parts above or below the melody. The sound produced is quite different from the familiar S A T B voice spacing of the chorale-type hymn heard in our churches. In Doukhobor singing, the melody is seldom on top. Transcribing Doukhobor choral music into music notation is often a nightmare, especially since the microphone tends to pick up the higher contrapuntal voice parts more readily than the inner melody sung by the greater mass of the congregation. The solo, duet, and three-part renditions of Russian folk songs are much easier to transcribe, even when the melody is in the lower part. The variety and complexity of Doukhobor part-singing offers a fascinating field for future musicological studies, and it is for this reason that I have discussed their music at some length.

Folk part-singing on a more modest scale was also practised in certain parts of the Ukraine. A few survivals were found in Canada by the late Mrs. T. Koshetz, former curator of the museum at the Ukrainian Cultural and Educational Centre in Winnipeg. In 1950 Mrs. Koshetz visited several Ukrainian communities in central and western Canada and collected about two hundred folk songs, noting both texts and melodies. A photostatic copy of her pioneering collection is in the manuscript archives of the National Museum. In the 1950s Professor Jaroslav Rudnyckyj began publishing a series of linguistic and dialectological studies on Ukrainian folk-song texts, a valuable reference work for folklorists despite the omission of musical transcriptions.

It was not until 1963, however, that Robert B. Klymasz began large-scale folk-music and folklore researches in the Ukrainian communities of the prairie provinces. Since then he has recorded well over a thousand folk songs on tape from about one hundred and seventy-five individual informants living in the Dauphin, Yorkton, and Vegreville areas of Manitoba, Saskatchewan, and Alberta respectively. His research was sponsored by the Canada Council and the National Museum. He has provided the National Museum with three excellent monographs on various aspects of his Ukrainian research—*A Bibliography of Ukrainian Folklore in Canada, 1902–1964*, *The Ukrainian-Canadian Immigrant Folksong Cycle in Canada* and *The Ukrainian Winter Folksong Cycle in Canada*. Musical transcriptions accompanying these monographs have been done by Walter Kymkiw and myself. The monographs will be published by the National Museum in the near future.

The Ukrainian research conducted by Robert Klymasz has revealed a wealth of folk-music material of surpassing significance. Ukrainian folk music is especially rich in ritual survivals. Songs connected with the wedding ritual are particularly numerous and varied. So are those concerned with the winter cycle (Christmas carols, New Year's songs), the spring cycle (Easter songs), healing rituals (incantations), and mortuary rituals (funeral laments). The survival of these and other archaic items, many of them traceable back to pagan times, has been facilitated by the absence in the Ukraine of broadside presses which in Britain and France submerged much of the ancient lore under a flood of printed material, much of it of poor quality. There is also a large body of Ukrainian ballads and historical songs, as well as numerous immigrant and macaronic songs of recent Canadian origin. The musical significance of this large and varied Ukrainian collection is beyond my knowledge at present. However, the relatively small portion of the collection I am familiar with would lead me to place it on a par with anything yet recorded in Canada.

Ideally, each ethnic community should be researched by a highly trained person who, like Robert Klymasz, speaks the language of the culture and has a good background knowledge of its folklore. In the absence of such qualified researchers in Canada, I have undertaken folk-music surveys for the National

Museum in several ethnic communities with the assistance of local interpreters and translators. The method is slow and far from perfect, but at least it does permit the recording and documentation of folk-music items for a variety of ethnic archives which, hopefully, will be researched by qualified specialists in the future. The important thing at the moment is getting the material on tape before it disappears. Our programme at the National Museum also involves the transcription of music and texts, the latter in both the original languages and in English translation. A series of small publications devoted to the folk music of various cultures in Canada is also planned. Aside from my *Twenty Ethnic Songs from Western Canada* (which contains folk songs from several cultures), the first publications to be released will be the Doukhobor and Ukrainian studies mentioned above. In the meantime, folk-music research is being carried on in several other cultures.

In southern Ontario, I have recorded two hundred and sixty-five Lithuanian folk songs with the assistance of Danute Rautins. Careful selection of traditional singers and materials has netted a wide variety of genres, some of which are rare or non-existent in other cultures. Of special interest are the uniquely Lithuanian *sutartine*, polyphonic work songs performed in the old culture by several women as they did their daily farm chores together. Mostly in canonic forms, these "tonal games" are characterized by clashing and parallel seconds, that give them a remarkably "contemporary" sound. The male counterpart of the *sutartinė* is the "dissonant" polyphonic music performed on *skudučiai*, single-toned pipes of various lengths. A Canadian innovation in the manufacture of these folk pipes is the use of bamboo with its natural joints to provide closed ends.

Most of my Hungarian research has been done in Saskatchewan where the first agrarian settlements of any size were established before the turn of the century. Maria Trebuss and I have so far recorded about one hundred and fifty Hungarian folk songs. In Manitoba most of my Icelandic research has been confined to the "New Iceland" communities west of Lake Winnipeg where I recorded one hundred and thirty-four Icelandic songs with the assistance of Kristine Kristofferson. Japanese research has been conducted in Ontario and British Columbia, but most of the one hundred and eleven vocal and instrumental recordings come from southern Ontario where I had the assistance of Martha Takata. Other brief surveys have produced sixty-nine Finnish items from the Lakehead district of Ontario, sixty Mennonite songs of secular origin from southern Manitoba, thirty-one Negro spirituals and gospel songs from southwestern Ontario, twenty-five Norwegian items from Alberta and British Columbia, and a smattering of vocal and instrumental pieces from various other ethnic groups. The total National Museum archive of ethnic folk music comprises about 2,400 items at present.

A significant development at the National Museum is the recent establishment of a new ethnic folklore research programme under which specialists for each ethnic group are being imported to conduct scholarly research in specific areas and cultures. The programme was initiated in 1967 with three projects: Finnish folklore in the Lakehead area investigated by Matti Salo of Finland, Icelandic folklore in Manitoba by Magnus Einarsson of Iceland, a Macedonian-Bulgarian survey in Toronto by Philip Tilney of the United States. This new programme is under the direction of Robert Klymasz, who recently joined the staff of the National Museum to assist Dr. Carmen Roy in the expansion of the Folklore Division's research activities. If the reports submitted by the initial researchers are an indication, then this new programme heralds a whole new era of folklore and folk music research in Canada.

MUSICAL INSTRUMENTS

Musical instruments play an important role in the folk music of many Canadian cultures, especially Indian and Eskimo. The National Museum began collecting aboriginal instruments early in the century when they were comparatively numerous. Its Indian collection now consists of nine hundred and eighteen musical instruments, most of them whistles, rattles, and drums. The Eskimo collection is much smaller, forty-four instruments. In 1964–65 Margaret McTaggart catalogued for the first time the large collection of Indian musical instruments in the Anthropological Museum of the University of British Columbia. This was done for the Canadian Folk Music Society's *National Bibliography of Canadian Folkmusic*, a card-index file in the National Museum which is being expanded considerably and prepared for publication by the Canadian Folk Music Society.

In English and French Canada the violin is the principal folk instrument and is used mostly for dancing. Traditional songs are usually sung unaccompanied. Other cultures have richer instrumental traditions. To conserve space I give the following list of musical instruments that have been noted during the course of folk-music research among various cultures in Canada. Recent additions to the National Museum's collection of musical instruments, acquired mostly through donation, are marked by an asterisk (*).

Drums: Indian, Eskimo, Chinese, Sikh (*tabla*)

Rattles: Indian, Eskimo, Sikh (*khartal*)

Sticks: Indian, Eskimo

Bullroarers: Indian, Eskimo

Snappers: Indian

Horns: Indian, Eskimo, English, Finnish, Lithuanian

Whistles: Indian, English

Gongs and cymbals: Chinese

Flutes and pipes: Indian, Ukrainian (**sopilka*), Japanese (**shakuhachi*), Hungarian (*tarogato*), Yugoslavian (*frula*), Polish (*fujarka*), Finnish (*kukkopilli*), Lithuanian (*skudučiai*) nian, 7 (*skudučiai*)

Bagpipes: Scottish, Czechoslovakian (*dudy*), Polish (**dudy*, **koziol*, **siesienki*)

Violin: French, English, Scottish, Norwegian (**8-stringed Hardanger fiddle), Métis, Indian, Eskimo

Zither (plucked): Finnish (**kantele*), Lithuanian (**kanklés*), Japanese (*koto*)

Dulcimer (played with hammers): Ukrainian (*cymbaly*), Hungarian (*cimbalom*)

String instruments (bowed): Ukrainian (*lira*), Polish (**gesle*), Yugoslavian (*gusle*)

String instruments (plucked): Ukrainian (**kobza, bandura*), Japanese (**shamisen*), Chinese (moon "harp")

CONCLUSION

The musical life of a nation depends heavily on its folk-music resources. We in Canada have been blessed with a particularly rich array of folk-music materials. First there is the music of our original Indian and Eskimo cultures; then the traditional music of our two founding races, French and English; and finally, the folk music of all the European and Asiatic peoples who have come to Canada in more recent times. The preservation of these musical resources is something of which we can be justly proud. Our French collections are unrivalled anywhere, and our English and aboriginal collections rank with the finest in the world. And the researches currently being pursued in our smaller ethnic communities are beginning to illuminate vast new areas of our folk-music resources.

However, the mere preservation of a resource has no significance in itself. The resource must be used constructively and creatively on a national scale. Only a small proportion of our traditional folk music has been made available to the academic community, the creative musician, and the public at large. The problem is one of communication. The relatively few books and recordings that have been published on authentic Canadian folk music give little indication of the wealth of material that lies unexamined in our archives. This also raises the problem of manpower. Up to the present, folk-music research in Canada has largely been carried on by a few dedicated individuals working in comparative isolation. Few institutes of higher learning offer courses where students may learn the techniques of collecting, documenting, archiving, transcribing, analysing, and publishing folk-music materials. There is no institute of ethnomusicology. The miracle of it all is that we have done as well as we have in preserving and disseminating our traditional folk music.

This miracle has been wrought largely by dedicated individuals and by the National Museum, the only institution in Canada conducting folk-music studies on a national scale among all ethnic communities. Les Archives de Folklore at Laval, probably our most sophisticated laboratory for the study of folk-music materials, has conducted excellent research on French folk music. The Canada Council has been an active sponsor of folk-music projects. The Canadian Folk Music Society recently has launched a national programme of folk-music research and publication under a series of grants from provincial governments. All these individual researchers, institutions, and organizations have brought Canadian folk-music research to its present level of achievement. What we need now is not only a continuation of basic folk-music research but the establishment of some sort of network of communication whereby the results of these researches can be made available to institutes of higher learning, to creative musicians, and to the public at large. Only then will the folk music of our disparate cultures receive the scientific, creative, and popular attention it deserves.[1]

1. I should like to thank Helen Creighton, Louise Manny, Edith Fowke, Father Germain Lemieux, Barbara Cass-Beggs, Robert Klymasz, Ida Halpern, and Margaret McTaggart for sending me the latest information on their folk-music researches and collections. I am especially indebted to Carmen Roy for her kind co-operation in providing information on the folk-music archives at the National Museum.

The History of Canadian Composition 1610-1967

ANDRÉE DESAUTELS

"La tradition, n'est pas de refaire ce que
les autres ont fait, mais de retrouver
l'esprit qui a fait ces grandes choses,
et qui en ferait de tout autres en d'autres
temps."

Paul Valéry

THE FIRST PERIOD
1610–1760

Canadian composition is largely influenced by the ethnic background of the people who created the country both physically
and spiritually. It is also deeply affected by geographical factors, by the sheer size of a country that is smaller only than
Russia, by wide open spaces where silence reigns and loneliness
descends upon the settler. Vast landscapes, not to be measured
on any human scale, impress themselves on painters, poets and
musicians. Engraved on the memory, such impressions—or

"inner landscapes" if you will—contribute their share to the musical awakening of the country and offer in part an explanation for the diversity of our musical idiom. Neither European (in the Continental sense of the word) nor American (as the term is understood in the United States), yet Europeans of this country and Americans in their own right, Canadians are the fortunate heirs of ethnic traditions which are the guarantors of independence and originality.[1]

Canada is a young country where present and future loom larger than the past; it has nevertheless four hundred years of music-making to its credit—while the first hesitant efforts made in the United States date only from the beginning of the eighteenth century. To come to grips with our own time we must adopt a wider view. Whether we turn to history proper, to ethnomusicology or stylistic analysis, they all bear out the contention that our musical history is the story of conquests and retreats, of withdrawals and delays, sometimes also of re-discoveries.

Even to-day we are overshadowed by the past, in all our artistic endeavours—by a past that was a perpetual challenge to our political destiny. Before the Treaty of Utrecht, New France (consisting of the French part of Newfoundland, Acadia, Hudson Bay, Louisiana and Canada itself) had been a political and economic entity of surprising proportions and importance. "Seventeenth and eighteenth century Canada is not at all a feudal colony, but the land there is possessed by seigneurial right; as a result of this regime two social classes that are practically unknown in the English colonies exist in Canada: the seigneurs and the copyholders," writes Guy Fregault.[2]

No wonder that the French influence was the first to be felt in the history of Canadian composition. Around 1610–1612 already, the first page of music to be written on Canadian soil, the first composition to see the light in North America, appeared at Port Royal. It bears the signature of Jean Biencourt,

1. Andrée Desautels, "Les Trois Ages de la Musique au Canada," in *Larousse de la Musique*, Tome II (Paris, 1965), p. 314.
2. G. Fregault, *La Société canadienne sous le régime français* (Publication de la Société historique du Canada, No. 3, 1954).

called "Baron de Poutrincourt," Lord of Picardy, who had explored the coast with Champlain in 1604 and 1606. It is important to emphasize that the brilliance of seventeenth-century France was to leave its mark on this first period of artistic life in Canada. It is also significant that music written during the seventeenth and early eighteenth centuries was of the ecclesiastical variety and predominantly modal such as the Prose Sacrae Familiae by Amador Martin (1684).[3]

The exceptionally high quality of French-Canadian musical culture during that period can be inferred from a list of works performed in the first basilica of New France; the School of Versailles was represented as well as the Chapel Royal. Among those whose works were heard on the banks of the St. Lawrence were Henri Dumont (maître de chapelle of Louis XIV) and Jean Baptiste Morin (1677–1745) attached to the household of the Duke of Orléans. Morin was one of the earliest composers to write French Cantatas; in 1708 when Louis XIV visited Fontainebleau he produced a *Chasse de Cerf*. André Campra must also be mentioned, he was one of the leading figures in the School of Versailles; it seems that his works were quite frequently performed in Quebec.[4]

No doubt our history is deeply influenced and vitally affected by the music of France so characteristically French in style and content. Modal traditions (Gregorian in origin) re-appear time and again, always a fructifying source of music written in Canada. They left their imprint on French-Canadian folklore and on the first scores written in North America; we re-discover them in the works of French-Canadian composers from Guillaume Couture to Claude Champagne (*Suite Canadienne*) and François Morel (*Antiphonie*), to name only those few. A preference for modal writing, for an ambiguity of tonal functions due to modal inflections, for rhythmic subtlety (a hallmark of French mediaeval music, a distinguishing trait of Fauré, Debussy and Ravel) are conspicuous characteristics of some

3. E. Gagnon, *La Musique à Québec au temps de Mgr de Laval* (la Nouvelle France, 1908).
4. Andrée Desautels, "Les Trois Ages de la Musique au Canada," in *Larousse de la Musique*, Tome II (Paris, 1965), p. 314.

French-Canadian composers. To which we might add that the neo-modalism of a Messiaen or a Jolivet (a modalism with polyharmonic tendencies) finds many disciples in Quebec, who are no less interested in recent discoveries concerning rhythm, timbre and dynamics.

Thus it is French modal writing that dominates our musical history from the start.

THE SECOND PERIOD: A MUSICAL COLONY
(1763–1918)

In 1759–1760, New France was conquered by the English, to whom she was formally ceded by the French according to the Treaty of Paris (1763). Its political, social, and cultural fabric was adversely affected by this defeat. Although the two predominant ethnic groups were of French and Anglo-Saxon origin, certain minority groups, composed of Germans, Ukrainians, Scandinavians and Dutch—whose diversified cultures had no common denominator—nevertheless helped to build musical life, if not at the level of composition, at least in that they made European music take root on Canadian soil.

The ethnic and political complexities prevalent in Lower Canada around 1800 stimulated and paralyzed cultural developments in turn. We must remember that Lower Canada in 1800 corresponded roughly to the present-day Province of Quebec, including the coast of Labrador (some years ago ceded to Newfoundland) but without the territory belonging to the Hudson's Bay Company.

What was Lower Canada really like in 1800? A society à la Rousseau? Or a prudish one, severe, rigid like a Quaker colony? Should we think of Quebec and Montreal as of flourishing cities harbouring merchant princes comparable to those of Genoa, Florence or Antwerp at the time of the Renaissance, inhabited by rich, intelligent and sophisticated people surrounding themselves with art treasures imported from Europe at great expense? Nothing could be further from the truth. Lower Canada was as yet a small colony of slight importance with a population of approximately two hundred thousand, there were only three cities worth mentioning: Quebec, Montreal and Trois-Rivières. Toward the end of the 18th century

Quebec had fourteen thousand inhabitants, Montreal eighteen thousand and Trois-Rivières twelve hundred. . . . In Quebec we find artisans of every description: harness makers, blacksmiths, carpenters, carters, tanners, painters, bakers, mattress-makers, barbers, perfumers and spruce beer merchants—a host of unhurried craftsmen, skilled and compliant. Architects who had no formal training erected buildings that were solid as well as beautiful; small shipbuilders, goldsmiths and sculptors without any letters of patent knew their metier and exercised it with consummate taste. A dancing master was also there—a few schoolmasters, the professors teaching at the seminary and the convent of the Ursuline sisters, and two music masters. But what on earth can they have taught, seeing that Philippe Aubert of Gaspé tells us that there existed no more than three pianos in Quebec city, one belonging to bishop Mountain, the other two owned by the Lanaudières and the Babys? The violin no doubt, also singing, harpsichord, harp and guitar.[5]

It was an important event in Canadian musical history when our first comic opera appeared. Its author—Joseph Quesnel (1749–1809)—was rather a strange character. He composed an opera called *Lucas et Cécile*, wrote a one-act play entitled *Le dîner à l'anglaise* (a satire on English manners); his best known work, however, is *Colas et Colinette*, a comedy à la Molière turned into a comic opera. In his works one finds reminiscences of Grétry, Philidor and Monsigny, whom he tries to imitate. *Colas and Colinette* includes airs and duets; only the vocal and second violin parts have been preserved; the style resembles the "comédie mêlée d'ariettes" much favoured in Paris during that time, a time which marks the beginning of a decline in French music. *Colas et Colinette* was composed in 1788 and first performed in Montreal in 1790.[6]

One of the dominant figures in this second period of Canadian composition was Antoine Dessane (1826–1873). He was born in France and studied at the Paris Conservatoire before becoming the organist of the Quebec Basilica. It was Dessane—a highly cultured musician—who made Canadians familiar with the work of César Franck. His manuscripts reveal a composer

5. Gérard Parizeau, *Mémoires de la Société Royale du Canada*, Quatrième série, Tome I (1963), pp. 188, 190.
6. Helmut Kallmann, *A History of Music in Canada 1534–1914* (Toronto, 1960), p. 65.

of quality and a skilled craftsman. His output, one of the most considerable of the period, includes several settings of the mass and a Suite for large orchestra (1863) which places him in the tradition of Franck; the Suite is remarkable for its vivid expression and subtle modulations.

At the turn of the century we encounter three men who had much in common: they were ardent patriots eager to develop Canada's musical life as a whole; yet they were also composers of note—Calixa Lavallée (1842–1891), Guillaume Couture (1851–1915) and Alexis Contant (1858–1918). These men were responsible for a return to the French tradition in music education as well as in writing. Although musicians of Anglo-Saxon and German origin, such as Glackemeyer (1751–1836) and Théodore Molt (1796–1856), had made an exceptional contribution to the musical life of French Canada, there is no doubt that we must pay homage to Lavallée and Couture for leading the fight for better education and for restoring French supremacy in the field of composition. They fought on several levels, just as Saint-Saëns and Theodore Dubois did in France. In one sense their work marks the end of a period; in another it signals the beginning of a new age.

It was only natural that composers born in Canada and raised in the French tradition would wish to write music in the French style, just as certain composers of the Boston group of the same period patterned themselves directly on European models. The same is true of certain composers born in the province of Ontario, such as Wesley Octavius Forsyth (1859–1937) who studied in Vienna and Leipzig and whose works, which were numerous even for the period (more than seventy opus numbers), are in the Austrian romantic tradition. A skilful contra puntist whose compositions reflect the rigorous application of scholastic fugal writing, Forsyth had the privilege, rare among Canadian composers, of being published not only in his own country, but also in Germany, England and the United States.

French masters such as Bazin, Boieldieu the younger, and Marmontel left their mark on Calixa Lavallée. It is said that in

1874 a symphony of his, of which all trace has been lost, was performed in Paris. During the time he spent in Boston as organist and choir master of the cathedral, he devoted himself more and more to composition. Several of his works were published in Boston, such as pieces for piano, band music, works for the theatre, and finally a comic opera, *The Widow* (1882), which was successfully presented in a number of American cities. The next year, as a gesture of thanks to the City of Boston, he dedicated to it a symphony for choir and orchestra (it has also disappeared).

Lavallée's work as a dedicated musician and patriot is just as important as his work as a composer. His output reflects the taste of the period as well as the demands of his public. He tried his hand at all forms of music, from simple songs to piano pieces, cantatas, symphonies, and comic operas. His knowledge of instruments, his experience as a performer, his travels, his endeavours to raise funds and his efforts towards building an organized musical life in Canada make him an important figure in this second period. Though somewhat superficial at times, he was certainly a devoted and sincere musician.

Among the composers who dominate the scene during this last part of the nineteenth century, Guillaume Couture deserves a special place. There is a marked difference between his early pieces written in Paris and the works of his maturity. Among the latter one could mention *Memorare*, *Rêverie*, *Fugue for Quartet*, *Grande Fugue* for organ with harmonies reminiscent of Franck, and a cantata, *Atala*; three religious works: *O Salutaris*, *Adorate*, and *Tantum ergo*, which he wrote between the ages of 23 and 26. When he was over fifty he composed a Requiem Mass, but four years before his death he had doubts about its orchestration. Théodore Dubois reassured his disciple: "You speak to me about your Requiem. Yes, your orchestration need not be changed; it is simple and will sound well. The feeling of this Requiem is excellent, it should be very effective in performance if care be bestowed on it."

It is undeniable that Couture owes the faultless elegance of his style to the French school, but he was not insensitive to

Handel's large frescoes of sound nor to Franck's exhilarating harmonies, as some passages in his work readily show. An ardent defender of Wagner, he became keenly interested in certain problems of musical aesthetics and discussed them with Fauré, Massenet, d'Indy, Saint-Saëns, Lalo and Bizet at their Monday evening gatherings in Paris. This group, which considered as its mission to liberate French art from the "Meyerbeerism" which had besieged Paris for more than half a century, did not prevent Couture from becoming an enthusiastic Wagnerian upon his return to Montreal.

His last work, *Jean le Précurseur* (composed between 1906 and 1911) is a religious poem divided into three parts. The first, "The Nativity," which is pastoral in character, is based on a Gregorian melody; the second one "The Prédilection," begins with the liturgical theme—*Attende*. The last part is entitled "The Martyrdom." The contrapuntal writing shows great skill, the choruses are not lacking in vitality or dramatic power, but the work as a whole is not sufficiently focused and is rather verbose. Because of the composer's failing health, the orchestration had been entrusted to Paul Puget, a French musician chosen by Dubois.

The exploits of Debussy—a turning point in the history of harmony, of texture and form—made little impression on Couture. His models were Théodore Dubois, Vincent d'Indy and several German-oriented composers, all of them rather academic in outlook. It was left to the next generation to make use of Debussy's and Ravel's vocabulary, to explore the newly created world of harmonies and tone colours. Yet in spite of his adherence to tradition, in spite of his academic, almost scholastic attitudes Couture commands admiration and respect.

Also in the European tradition is the work of Alexis Contant (1859–1918). He took some lessons from Couture (a few years his senior) but they soon separated; the pupil rejected the master's approach to harmony and counterpoint. Contant went to Lavallée for advice, but on the whole he was an autodidact, acquiring his craft by studying Bach, Weber, Wagner, Saint-Saëns, Gounod, Massenet and Franck. A man of integrity, he was not afraid to confess "I find too many imperfections in my previous masses, too many reminders of my studies." And to those who were critical of his cautious conservatism, he replied: "It seems that our people are still unprepared for the audacities sometimes to be found in modern writings." "And," he added, "I prefer to follow masters of melody such as Gounod, whom I shall always admire." It must be admitted that certain of his melodies reveal too much of Gounod's influence.

His most important works are, without doubt, his large frescoes for choir and orchestra. In 1903 he wrote a concert mass—his first great success as far as the public was concerned. The mass follows the tradition of his European masters; he admits it himself: "My mass does not have those modern characteristics which I sometimes admire in others." However, Achille Fortier (a musician as well as a critic) wrote in *La Patrie* (January 1903): "The Agnus Dei, to my mind, is the best part of this Mass. The harmonies are rich and skilfully arranged; the orchestration is successful and the movement makes the kind of impression which only true Art is able to produce." The critic concludes: "A solidly constructed composition; a work of sterling quality full of inspiration that produces highly expressive, beautifully balanced melodies supported by harmonies that are both eminently suitable and restrained."

Cain, first performed in 1905, marks an important date in our history, because it is the first Canadian oratorio. A choir of two hundred and fifty voices, five soloists, and an orchestra of fifty formed an ensemble which was quite astonishing for the period. The work contains three parts: "Hate," "Blood," and "The Promise," preceded by an overture.

As Romain Gour observes, in addition to retaining in this first oratorio the religious feeling which animated his earlier masses, Contant reveals a feeling for dramatic expression which he had not shown before.[7] It contains striking polyphonic contrasts in the manner of Verdi or Berlioz, and consists of fugues, canons, and grandiose ensembles in which the orchestra, complemented by the choral sections, has the largest role. It also

7. Romain Gour, *Alexis Contant* (Ed. Eoliennes, 1951), Vol. V, No. 1.

shows a certain Wagnerian influence and a marked operatic bent. In the overture, after a short fugue, there appears a melody that reminds one of Massenet. But in the second section, "Blood" (the climax of the oratorio), the murder of Abel is vividly expressed by a clash of cymbals after the fashion of Berlioz in the "Marche au Supplice" in the *Symphonie Fantastique*. Charles Harriss (who founded the McGill Conservatorium) wrote to Contant shortly after the première of *Cain*: "The time has certainly arrived for Canada to show signs of creative talent in musical composition."

After *Cain*'s success, Alexis Contant wrote a second oratorio in 1909, *Les Deux Âmes*, based on a poem by Henri Roullaud, a French writer who had settled in Canada. Before presenting the work, the composer (not quite sure of himself) submitted the manuscript to the renowned conductor, Walter Damrosch, who happened to be in Montreal at that time. "The score shows great powers and skilful work," said Damrosch. "It should have a hearing." Reassured, Contant had his work performed on November 16, 1913. It is different from *Cain*, closer to a symphonic poem. There is greater continuity in the development of the themes and the work generally reveals greater maturity. The chorus plays a vital part, while the two soloists serve as a link only between the different sections. Although *Les Deux Âmes* is sometimes reminiscent of Elgar's *Dream of Gerontius*, based on Cardinal Newman's poem, it is definitely Alexis Contant's masterpiece.

In the same year that he was working on *Les Deux Âmes*, he composed the symphonic poem *L'Aurore*. A new stage is reached: borrowings from Wagner, Gounod and Franck are replaced by original ideas. "In this work one finds dissonant textures close to Sibelius and Richard Strauss," writes Jean-Yves Contant, "although these composers were still unknown in Montreal at the period in question."

In the sphere of chamber music, Alexis Contant has left us a trio for piano, violin and cello (1907). This is one of the first chamber music works ever composed in French Canada. Shortly before his death, he conceived the idea of writing an opera based on a play by Louis Fréchette called *Veronica*, but illness was to interrupt the creation of a work that might have become the first opera composed by a French Canadian.

Between 1816 and 1914 an impressive number of English immigrants had come to Canada to settle in the different provinces. One of them was Healey Willan (1880–1968), a very prolific composer; as to quantity, his work is certainly unsurpassed. His musical studies at St. Saviour's Choir School and those he pursued with William Stevenson Hoyte seem to have had a decisive influence on his organ and religious works of which there are about two hundred extant. With the help of Francis Burgess, he gained a deep understanding of plain-song.

Towards the end of the nineteenth century, London was the scene of a veritable renaissance of English music. The German domination to which it had been subjected came to an end and national sources were rediscovered; the return to folklore, to the Golden Age of Elizabeth, produced a style of writing far removed from German chromaticism: it was diatonic and modal. Because he was attached to the choral and religious tradition of his native country, Willan's religious works came under the extremely strong influence of the polyphonic works of the Renaissance. If he seems sensitive to the mystic and meditative polyphonies of William Byrd or Palestrina, the harmonic results of his counterpoint nevertheless remain modern. It is not rare to find archaic parallel organum effects in *Apostrophe to the Heavenly Hosts* and in the motet *Hodie Christus Natus Est*.[8] However, in the manner of certain English polyphonists of the Renaissance, he weaves a counterpoint quite independent of vertical sonorities which lends his style a peculiar and archaic charm.

Willan's organ works are no less important than his religious ones; as many as one hundred and twenty-five have already been published, including chorales, preludes, hymns, passacaglias and fugues. "His *Introduction, Passacaglia and Fugue* is one of the most important works of our time," writes Godfrey

8. G. Ridout, *The Canadian Music Journal*, Vol. III, No. 3, 1958–1959.

Ridout. And the eminent French organist, Joseph Bonnet, adds: "This piece is the greatest organ work since J. S. Bach." Few musicians can pride themselves on having received such ultimate praise! In the *Passacaglia* itself, Willan is not afraid to use the traditional ostinato on which he builds admirable variations. The fugue, because of its chromatic subject, is highly dissonant; the work as a whole is suffused with a Bachian atmosphere.

In his symphonic works, which he started writing at the age of fifty-five, Willan was more dependent on his models; his first symphony lacks originality. A master of polyphony, he obviously wants to impose upon the orchestra stylistic peculiarities typical of organ music, of contrepuntal textures. Reminiscences of Tchaikovsky's *Symphony in E Minor* are also evident. The *Second Symphony in C Minor* reveals his neoclassic spirit and his affection for Elgar's grandiloquence and sumptuous orchestration. The first movement is noteworthy for its tragic theme, which appears in the cellos, to be repeated and developed by the orchestra; and for the fugal section, which once more shows his mastery of counterpoint. The solemn, grave second movement is meditative in character—too lyrical perhaps and somewhat banal in spots. Yet it is a highly poetic movement, followed by a *scherzo* full of wit, worthy of the best English humour. Both symphonies show a preference for classical form and an affection for traditional writing. Willan seems to shy away from contemporary language: "I dislike modern music as the term is generally understood today. I find it frightfully monotonous and tiresome."

In 1944 he wrote a piano concerto in one movement, which nevertheless has a tripartite structure. It is a well-constructed and skilful work, clear in design and very well balanced. Classic in spirit, but romantic in style, the concerto uses, on occasion, Wagner's harmonic vocabulary. The contemplative *Adagio* is full of phantasy and displays the poetic qualities which one so often finds in the work of the master who remained unalterably faithful to his native traditions. Nobody could define himself more aptly than he did when he wrote the following quatrain:

> Irish by extraction
> English by birth
> Canadian by adoption, and
> Scotch by absorption.

An excellent cocktail, highly flavoured, it sometimes produced heady harmonies, especially in Willan's opera *Deirdre* (1943) based on a libretto by John Coulter. This is a most poetic work, inspired by Nordic legends such as *The Red Branch Knights of Utter*, the work of a Celtic Romantic who is still under the influence of Wagner; the work of a musician who is less eager to surprise his audience than to move it, less eager to speak the language of his time than to express himself well. Willan gives one the impression sometimes of belonging to another age, dedicated to his task as chapel master and organist, like the cantors of the time of Bach.

Like Ralph Vaughan Williams, he always remained deeply attached to Nordic folklore, with its ancient legends, as well as to the religious heritage of his native country. Like Gustav Holst, he had difficulty in escaping the Wagnerian influence. To the end of his days he remained a leader among Canadian musicians, a master of traditional writing to whom more than one generation of composers owe their training and their conscientious approach to their profession.

To Healey Willan who guided almost all the composers of the Toronto Conservatory and Faculty of Music between 1910 and 1930, there corresponds another great figure in the history of composition in Canada: Claude Champagne.

What we called the second period of composition in Canada was marked deeply by foreign influences on a country which was looking for its identity and for stable foundations. Complete isolation between the provinces paralyzed artistic creativity. But out of this solitude rose a few voices: those happy few who have been mentioned deserve the credit for breaking the silence; their efforts represent a victory of light over darkness.

The period extending from 1763 to the dawn of the twentieth

century was a time of transition; for music, like a developing civilization, is conceived and formed in successive stages. Re-evaluation becomes necessary, of basic concepts as well as of the means at our disposal to attain our objectives. Twentieth-century composers will make a critical inventory of the past, they will form their own aesthetic convictions, will develop a style of their own—a style based on a free choice of materials, techniques and forms of organization. The erstwhile imitators of Europeans will soon be their equals.

THE TWENTIETH CENTURY

"L'originalité est chose d'apprentissage."

Baudelaire

Canadian musical culture as it existed at the beginning of this century was a mixture of many ingredients; it could not have been more diversified than it turned out to be. Even today, there is no such thing as Canadian music; what we do have are various kinds of music written in Canada perpetuating West-European traditions. Borrowings from different folklores—Indian, Eskimo, French, English, Scottish and so on—were superficial and rather few in number. Canadian folksong did not contribute to a renewal of rhythmic and melodic textures as had been the case with Kodaly and Bartok.

The essential characteristics of this new period are, chiefly, the progressive mastering of objective problems and the integration of musical concepts expressed in and developed by an original technique. The supremacy of present-day Western music rests on its intrinsic universality; nevertheless, nobody would dare to deny the presence of essentially French elements recurring constantly in the work of Pierre Boulez or Olivier Messiaen, which distinguish these two from present-day German or Italian composers. The same can be said of several Canadians whose original concepts enable them to develop a personal style.

Some of our composers follow classical precepts of universal validity. Other, younger ones, avoid them; they prefer newer, more contemporary procedures; they are determined to find their own way. They seem to regard it as their main task to base their work on novel concepts concerning the nature of music—the most significant compositions written during the last thirty years are precisely those whose outward appearance (or style) is derived from inner convictions.

While Healey Willan dominated the Toronto group of musicians, Claude Champagne (1891–1965) shaped a whole generation of French-Canadian composers in whom he inculcated a desire for perfection and for the discipline that their profession demands. He is indubitably the most Canadian among our composers by virtue of his rhythmic accentuation, and the most French by virtue of the perfection of his style and the lucidity with which he expresses himself. It is through him that French musical culture attained new heights on Quebec soil which, in the seventeenth century, had been the cradle of our musical civilization. Claude Champagne believed that personal expression should be subordinated to the discipline of a particular style without sacrificing emotional power. He proved by his work (the result of introspection and deep meditation) that a new artistic consciousness had developed in Quebec, that Canadian music was at the threshold of a new age.

Claude Champagne was born in Montreal in 1891. To his paternal grandfather (who at times played the role of "violoneux") he owed his taste for peasant gigues which gave to some of his compositions such a distinctly Canadian flavour; from an Irish grandmother he inherited his fondness for day-dreams and poetry as well as his gift for thought and reflection. As an adolescent, he taught himself the violin while at the same time pursuing his piano studies. For his first harmony lessons he was indebted to Rodolphe Mathieu, a self-taught composer whose knowledge of the secrets of harmonic chemistry stemmed from Rimsky-Korsakov's treatise. But it was Alfred Laliberté who encouraged him to become a composer. Thanks to him Champagne fell under the magic spell of Tristan and became acquainted with Scriabin's harmonies which he greatly admired. Laliberté submitted his first important work to Rachmaninoff, then visiting Montreal; it was *Hercule et Omphale* (1918), a symphonic poem—its successful performance by the Société des Concerts du Conservatoire in Paris (1926) brought him a great deal of recognition.

During this first period Champagne fell under the influence of the Russian school—Moussorgsky, Borodin and Rimsky-Korsakov. Their poetic intensity, the freedom of their brilliant colour schemes, the modal nature of their work, their supreme mastery of orchestration so full of light and shade, their predilection for ancient legends made a deep impression on his subconscious. While he was writing *Hercule et Omphale*, he became acquainted also with Russia's great novelists Gorki and Dostoevsky.

In 1919, however, Champagne discovered the lasting values of the French tradition. The mysterious power of Russian art had enchanted him; yet in the music of France he discerned a rigour, a purity, a luminosity to which he was spontaneously attuned. It was as if invisible hands beckoned to him across the centuries; he felt a powerful urge to return to his own heritage that was in danger of being lost and forgotten.

Champagne sought advice from Paul Dukas (a French master whose logical mind and sensitive nature seemed always to be in perfect equilibrium). Dukas advised him to work with André Gédalge (a former fellow student of Debussy's in Massenet's class). With Gédalge—the teacher of Ravel, of Milhaud and Honegger—Champagne studied counterpoint and fugue. He is certainly indebted to him for his mastery of inter-weaving melodies. It was during that time Champagne discovered Renaissance polyphony which came as a relief after the aridity of his academic studies. He even sang in the *Schola Cantorum*. He was completely won over by the poetic quality of the modal music of the renaissance and by that of Gabriel Fauré, whose subtlety, whose delightful and sensuous arabesques, appealed to him particularly.

But the strongest influence during the seven years Champagne spent in Paris was that of Debussy: "The music that made the greatest impression on me was Debussy's," he confided to us shortly before his death. Delighted at being able to free himself from tonal tyranny, Champagne established, in a completely natural way, a link between the modal character of our folklore (French in origin) and that of the new musical renaissance to which the names of Fauré, Debussy and Ravel add so much lustre. Dazzled by all this Mediterranean brilliance, but without ever losing touch with his native country he embarked on a search for his own identity. He became intensely interested in the freedom of the French school, its unusual sonorities, its sheer poetry which corresponded to his own.

In the *Suite Canadienne* for choir and orchestra (1928) he integrated these various elements; he also demonstrated his enthusiasm for Canadian folklore. The Concerts Pasdeloup orchestra, under the direction of Rhené-Baton, presented the work in Paris where it was warmly received. His contrapuntal writing seemed to be a return to the admirable French polyphonic compositions which characterized the Golden Age of music in the sixteenth century. The work was published by Durant, and was one of the first Canadian compositions for choir and orchestra to be given a première performance in Paris. It seems that Champagne had taken to heart Jean Cocteau's: "Plus un artiste chante dans son arbre généalogique, plus il chante juste."

Upon his return to Canada after an absence of eight years, he wrote the *Danse villageoise* whose lively rhythms were to be heard around the world. Its rhythmic inflections are inspired by French-Canadian folklore and have a charm all their own. Two elements which are blended in the work seem to symbolize the composer's French and Irish backgrounds: the upper melodic part, so reminiscent of the French *rigaudon*; and the accompaniment, which reminds one of the bagpipes of Scotland and Ireland.

In 1943 Champagne wrote *Images du Canada français*, for choir and orchestra. The *Images* are real musical engravings in which the composer reveals his mastery of the orchestra and his knowledge of the particular requirements of the different instruments. No doubt he owes the clarity of the orchestral design to the French school. In "Marines" the listener detects with delight the familiar voice of Debussy, that "Claude of France." But the French influences are so perfectly assimilated in Champagne's works that they do not affect the originality of his art in any way. The *Images du Canada français* had their first Canadian performance in Montreal under the direction of Jean-Marie Beaudet in 1947. They were presented in Paris in 1956.

In 1945 one of Champagne's master works appeared: the *Symphonie Gaspésienne*. The work is particularly remarkable for its scoring. The infinite possibilities of the orchestral harmonies are contrasted with the intricate play of timbres; the ensemble coalesces into one great instrument capable of expressing every nuance of poetic intent. The *Symphonie Gaspésienne* may indeed be considered to be a vast impressionist poem. As Champagne explained: "As far as my music is concerned, it is nature which made the greatest impression on me." Like Debussy, Champagne seems to cherish the dream of expressing "the mysterious harmonies existing between nature and the imagination, and to decipher the music which is written in nature." Like his Celtic and French ancestors, he is in his element in a cloud-filled atmosphere and enchanted by the poetry and mystery of morning mists. In this work, whose contours are inspired by the topography of the Gaspé Peninsula, the composer creates an evocative atmosphere; an oboe solo conjures up the melancholy and the infinite solitude of the Gaspé fisherman.

Like Debussy in *La Mer*, Champagne found pleasure, as A. Schaeffer has noted, in "drawing in clear lines the elusive contours of the moving sea, the continuous ebb and flow of the waves, the splendid crashing of the watery masses." Yet the sea of Champagne's is not that of Balbec or Etretat—he dreams of our own majestic St. Lawrence, with its mists at dawn and the flight of gulls over the rock at Percé. A visual image often gives rise to the use of analogous devices. Thus the movement of the work is free, like the movement of the waves in ceaseless motion and ever changing shapes, making us forget the tyrannical pulsation of the beats. Such metric freedom is typical of Champagne; like Debussy, he endeavoured to free rhythm from the division into bars. The form renews itself at every moment; it progresses according to associations with musical landscapes, by a play of perspectives corresponding to those found in the panorama of the Gaspé coast, and in accordance with a series of contrasts in instrumental colour. The composer of the *Symphonie Gaspésienne* is certainly the greatest impressionist poet of our Canadian landscape. After its first performance by the orchestra of the Concerts Symphoniques de Montréal in 1949, under the direction of Désiré Defauw, it was presented in Paris in 1957 at the Théâtre des Champs-Elysées with the orchestra of the Radio Diffusion Française under Gaston Poulet.

After writing a piano concerto in 1950 Champagne completed one of his profoundest works: his *String Quartet*. That was in 1951—an important date in the history of Canadian music. Wisely, he had waited until his last years before approaching the most difficult task a composer can encounter. The quartet contains elements of both sonata and fugue. Expert in the most rigorous aspects of counterpoint, Champagne reveals his innermost personality by means of the most admirable and sparing polyphony, highly dissonant at times. It is a unique work pared down to essentials, growing out of, and reflecting, a solitude that seems to be the lot of the best of our poets and painters.

Claude Champagne's *magnum opus* is *Altitude* (1959), perhaps one of the most important works of this new age by virtue of its proportions and the audacity of its style. It is a vast musical fresco inspired by the grandeur of the Rocky Mountains. Here again the composer identifies visual images with the structural components of a symphonic work that is divided into three parts: "Primitive Times"; "Meditation"; and "Modern Times." We are in the presence of a poetic and mystic vision no less grandiose than Nature herself. The intersecting lines of mountain landscapes (seen as a sensitive painter would see them) are reflected in a technique that could only be compared to film-cutting; yet contemplation leads the composer to group the elements so as to reveal their secret unity. There is a concordance between the world of the mountains in all their mystery and silence and the spiritual world of the artist. Here is John Beckwith's description:

The work, inspired by the Rockies, is both descriptive and reflective: it evokes the rise and fall of mountain slopes and the mountain-top atmosphere; it also looks spiritually inward and reflects on that communion with time and space which mountain-top sojourns so often arouse. The score calls for a mixed chorus in two passages, on a Huron-Indian prayer and a text from St. Francis of Assisi. It is one of the first Canadian works to give solo prominence to the Ondes Martenot. Its "program" involves topographical and historical considerations. The first and third sections are subtitled Epoche primitive and Epoche moderne. The first has a prelude and "ascent" based on the juxtaposition of strangely Bach-like tonal counterpoint and atmospheric effects for the ondes and high strings; then the Indian prayer; then a depiction of an avalanche. An orchestral meditation forms a link to Part Three. Part Three praises God for the sun, for fire, for the moon and stars, and for the seasons, and concludes with a reminder of geological sources in another mountainous "ascent."

The orchestration of *Altitude* is powerful, at times making use of all the possibilities of a great orchestra, combining the various sections with the ineffable sounds of the Ondes Martenot; at other times it is sparse (in the contrapuntal passages for strings, for instance). Recitation is judiciously employed, embued with a sense of magic reminiscent of mystical incantations. The work was first performed in Paris (1964) by the Orchestra Pasdeloup under the direction of Remus Tzincoca.

Among Champagne's contemporaries there existed a number of Canadian musicians who (from 1918 on) acquainted Montreal with the brilliant achievements of the French school; these courageous pioneers deserve a place in our narrative. Léo-Pol Morin (1892–1941), a refined and highly cultured artist, presented the works of Debussy and Ravel to the Canadian public for the first time, in collaboration with the eminent singer Cédia Brault (1894). This singer had the distinction of being the first Canadian to sing the role of *Carmen* abroad with world-famous artists such as John Sullivan of the Chicago and

Paris Operas, Robert Cousineau of the Metropolitan and Léon Rothier of the Paris Opera. She was also a remarkable Dalila under Pierre Monteux's direction in Worcester in 1923.

Thanks to distinguished and dedicated artists such as these, as well as Victor Brault, Arthur Laurendeau and others, the most significant works in the French repertoire were, for the first time, performed on Canadian soil. Cédia Brault and Léo-Pol Morin gave first performances in Quebec of Claude Debussy's *Proses lyriques* (1918), *Shérérazade* and Maurice Ravel's *Chansons madecasses,* for the rehearsals of which Ravel came especially from New York (1928). Darius Milhaud's *Poèmes Juifs* were also first performed in Montreal by Cédia Brault (1926), with the composer at the piano. (He acknowledged that he had found "an excellent performer and a musician of quality," whose voice was both warm and vibrant.) It was due to their efforts that the works of Fauré, Debussy, Ravel, Milhaud, Roussel and Honegger (to name only these) were presented so early in the century. As a result of their efforts also, Montreal experienced a renaissance of French musical thought destined to have a profound influence on the composers of that city.

Among the Canadian composers who, like Claude Champagne, have a well-defined style, and whose works mark a turning-point in the history of composition in Canada, John Weinzweig (b. 1913) is outstanding. A true leader, he trained a large number of young composers from Toronto and western Canada. After studying the romantic repertoire, he became one of the first musicians in Canada to abandon traditional tonality and to use first atonal, and then serial, language. Through him, young composers of Toronto and western Canada (well in advance of Montreal composers) became acquainted with the new Viennese school of Schoenberg, Berg and Webern.

Twelve-tone technique has been the basis of my art since it appeared in my *Suite for Piano* in 1939. I believe I can be considered responsible for introducing this manner of writing into Canada. I made contact with it during my stay in Rochester when I heard Alban

Berg's *Lyric Suite*. In this music I found what I needed. It made a deep impression on me.

After various attempts to work within the framework of North American idioms, he felt free to express himself within a system without being enslaved by it. This enabled him to develop a personal and highly versatile style. He makes use of the rhythmic and melodic elements of Eskimo songs and dances in his symphonic poem *The Edge of the World* (1946); of the rhythmic structures of swing-style jazz, blended with serial writing, in the *Divertimento* for bassoon and string orchestra (1959); and of Indian chants and French-Canadian folksongs in *Red Ear of Corn* (1948–49). But by 1943 he seems to have found his true voice in *Interlude in an Artist's Life*, a significant work whose psychological theme is solitude—the solitude experienced during the war when the composer served in the Royal Canadian Air Force. The *Interlude* is a string quintet in ternary form whose style—characterized by rhythmic and thematic textures—is already very personal. The unifying factor of the work is a twelve-tone subject in which the interval of a perfect fourth is predominant. It is transformed in the middle section and restated afterwards in its original form.

One of Weinzweig's major works is, doubtless, his *Violin Concerto* written between 1951 and 1954. It is neo-classical in structure, neo-classical in scoring; the first movement makes use of sonata form introducing two subjects; the orchestration (double woodwinds and brasses) follows classical examples. Lucidity of texture, masterful treatment of a well-balanced orchestra are outstanding characteristics. At times one feels that the composer is very well acquainted with Mozart's and Prokofiev's violin concertos. Yet whatever can be traced to these sources is so completely integrated that it is hardly perceptible: which distinguishes Weinzweig (as well as Claude Champagne) from some of the younger composers in whose works reminders of their studies are only too apparent. The second movement begins with an ostinato motif consisting of two notes (E flat, D) first appearing in the basses. The composer's mastery of contrapuntal writing manifests itself in the canonic treatment of the soloist's theme in the strings. The third movement is freer in form, combining the characteristics of rondo and variations. The proportions of the concerto, the perfect balance between solo sections and orchestral tutti, the charm of those passages that seem to be suspended between tonality and atonality contribute to the importance of a work that enhances the Canadian repertoire.

In 1957 Weinzweig wrote *Wine of Peace*, a remarkable score, both solemn and profound. Dedicated to the United Nations, it bears the subtitle "two dramatic songs for soprano and orchestra." The first song, "Life is a Dream," is inspired by a Spanish play by Pedro Calderon de la Barca reminding man that glory and riches fade like dreams. The second one, called "City of Brass," is based on an anonymous poem translated from the Arabic: a city's glorious past is evoked in it, but also its conquest leading to death and destruction. The poet counsels all men to drink of the wine of peace. The choice of texts bears witness to the composer's preoccupation with the problems facing man confronted by the contemporary world. His willingness to adapt his language (however free in itself) to the requirements of a deeply human message in which he is involved tells us a great deal about his artistic convictions, about his search for integration.

As the composer Kasemets appropriately says, "*Wine of Peace* comes closest to summing up Weinzweig's concepts of musical expression. It displays formal clarity and warm emotions; its orchestration is both consistant and specific. It shows the composer's personal views on the burning question of humanism in the twentieth century. Through every bar of this composition shines John Weinzweig as we know him now, a profound thinker, a mature craftsman, a sensitive and warm man."[9]

The instrumentation of this work is one of the most remarkable in Canadian music, and one of the most poetic. The composer does not hesitate to divide his orchestra occasionally into

9. Udo Kasemets, *The Canadian Music Journal*, Vol. IV, No. 4, 1960.

small groups, thus subtly creating a sort of "aura of sound" around the poem and allowing the voice to bring out the full value of the text, without ever allowing it to be submerged by a heavy orchestral mass. In making judicious use of very colourful instruments such as the piccolo, flutes, glockenspiel, vibraphone, bells, harp, or of special combinations. Weinzweig shows himself to be a master of an instrumentation containing unusual timbres. The work is sometimes serial, not in the sense of certain twelve-tone composers given to strict observance of the rules, but in a style that reveals a more flexible, more personal conception of tone-rows. Thus, the composer informs us that the E flat, D, B flat motif that one finds constantly in Spanish music has its origin in Arab song. "I included this motif in the tone-rows on which this work is based in order to attain total integration of the poems."

One of his latest works (his greatest achievement in the field of chamber music) is the *Quartet No. 3*, first performed on February 28, 1963. The composer has entered a new phase of development, at least as far as concepts of form and serial textures are concerned. Until 1961–62, Weinzweig had used twelve-tone technique only, horizontally, melodically; in the quartet, however, it affects harmony and polyphony as well, although he does not employ the generalized series.

Influenced by the flow of free associations in *Finnegan's Wake*—the composer admired Joyce's masterpiece—the quartet has the distinction of being one of the first Canadian works to be based on the manifestations of the unconscious mind which demand complete freedom of form comparable to that of the surrealist poets. No doubt the neo-classic side of Weinzweig needed to react against the traditional rules of composing. "I allowed my feelings to exceed the bounds of logic," he told us. In any case, are our lives not determined by periodically recurring events as well as chance? "Harken to the advice of the passing wind," said Debussy. The contemporary artist, it seems, seeks to express his innermost self; but he can do it only by using a formal language forever shifting from the irrational to the rational.

"The quartet," writes the composer, "is a work of changing moods and phantastic images freely emerging from the subconscious." For all that, it is neither chaotic nor structurally disorganized; on the contrary, the *Quartet* is Weinzweig's most rigorously constructed and most accomplished composition. At times it seems to hark back to German expressionism, to Webern's pointillism; such incidental similarities, however, are largely superficial. The five movements are based on a twelve-tone row; the first five notes are always present; the seven remaining ones appear in a different order after the third movement. All five movements use complex time signatures such as 9/8, 8/8, 7/8, 15/8, etc. The last movement—it bears the title "In Memoriam"—is dedicated to the composer's mother who died while he was working on the *Quartet*. It is an *adagio* and uses the Hebrew prayer *Kol Nidre* as a fundamental motif. One senses the author's determination never to exclude the human element. In fact, Weinzweig's whole *œuvre* bears witness to his desire to integrate human values and music, to "re-humanize" the art. It is this, perhaps, which makes his work so appealing, this which distinguishes him from those of his fellows who prefer abstraction to integration.

Barbara Pentland (b. 1912), to whom we now turn, belongs to a group of composers who make use of different styles, changing from one to another with remarkable facility. This seems to be the outstanding characteristic of the American School, a product of a geographically and demographically diversified continent.

Although she is very little influenced by folklore, she nevertheless uses three French-Canadian folk songs in her violin sonata. It is quite obvious also that the vigorous rhythms of Indian dancers (she hails from Winnipeg) must have made an impression on her; it may well be that such memories (unconscious ones perhaps) are responsible for her rhythmical vivacity. Here are her own comments with reference to the sonata:

There are certain basic sounds in all very old folk songs from almost any land which transcend race, colour, or creed, and make it the common heritage of all peoples. My share of French ancestry may make me rather partial to these particular songs of our early settlers and voyageurs, but it was their purely musical qualities and possibilities which influenced my choice.

When she was studying in Europe under Cécile Gauthiez (a professor at the *schola cantorum* and a disciple of Vincent d'Indy), she came under the influence of César Franck, an influence quite apparent in her *Five Preludes* (1938), her *Rhapsody for Piano* (1939) and her *Piano Quintet*.

Her style changed somewhat while she was studying in New York. Her works make use of a more contemporary vocabulary; echoes of Bloch, Prokofiev and Stravinsky are prevalent. Aaron Copland's pre-eminence in the American school is well known, and it is hardly surprising that several composers of Anglo-Saxon background—Pentland among them—were inspired by him. Her works written after 1942 prove the contention. The characteristic traits of her style, such as lively, spontaneous and often syncopated motifs, show the influence of Copland, Stravinsky and the American school in general. Numerous examples can be found in the *vivace* of her *Violin Concerto* (1942), in the *allegro animato* of her *First String Quartet* (1945), in the *Organ Concerto* (1949) and in the *presto* of her *Second Quartet* (1953).

Pentland spent seven years in Toronto teaching at the Royal Conservatory (1942). Being in contact with her colleague John Weinzweig, she became keenly interested in atonalism and serialism. But it was not until 1948 that her talent as a contrapuntist manifested itself in the brilliant use she made of the vocabulary and the artifices of twelve-tone technique, such as inversion, augmentation, canon, etc. Tonal implications, however, are not completely avoided; the composer seems to have made a "lady's agreement" with tonality.

Although counterpoint seems to be her most successful medium, we must draw attention to Pentland's admirable treatment of variation (*Variations on a theme by Boccherini*, 1948) and of neo-classical forms in general. Her orchestral writing, however, particularly in her symphonies where contrapuntal textures are predominant, lacks transparency; single lines are less clearly perceived if the orchestration is too heavy.

One of the most notable scores in the Canadian chamber music repertoire is Pentland's *Second String Quartet* (1953), chosen by the International Society for Contemporary Music to be performed at the Stockholm Festival of 1956. "The five movements of this quartet," says Robert Turner, "remind one of Bartok's quartets up to a certain point, particularly in the way the instruments are used."[10]

The main characteristic of the work (constantly recurring in Pentland's compositions) is a passion for linear textures; examples can be found in the retrograde writing of the first movement, in the contrapuntal aspects of the second where fugue and sonata form are ingeniously combined, in the linear complexity of the double fugue of the fourth movement—altogether a display of splendid craftsmanship.

During the last few years Pentland seems to have followed the contemporary trend that can be traced to Webern—one more indication of her versatility and the ease with which she adapts herself to changes of style and musical thought. Her *Symphony in 10 parts*, for instance—so concise, so economical in its means, so rigorously structured—is modelled after Webern. A lively *scherzo* uses the retrograde as a constructive device with great skill; it is "folded over," so to speak, since the first part of the movement is repeated in retrograde form.

Endowed with a high degree of intelligence, Barbara Pentland is perfectly conscious of her own development and under no illusion as to the place occupied by contemporary Canadian composers when she writes:

There are the few fortunately who have evolved with the music of our time, taking as our national heritage the great trends of the century inherent in the work of Schoenberg, Bartok, Stravinsky, Hindemith in touch with the young American Music, and yet slowly bringing forth our own manner of speech. At last we've started

10. *The Canadian Music Journal*, Vol. II, No. 4, p. 24, 1958.

Vol. X.—No. 9.   MONTREAL, SATURDAY, AUGUST 29, 1874.   {SINGLE COPIES, TEN CENTS.
$4 PER YEAR IN ADVANCE.

THE NEW GRAND OPERA HOUSE, TORONTO.

Left
The New Grand Opera House,
Toronto, 1874

Below
National Arts Centre in Ottawa,
under construction

Upper left
Igor Stravinsky meditating during a
CBC rehearsal

Lower left
Doreen Hall instructing an Orff class
in Toronto

Upper right
Electronic music studio, University of
Toronto

Lower right
Orford Quartet of the University of
Toronto

Orford JMC Centre for Music and the Arts, Mount Orford Provincial Park, P.Q.

National Youth Orchestra

The Canadian Opera Company performing *Louis Riel*, III, 3

The Royal Conservatory Opera School production of Carl Orff's *The Wise Woman*

Scene from the Royal Winnipeg Ballet's *Les Patineurs*. Shown
here are Antony Greeves, Joan Askwith, and Paul Blakey

Leslie-May Downs and Richard Beaty of
Les Grands Ballets Canadiens in *Carmina Burana*

something even if it still leaves our generation in the difficult role of pioneer.[11]

Speaking generally, one would have to say that talent and skill are more in evidence in Pentland's work than that depth of thought that ought to underline the complexities of "the game." Yet enjoying the game, enjoying the technical mastery with which she is able to play it, she is certainly very successful in that dynamic and, often enough, aggressive style of hers.

The work of Jean Papineau-Couture (b. 1916) reflects his need to attain a deeper knowledge of musical problems that interest him. Given to research into extra-tonal possibilities with a view to comparing them with his own ideas regarding musical means of expression, he never tires of exploring new universes; but he selects them carefully before assimilating them into his own work. Enamoured of logic, a pure Cartesian, who does not believe that one can make great use of an art before having acquired a clear knowledge of it, Couture is certainly one of the most genuine disciples of Nadia Boulanger. When he studied with her in Cambridge, Massachusetts, she guided him in his career as a composer, developed his taste for writing and encouraged what could be described as a synthesis between Latin neo-classicism and Stravinskyan rhythmics.[12]

There is no doubt that his studies in the United States left their mark on him; the sources of his language may equally be traced to the American School (Aaron Copland, Chandler) and to Stravinsky, his model.... As neo-classicist Couture is fond of traditional forms such as the suite, sonata, concerto, symphony, variation, rondo, aria da capo, and fugue.

But his diversified language implies unresolved problems which oblige him to reconsider the dialectic of texture and form. Moreover, the neo-classicist in him is not afraid to make use of harmonic and rhythmic audacities that are acceptable nowadays; yet they are subordinate to the logic of a highly-

11. *Ibid.*, p. 24.
12. Andrée Desautels, "Les Trois Ages de la Musique au Canada," in *Larousse de la Musique*, Tome II (Paris, 1965), p. 322.

organized, essentially Cartesian mind. Employing textures that are sometimes tonal (*Concerto grosso*, 1943), sometimes polytonal (*Suite for Flute*, second movement), sometimes atonal, as in his ballet *Papotages* where certain chords become centres of reference replacing those of the tonal system, Couture seeks solutions to the problems besetting our time.

For a long time he was rather reluctant to accept the serialism of the new Viennese school, particularly the serialism of strict twelve-tone composers. Finally, however, he entered into a gentleman's agreement with total chromaticism retaining some tonal implications (in the *Suite for Solo Violin*, for instance, that dates from 1956). A few years earlier Stravinsky, his master, had taken the same step. Among the masterpieces of Couture's first period we would single out the *Concerto Grosso* (1943) and the *Psalm 150* for soprano, tenor, mixed choir, organ and orchestra (1954), one of his most successful works. Stylistically as well as spiritually the Psalm harks back to Bach's cantatas and chorales. Occasional reminders of Stravinsky's *Symphony of Psalms*—harmonic and rhythmic reminiscences—do not detract from Couture's achievement.

The fundamental problem that confronted him from 1956 on was the problem of structural logic. As a result of an instinctive reaction against the dangerous dissolution of form, he entered upon a period of what one could describe as constructivism: the pleasure of playing with shapes and forms, composing in the full light of consciousness became more important than explorations of the realm of poetry hidden in the recesses of the mind; the five *Pièces Concertantes* for various chamber music combinations exemplify Papineau-Couture's new approach:

Pièce Concertante No. 1 for piano and string orchestra—its title is *Repliement*—is reminiscent of the fourteenth-century composer Guillaume de Machault, particularly of his rondeau *Ma fin est mon commencement*.

Pièce Concertante No. 2 for cello and chamber orchestra, entitled *Eventails*, is harmonically and polyphonically more advanced. It could be described as a *rondo varié* with a harmonic rather than an essentially melodic refrain. Short retrogrades are being employed, also the device of increasing and decreasing the density of sound. The fluctuations in density which explain the title (*Eventails* means "fans") depend on the quantity of sound or on the textural design.

Pièce Concertante No. 3 (1959), scored for flute, clarinet, violin, cello, harp and string orchestra, is a set of variations in which the composer seems to explore new facets of twelve-tone technique. In his *Suite for Violin*, he had already shown an interest in serialism, but only in its linear aspects. Here, however, he pays attention to the harmonic possibilities inherent in the series, employing them in the framework of variations.

Pièce Concertante No. 4 (1959) for oboe and string orchestra is called *Additions*. The structural organization reminds one of the *Schola Enchiriadis* of the ninth century that defined music as the daughter of mathematics. The work is based on the following mathematical schema:

1st fragment	2nd fragment	3rd fragment
1 note $+ 1 =$	2 notes $+ 1 = 3 + 1 =$	4 notes $+ 3 = 7$
	4th fragment	
	8 notes $(+7) = 15$	

Toward the end of the *Pièce* the intervals appear in retrograde form while the note values remain unchanged. The music seems to determine its own development, seems to create itself while it unfolds in time.

Pièce Concertante No. 5 (1963) is scored for orchestra and bears the title *Miroirs*. It is a study in mirror devices affecting not only melody but harmony as well. Couture enjoys such experiments; in this respect he is just like Stravinsky who would rather be a craftsman than an "artist," who takes great delight in organizing musical material, in building structures whose *raison d'être* is beauty of form.

One of Couture's latest works is the *Piano Concerto* (1965). It shares some of its harmonic characteristics with the *Pièce Concertante No. 1*. In the Concerto, they are, however, further elaborated and perfected. Alternating harmonic schemes are being employed, comprising:

1. a chord consisting of 6 tones, symmetrical in itself, also using the principle of mirror reflection, namely D flat, F, E flat—F sharp, E, G sharp = 6 tones (if the chord is transposed to the augmented fourth the whole of the chromatic scale is covered);

2. three chords of 4 tones each, again involving all 12 tones of the chromatic scale.

The two schemes enable the composer to explore a variety of possibilities of chord formation.

The *Concerto* is in one movement in which two contrasting tempi alternate. The *cadenza*—it appears in the middle of the work—is integrated into the form as a whole. The *Finale* could be described as a synthesis (in vertical order) of all that went before.

Surveying Papineau-Couture's work as a whole, we realize that he explored various approaches to composition, in every case pursuing his investigation to the end, never tiring in his zeal for perfection, and working with a thoroughness that is typical of him. Like Stravinsky, he became a champion of pure music, i.e., music devoid of emotion. A work of art, according to Couture, is nothing but an order imposed on time, autonomous in form and free of purely human concerns—a conviction that he shares with Eduard Hanslick.

Godfrey Ridout (1918), a disciple of Healey Willan whose own tastes resemble his in some respects, is a remarkably gifted musician—sincere and honest enough to admit quite candidly from what source he derived the greatest inspiration for his work: from Gustav Holst's symphonic suite *The Planets*, whose brilliant orchestration is on a par with the great romantics. "This was the first contemporary music that appealed to me and made a tremendous impression on me," Ridout confessed. And he added, "if there is any single influence in my music that has been uppermost it has been Holst."

After writing a *Ballade* for viola and string orchestra (1938) he composed a *Festival Ouverture* (1939). Based on a poem by

Walt Whitman and classical in form, the ouverture is permeated with all the anguish that afflicted the world at the beginning of the Second World War. His first mature work, however, and rather an important one, was *Esther*, a dramatic symphony, first performed by the Royal Conservatory orchestra under the direction of Ettore Mazzoleni. In addition to Holst, Ridout's models here are Walton and Elgar; he is also deeply influenced by the music of the Anglican Church: ". . . being an Anglican and being brought up quite solidly in the Anglican tradition, the Anglican music left a very strong mark on me," he wrote. In this context, it is not surprising that Ridout's vocal composition seems best to express his poetic nature and meditative sensitivity. He is particularly successful in treating religious subjects that inspire him, witness his admirable settings of John Donne, called *Holy Sonnets* or *Cantiones Mysticae* (1953), premièred by Lois Marshall under the direction of Stokowski. They are most valuable additions to the Canadian repertoire of sacred music.

Ridout obviously needs a poetic stimulus in order to compose (as does John Beckwith). It is the perfect blending of poetry and music that makes the *Cantiones Mysticae* so outstanding. In the second song, "Thou Hast Made Me," both the melodic line and the accompaniment are profoundly moving; the accompaniment of Bach Cantatas come to mind, their rhythmical character, their symbolism. In the third song, it is as if a sudden gust of wind enlivened the rising melodic line, turning it into a sounding symbol of the words "at the round earth's imagin'd corners blow your trumpets Angels, and arise, arise from death." The music is meditative in character, highly poetic, emotionally charged as well as spiritually profound. The scoring is effective and testifies to the composer's sound craftsmanship.

His *Four Sonnets* for mixed choir and orchestra date from 1963; they are based on the Epistle of St. Paul to the Galatians v.22: "but the fruit of the Spirit is love, joy, peace." Here again we feel the impact of the composer's personality expressing itself in a highly original way. Ridout has a rhythmic style all his own, characterized by dynamic energy; he is not at all afraid to use Stravinskyan syncopations or *contrattempo*.

His choral writing is often homophonic, formed by an affinity with the psalms and hymns of the Anglican Church. The melodic texture, frequently of great simplicity, springs naturally from the poetic context. Imbued with the spiritual meaning of a sonnet, he works like a poet rather than like an organizer of sound material or an architect of structures. His music always reflects an inner need to write; meditation and devotion are more precious to him than the pleasures of playing with shapes and moulding material.

Ridout excels in writing for voice, while Harry Freedman (b. 1922) is more successful in the instrumental field. This is not surprising. During the years of his apprenticeship he mastered clarinet, oboe and English horn and acquired a sound knowledge of instrumentation. Born in Poland, Freedman came to Canada in 1925; he pursued his musical studies in Winnipeg and at the Royal Conservatory of Toronto where he became a pupil of Weinzweig. He excels in the art of suggesting colours and lines; thus his music is enriched by his sensitivity toward visual art. After working with Weinzweig he sought instruction from Ernst Krenek—the same Krenek who rather wittily described himself as "sitting between two chairs"—which refers to the fact that he had absorbed such an impressive number of disparate styles. Weinzweig and Krenek were Freedman's mentors in his approach to atonality.

To complete his studies, however, he went to Tanglewood where he followed the courses of Olivier Messiaen and Aaron Copland. He is strongly influenced by jazz (much more so than by Weinzweig or Somers). Rhythmic irregularities seem to inspire him. Sometimes, in his slow movements, Freedman uses the formal outline of the blues that consist of three four-bar periods (AAB); the harmonic scheme underlying the resulting twelve-bar period serves jazz players quite frequently as a basis for improvisation. It seems to have left an imprint on Freedman, giving his music a typically North-American flavour.

In *Tableau* (1952) the composer evokes the immensity, the austerity, the solitude of the Arctic, communicating the feeling of helplessness and awe that overpowers man contemplating vast landscapes not to be measured on any human scale. Using atonal and rigorously polyphonic textures he succeeds in conveying the emotions of a poet, of a painter confronted by the cruel emptiness of those icy deserts (which are also a harrowing symbol of spiritual loneliness).

This *poétique visuelle*, so typical of Freedman, pervades also his *Images* (1957–58). His outlook, his reactions are those of a painter; visual associations are identified with their musical analogues and transformed into sounds. *Images* draws its inspiration from Canadian paintings. The first, Loren Harris' *Blue Mountain*, invites the composer to turn himself into a landscape painter as it were; the stylized contours of the mountain are alluded to; the scoring—for English horn, bass clarinet, bassoons, French horn, trombone and low strings—evokes the blue of the night, the sombre hues of the picture. Two-part writing predominates, "perfect intervals play an important role," the composer told us.

The second painting is markedly different from the preceding one: it is Nakamusara's *Structure at Dusk*. The music that corresponds to it—fragmented lines rapidly moving over a background of veiled trills and murmuring strings—seems imbued with the qualities of Japanese prints, of oriental art in general: lightness of touch and transparency of form.

The third painting, an abstract work by Jean-Paul Riopelle, elicits from the composer an aggressive piece, replete with the most audacious harmonies, a violent rendering of the painter's brush strokes, of his free, bold lines. Fierce passages and brutal chords complete a sound picture in which the painter's influence is obvious even in the composer's technique.

Freedman has more to his credit: several works employing twelve-tone techniques (*Nocturne*, 1949), others in which he espouses serialism (*Five Pieces for String Orchestra*, 1949), also a symphony (1961) that displays a superb knowledge of orchestration and polyphonic artistry, which, however, would have profited by greater economy of means. The twelve-tone system Freedman finds "too restrictive."

One of the most remarkable personalities of the present-day generation is Harry Somers. No doubt he is indebted to his teacher John Weinzweig for his thorough knowledge of orchestration and for his sound craftsmanship. He continued his studies in San Francisco with the pianist Robert Schmitz, then for a year in Paris with Darius Milhaud. In his approach, however, he resembles Weinzweig rather than Milhaud who favours polytonality. The free atonalism that Somers uses in some of his works (without excluding diatonic implications, in the *Suite for Harp and Chamber orchestra*, for instance) proves his adherence to the Toronto rather than to the Paris school. An extremely versatile and highly gifted musician, he seems always on the lookout for new devices and unusual sound combinations, as seen in his *Fantasy for Orchestra* (1958) which is a veritable showcase of orchestral virtuosity. The composer had the privilege of hearing the work performed by the Orchestre des Concerts Symphoniques in Montreal under Igor Markekitch (1958).

In 1961 two significant works marked a new stage in the evolution of Somers' orchestral style—*Abstract* and *Five Concepts for Orchestra*. In *Abstract* (commissioned by CBC-Television) the composer set himself the task to produce quasi-electronic sounds by means of traditional instruments, i.e. strings, harp and percussion. "Lyrical, rhythmical and atonal in character, with colourful orchestration that exploits all the instruments both individually and collectively," the score displays an abundance of rhythmical and contrapuntal devices.

Five Concepts for Orchestra is an experimental work; its four movements are "short and atonal, veritable studies in orchestral sound," extending serial treatment to pitch, intensity and rhythm. The first movement is a study in different sound registers, the second a study in rhythm for percussion alone; the third movement is a study in line, the fourth a *scherzando* based on ornaments; it is sparse, light and condensed. Its linear austerity reminds one of oriental poetry. The fifth and last movement is a study in dynamics. The work as a whole is extremely interesting but it does not seem to have any significance other than experimentation for experimentation's sake.

One of Somers' most recent and most original compositions is unquestionably *Stereophony*. Toward the end of the sixteenth century, Andrea and Giovanni Gabrieli had discovered the importance of stereophony; they made use of it in their motets for double and triple choirs and various groups of instruments. The cathedral of San Marco in Venice had two organ galleries opposite to each other; performers stationed there were capable of producing antiphonal effects and the contrasting choirs constituted different sound sources.

Electronic music influenced Somers a great deal; he spent some time at the Electronic Music Studio at the Faculty of Music of the University of Toronto directed by Myron Schaeffer. In *Stereophony*, however, he had no recourse to frequency generators or any other kind of electronic machinery to aid him in his search for new ways of plotting sound against time. He uses traditional instruments but groups the players in different locations throughout the hall, thereby adding a spatial dimension to the sound perceived by the listener:

> The title refers to the distribution of the orchestral forces in order to utilize the stereophonic possibilities inherent in a concert hall, that is, the projection of sound sources towards different parts of the stage and the hall. This means that the work differs or varies according to the position of the listener. This also allows the composer to write a score that would be impossible if there was only one focus. For he can use space to create all kinds of anti-phonal and polyphonic combinations which might be far too heavy or too confused if they were produced by the orchestra seated in the usual way.

"I consider this score," adds the author, "as a work in progress."

Eventually, Somers would like to add a group of wandering musicians who would circulate throughout the corridors and even in the hall while performing their own "segment" of the work. The composer's problem was to find locations for the musicians that would allow maximum utilization of space in a circular direction as well as in height. At the first performance of the work in Toronto, he used the two balconies above the stage as well as those overlooking the hall; then he arranged the instruments in such a way that two identical instruments were never seated on the same level or on a level forming a circumference. The string orchestra was divided into two groups and used antiphonally. Four trumpets present the basic elements that are developed in the course of the work. A series of twelve tones divided into three groups of four appears in all serial combinations. An interesting feature of *Stereophony* is the deliberate lack of synchronization perceived by the ear; the time-lag consists of some fractions of a second. Even if the musicians responded instantly to the conductor, the listener would be left with the impression of a lack of synchronization, of a lack of symmetry of sound structures unfolding in time. This phenomenon, which, in certain cases, is considered "a fault, can be turned into a virtue," says the composer, "if it is taken into consideration while the work is being conceived."

Stereophony is certainly an exceedingly interesting and highly successful work, a veritable *résumé* of all the experiments conducted by the author; it excels in contrapuntal writing and shows a preference for unusual sonorities handled with exquisite taste. What materials were chosen, how they are employed, how they are related to each other and incorporated into the framework of serial structures—all these are significant factors enhancing one of the most original scores in the Canadian repertoire. *Stereophony* was premièred in Toronto; it was also performed in Australia in 1965.

His self-confidence, his technical facility, have made it possible for Somers to master a variety of forms. He wrote an opera, *The Fool* (1953), a *Passacaglia and Fugue* for orchestra (1954), a *Symphony* (1951), also a number of quartets; the second one (1950) is a very profound and introspective work. In all of his writings, Somers seems to strive for a perfect balance of rigour and freedom; he is certainly one of our most gifted and accomplished composers.

Clermont Pepin does not belong to those composers who are

influenced by and adopt one style after another; he follows the natural evolution of his thought. He has a great gift for improvisation. His Canadian mentors, Claude Champagne and Arnold Walter, taught him respect for writing and the self-discipline that goes with it; they helped him to develop his innate capacities. His early works are strikingly dynamic, having a profile all their own. His French teachers were Arthur Honegger and André Jolivet; thanks to them—thanks also to his own talent and temperament—he arrived at inner convictions that governed him between 1955 and 1963, during a time when personal and artistic problems overshadowed problems of craft and technique. His lyricism (romantic at times), his deep sincerity, show Honegger's influence. Jolivet aroused in him an interest in sacred ritual music, in its rhythms and modes. It was also Jolivet—a follower of Varèse in this respect—who encouraged his Canadian pupil to explore new sound sources and to free himself from the dictates of tonality.

The main ingredients of Pepin's style are powerful rhythms (they are quite obsessive at times) and strong polyphonic textures capable of evoking a world of magic and incantations, particularly in his symphonic poem *Le Rite du Soleil Noir* which won him, in 1955, the second prize in the International Competition of Radio Luxembourg. The work—it is partly atonal—displays all the peculiarities of his style (so does *Guernica*, a symphonic poem dating from 1952): the ability to produce telling effects, forceful rhythms, dramatic power and a contrapuntal web, reminding one of Honegger in its strength.

A new level is reached in the quartet called *Hyperbole* (1960); there, as well as in *Nombre* (1963) the predominant feature is serial counterpoint relentlessly applied. In *Monade*, his most recent work, Pepin creates quasi-electronic effects by using traditional string instruments.

Monade is written for an ensemble of fourteen string instruments, not for a "compact ensemble," but for fourteen sound sources that are sometimes independent of one another. In sum, *Monade* is scored for fourteen instruments whose timbres, although basically identical, here become truly diversified and as it were personalized by their different methods of attack, their respective rhythms and their differences in pitch.

No doubt we must consider *Monade* an experimental work characterized by effects particular to electronic music, teeming with rhythmic and contrapuntal complexities; one can only hope that the new trend will not obliterate the warmth, the very human qualities of the composer's earlier works.

For François Morel (1926) sensory impressions are of great importance. It was Varèse who kindled his love for sound material as such, who aroused his interest in hitherto unused materials, in the infinite variety of acoustical phenomena including evocative noises. Varèse's influence (though perfectly assimilated) manifests itself also in the structural procedures adopted by Morel, in the constant transformation of basic cells, of sonority, density and rhythmics. Varèse finally confirmed the composer in his belief that music should be associated with all the cosmic forces.

Morel—virtually self-taught—is one of the most gifted composers of his generation. His first public success came in 1953 when Leopold Stokowski conducted his *Antiphonie* in Carnegie Hall. Essentially of French culture by taste and sensitivity, Morel succeeds in creating an impressionistic score in which mediaeval and modern elements appear closely connected and perfectly blended. Morel himself explains:

The horn starts a Gregorian melopoeia as a counter-melody that is gradually integrated by means of complex neo-impressionistic chords often used in blocks. Chords in seconds and dissonant super-structures in thirds are also being used. Although the chords are not related to a tonal centre they are related to each other by the thread of the modal melody.

Already in 1947 Morel had revealed his impressionistic nature when he wrote *Esquisses*, modal in character. This work succeeds in evoking the sketches of Degas. He knows how to integrate the result of Debussy's, Messiaen's and Varèse's boldest experiments into his own writings in an original and highly personal manner. Varèse drew his attention to the possibilities inherent in sound material and provided him with new structural concepts. Being an indefatigable explorer (without being the slave of any system) Morel interests himself in all modern idioms; his taste, however, his keen intelligence, allow him to view them with discernment.

After an impressionistic period (if we may describe it that way), Morel moves in different directions; he writes a *Symphony for Brass* incorporating jazz elements into an idiom that has lost the modal flavour of his previous works. His studies of Stravinsky scores (*Le Sacre* in particular and *Les Noces*) and Varèse's work assisted him in his attempts to free himself of earlier influences, and led to the creation of *Rituel de l'espace* (1958–59), his first atonal work.

Previously unaffected by the Vienna School, Morel now turns to serialism, using it as a co-ordinating element in atonal textures. His first essay in serialism, entitled *Boréal* (1959), characterized by a constant oscillation of density, seems to hark back to Varèse. Boulez' influence must be added to that of Varèse; Morel seems to have been particularly impressed by *Les Improvisations sur Mallarmé*, by Boulez' highly original orchestration, by the almost magic effects drawn from harp, vibraphone, bells, percussion, snare drums and suspended cymbals. This was a score to which Morel's poetic nature deeply responded. In 1960 he wrote *Le Mythe de la Roche Percée* for two wind ensembles, where atonalism submits more and more to the organizing principles of serialism. In 1962 he paid his respects to one of our greatest painters, Paul-Emile Borduas by writing *L'Etoile Noire* or *Tombeau de Borduas*. The painting itself had received the Guggenheim prize of 1960 and was judged to be the best Canadian painting of that year. Thinking in terms of an analogy between the two arts involved, Morel establishes a play in contrasts between the sections, starting with the "blot" of the technique known as tachism. For this he uses the three traditional divisions of the orchestra. There is an affinity between this work and Mondrian's neo-plasticism with its "immobility in the manner of Vermeer." One might say that the techniques involving the generalized series enable the composer to reproduce the impression of a mysterious silence given by the painting. The generalized series becomes a means of exploring the totality of tonal space and opens new perspectives within the sections. The painter plays with the imponderables of space; the composer—by osmosis as it were—identifies himself with the material, impresses his musical personality upon it. He uses stereophonic devices in the work; not in the placement of players, however, but within a given instrumental section. Here are his comments:

. . . the basic material of the work is provided by a series of twelve tones, without, however, being written in constant twelve tone style. Within this series two segments contain a quotation from Beethoven's Quartet in F Major Opus 135: "Muss es sein? Es muss sein." The work starts with a dramatic introduction that establishes a connection with Borduas' painting. It communicates a feeling of grandeur, of shock, even of violence reflecting the contrasting *valeurs* of the painting itself.

In l'Etoile Noire there is no theme as the term is commonly understood. A dramatic introduction is followed by the first part, containing a fugal section. This climax is succeeded by the second part, containing material previously presented which leads into the coda. The Coda itself, formed like question and answer, is based on one and the same motif presented in a single melodic line. L'Etoile Noire ends in an atmosphere of profound calm engendered by the intuitive comprehension of space. It is like the contemplation of a new dawn that, moment by moment, creates its own light.

One of Morel's most recent works of import is his second string quartet (1962–63). It is here that the composer is at his best as far as polyphony is concerned. No doubt it makes the least concessions of all of his works. In his first quartet the influence of Bartok can still be detected; the second one, however, bears witness to the composer's evolution; it shows splendid craftsmanship and captivates by its intrinsic logic of design. Morel is a man of talent, of high intelligence and great sensitivity; a composer who loves to experiment—a representative figure of our age.

One could also emphasize the genuinely high quality of Roger Matton (1929) whose rhythmic accent is very typical of our country. The accurate expression of a certain violence and his aggressiveness are psychological elements that Matton has been able to render with all the dynamism that characterizes a young nation. Certainly, he is less concerned with nationalism in music than with authenticity and he tends to yield under stress of necessity. This seems evident in *Horoscope*, a choreographic suite (1958) based on an Acadian legend. In *The Forge*, a work in which he obtains evocative sound effects from the percussion instruments, Matton demonstrates that he is quite capable of achieving striking effects.

Deux Mouvements Symphoniques I and II (1960–62) indicate a new integration of the rhythmic elements of his language: on the one hand the syncopations derived from jazz (*Mouvement Symphonique I*), on the other, the obstinate and percussive rhythms in the manner of Bartok (*Concerto for two pianos*).

Roger Matton's work, as a whole, has a style, an atmosphere all its own. This is certainly more than can be said of the writings of many of his contemporaries which depend rather heavily on borrowings from chosen models. His inner freedom, his absolute sincerity are guarantors of his originality, of the high quality of his work.

THE AVANT-GARDE ON THE WAY TO BREAKING THE SOUND BARRIER

"Ni la matière, ni l'espace, ni le temps, ne sont depuis
vingt ans ce qu'ils étaient depuis toujours."
                                        Paul Valéry

Our younger composers belong to an *avant-garde* eager to contribute its share to the discovery of new perspectives of sound. Most of them are twelve-tone composers. Following in the footsteps of Boulez or Stockhausen, they set themselves the task of exploring the possibilities inherent in a generalized series without shying away from the final consequences of such investigations; the act of composing itself needs to be re-thought. The magical results of sound transformation by electronic means—so apt to drive the audiences of our subscription concerts into a panic—enable the fiercely *avant-gardistes* to determine how the sound material manifests itself in time and space, allowing the musical flow to create its own shape in the unfolding.

The first electronic music studio appeared in the National Research Council in Ottawa. The University of Toronto, and later on McGill University, followed suit; the number of studios is steadily on the increase. Following Stockhausen's visit to Montreal in 1964, several composers changed their outlook. A whole new world of sound opened up, new concepts of content and form changed musical perception itself and influenced creative thought. In Canada as everywhere else, Webern, Varèse, Messiaen, and their disciples Boulez and Stockhausen, were the recognized leaders of the movement.

Some of these progressive composers favour improvisation and chance, appearing within the various structures. Others explore the various parameters of the sound material, while most of them are keenly interested in indeterminacy which, in the case of Stockhausen, affects form itself, resulting in compositions giving free rein to interpretation: every performance will be a different entity: we are in the presence of a new philosophy of form. Boulez "poétique de l'instant" seems particularly fascinating. It embodies a new notion of time: moments of action are followed by moments of contemplation. "During the periods of contemplation sounds are being transformed without being modified [says Boulez], a musical entity already presented is prolonged by resonance that ought to be listened to. The musical event itself appears during the period of action."

An outstanding *avant-garde* composer who had the courage to defend modern music was Pierre Mercure. Born in 1927, he died in 1965; his last works gave ample proof of his talent, his daring, his indefatigable search for new horizons. In his earlier works (it happens to young composers generally) Mercure did not escape the influence of older masters; one is often reminded of Stravinsky (in *Pantomime*, 1948) or of Ravel (*Kaleidoscope*, also 1948). The *Cantate pour une joie*, however, for soprano, choir and orchestra based on a text of Gabriel

Charpentier and written in 1956, is of surprising originality, born of inner necessity and full of poetry. Only a year later, Mercure finished the *Divertissement pour Quatuor à cordes et orchestre à cordes*, a work admirably structured and very compact in style.

By 1951 Mercure had already shown an interest in serial techniques. Inquisitive by nature, he explored every contemporary idiom; in 1949 he discovered Pierre Schaeffer's *musique concrète*; which was a revelation rather than a simple discovery. The sorcery of Schaeffer's "sound objects" aroused his curiosity and stimulated his imagination. He began to use *musique concrète* most ingeniously, combining it with traditional orchestral timbres. Two of his last works are in that category: *Formes 64* (film) for *musique concrète* and wind instruments, i.e., saxophone, tuba and trombone written in 1964; and *Eléments 3* (film) for flute and *musique concrète*, composed in 1965. Sound materials stemming from disparate sources appear in masterful synthesis; no doubt Mercure, had he lived, would have become a leader in the realm of new music.

After 1961—at that time he was organizing *La Semaine de Musique actuelle* during the Montreal Festivals—he devoted most of his energy to *La musique expérimentale*. Whether he turned to *musique concrète* (films), *musique synthétique* (*Incandescence*, 1961) or to electronic music proper (*Psaume pour abri* 1963), he was never afraid to explore new worlds of sound, always hoping that the public would follow him; which it did not, excepting those few who believed in him. He did not shy away from the untried and the uncommon, he agreed with Otto Luening who had said that the new sound material, however strange, could be put to legitimate musical uses. From Boulez and Stockhausen he had learned how to organize the material; he followed their example—he would rather take risks than remain indifferent, inactive and secure. The present, to him, was a time of high adventure.

Among those who fight for recognition of new music in Montreal, Serge Garant (born 1929) deserves consideration.

In December, 1966, he established a Contemporary Music Society which might well do for Montreal what *Le Domaine Musical* does for Paris. *Musique concrète* made less of an impression on him than on Mercure. A follower of Boulez, he is mainly interested in serialism affecting all parameters; problems of structure appeal to him more than electronic artifices. While Boulez, however, rejects anything not rigorously controlled, Garant likes to experiment with chance music. No doubt Stockhausen's appearance in Montreal (already referred to) hastened Garant's development. Two of his works are the result of his pre-occupation with chance procedures: *Ouranos* and *Ennéade* (1964). *Ouranos* (performed by the Quebec Symphony orchestra) calls for an enlarged percussion section of twenty different instruments. The work consists of eleven sections; the conductor is free to start with any one of them but is asked to return to the sections previously omitted. In *Ennéade* —consisting of nine sections—the chance element is still stronger; the conductor may perform the sections in any order he wishes to (Ennéade means an ensemble of nine similar entities). It stands to reason that every performance creates virtually a new work. The composer provides a basic outline taking a future development into consideration that becomes ever more definite and compact in structure.

Chance music can be used in a number of ways. Stockhausen has provided us with a list of those he uses in his works; they range from strictly defined structures to others allowing a maximum of chance. Garant's most successful attempt in that genre is *Anerca* (for soprano and eight instruments, written in 1965), a work that—comparable to jazz—materializes and develops only in performance. Organized on the lines of *la peinture nonfigurative*, it relies a great deal on improvisation. "The musicians are given a rhythm pattern to improvise on," Garant tells us, "but they are, at least to a certain extent, guided and directed while improvising." The composer maintains, and rightly so, that musicians should not be afraid of the unknown; they should be prepared to come to grips with it whatever the outcome might be. He himself accepts the risks involved; every one of his new works demonstrates his courage to live in the here and now.

Among Montreal composers Otto Joachim is the most daring, the most advanced one. A violist by profession, he is both a clear thinker and a visionary, occupying a far-out position in the progressive movement. Deeply impressed by Webern's serialism, he explores the field of twelve-tone music to its last limits and, like Boulez, he is deeply convinced that Webern's music contains the seeds of hitherto unsuspected developments, that serialism need not be confined to pitch only. What distinguishes him from Webern, however, are his rhythmical procedures characterized by contractions and expansions derived from Messiaen; which brings him nearer to Boulez.

The particularities of his style are evident in his *Music* for violin and viola, in the cello sonata, in a piano piece called *Eclosion*. *Music* is the title of a work in five movements; the sections increase in complexity while diminishing in length so that the last movement is very concise and compressed.

Joachim has a great liking for unusual, for literally unheard-of sounds, drawn from traditional instruments; here we find him inspired by Varèse whom he greatly admired. The sound effects in *Eclosion*—pedal effects, staccati, harmonics, bell sounds—are all derived from the piano.

His interest in chance music led to the creation of one of the most original scores ever to appear in Canada. *Illuminations No. 1* (1966) for two percussion instruments, flute, guitar, piano and narrator. It is basically a twelve-tone work using aleatory combinations indicated on a special chart. The musicians are sitting in the dark. Above every one of them there appears a light wired to a control panel that is manipulated by the composer. The intensity of the light determines both tempo and dynamics. One concludes that chance music here is controlled or directed, even though the composer must be prepared for unforeseen happenings.

Following the lead of the universities of Toronto and McGill, Joachim established an electronic music studio of his own; it is worth mentioning that he was invited to write an electronic composition for the Canadian Pavilion at Expo '67: the inverted pyramid of the pavilion radiated strange sonorities that seemed to come from outer space, musical symbols of our scientific and industrial civilization. His raw-material consists of electronically generated sounds (some of the apparatus is of his own invention), sub-harmonics of saw tooth waves in particular. Neither *musique concrète* nor traditional instruments are being used; Schaeffer's *objets sonores* have no attraction for Joachim.

At the time of writing he is putting the finishing touches on an important orchestral work commissioned for the Centennial. It is called *Contrastes* and seems to benefit from all his researches in the fields of serialism, stereophony and chance music. It is worth mentioning that the two composers who were chosen to help celebrate the Century of Confederation were François Morel and Otto Joachim; certainly an honour to be proud of.

Among the younger composers Gilles Tremblay deserves a special place; although still very young he has important works to his credit: *Cantique de Durée* scored for an orchestra of fifty divided into seven groups, performed in Paris under Ernest Bour at the Domaine Musical; *Champs* (1965) for piano, marimba, vibraphone and percussion, performed in Montreal by the Ensemble de percussion de Paris; and an electronic composition for the Québec Pavilion at Expo 67. Twenty-four channels were used in performance, demonstrating the composer's interest in stereophonic devices and antiphonal effects. No doubt Tremblay is master of his métier; musical acumen and a high degree of sensitivity characterize his work.

Turning to Istvan Anhalt we find that he, too, is bent on exploring unknown regions in the universe of sound. Born in Budapest in 1919, he studied under Kodaly, Louis Fourestier and Nadia Boulanger; at present he directs the electronic music studio of McGill University. His Symphony (1954–58) is a serial work consisting of thirteen sections all based on a short motif of four notes. Anhalt's use of twelve-tone techniques is markedly different from Weinzweig's or Somers'; he is closer to Schoenberg in this respect. Like Schoenberg, he avoids the doubling of choral notes above or below, yet, true to Central European traditions, he has no hesitation to double in unison— in the *Sonata for Violin and Piano*, for instance, whose special flavour can be traced to that device. Anhalt's serialism is of Austrian persuasion, atonal and athematic. In order to avoid what might be construed as a compromise with thematic concepts derived from classicism, he generally shies away from the periodicity and prefers greater freedom in rhythmic structure. As a result of all this the emerging style is highly abstract and by no means easily grasped.

Comments is one of Anhalt's most original works. Scored for contralto, violin, cello and piano, it is a setting of three short clippings from the *Montreal Star* (they were distributed among the audience when the work was first performed). The first "comment," for instance, refers to the headline "Bali's leading dancer slain"; the music is inspired by the modes, the timbres, the intensely poetic atmosphere of Indonesian gamelan ensembles. The last of the "comments" shows that a true musician can use almost any text as a pretext for writing, even if it is only a weather report he is setting to music. It is not the subject matter that counts in art but the over-all achievement. Right now Anhalt is deeply involved in electronics, surrounding himself with generators, filters, modifiers, multi-track recorders and other kinds of apparatus, much of it invented by Dr. Hugh LeCaine of the National Research Council who gained a world-wide reputation as a pioneer in the field.

Murray Schaefer (born 1933, a pupil of Weinzweig) moved from polytonality (*Harpsichord concerto* 1954) to pantonality (*In Memoriam: Alberto Guerrero*, 1959); and finally, in *Protest and Incarceration* (1960) and *The Judgement of Joel* (1961), to atonality. In *Dithyramb* he espouses serialism. The various movements of *Dithyramb* are closely interrelated, each serving as antecedent for the following. In *Canzoni for Prisoners* we find him experimenting with timbres, mixing sounds derived from percussion instruments, vibraphone, celesta, harp and piano: the pieces are veritable studies in sonority. Sometimes they remind one of the *pizzicato* effects in Alban Berg's *Lyric Suite*, sometimes of the Ondes Martenot, their specific timbre and those half-tone glissandi which are rather tiresome if used in profusion. The work is atonal; its five sections are interconnected, they are variants of the basic material. The canonic devices and isorhythmic groupings employed in the score have rather a Stravinskyan flavour. Yet Schaefer is extraordinarily skilful in writing canons; he demonstrates his dexterity in the *Five Studies on texts by Prudentius*, each study being a canon either strict or free. The "studies" are to be performed stereophonically: a singer (soprano) occupies the stage; flute players are stationed in the four corners of the hall. Thus "the special movement of the music is accordingly centrifugal in 'Adam and Eve'," writes the composer, "diagonal, in 'Moses has received the law', circular in 'The City of Bethlehem' ".

But it is in *Loving* or *Toi*—a veritable audio-visual poem—that Schaefer explores further possibilities. *Toi* is a television opera in which he uses every technique at his command—rapidly alternating scenes, superimposed images, a multitude of actors appearing and disappearing at a pace that would be quite impossible on the stage. Electronics play their part; video-tape montages are put to good use. The final results are what we might call a functional opera whose technical aspects serve the purpose of illuminating a highly ambiguous and complex subject: love, for that is what the play is all about. "*Toi*," says Schaefer, "has no plot in the usual meaning of the term, that is no situations arranged in logical order proceeding from Point A to Point B. On the contrary, the scenes are interrelated regardless of time and space, without any specific chronology or topography." To find a musical equivalent for the subconscious manifestations of love in dreams and hidden yearnings the composer uses *Sprechgesang*. No matter that some words, some phrases are quite incomprehensible—they are symbols for psychological forces concealed below the threshold of consciousness. The work makes a powerful impact. With its

Freudian implications and the apparent lack of coherence, it owes its existence to a dynamic conception of time and space in relation to the conscious and unconscious aspects of love.

Thanks to the creation of the Canadian National Film Board in 1939, film music gained in importance. Outstanding composers (Robert Fleming, Maurice Blackburn, Eldon Rathburn) wrote scores that were both effective and significant, relating image and sound in an artistically satisfying manner. They disproved the notion that film music plays only a subordinate role, that it necessarily restricts the freedom of the composer.

In the case of Blackburn, for instance, the limits imposed merely enhance his powers of invention (though he may have had to revise his classical equipment and to change his outlook). "If you work with a stopwatch in hand you learn to cut out all padding," says Henri Sauguet. Canadian films helped to bring a special brand of film music into being—concise, compact and smoothly integrated into the rhythmical flow of images.

A successful dialogue between music and film obviously depends on the sound materials used, on the techniques employed, the experiments conducted. Blackburn's and Norman McLaren's experiments gave splendid results, they could be called revolutionary; signs for sounds were directly drawn on celluloid; thus they were automatically synchronized with the picture. Such sounds, particularly those that appear in animated design, have a great affinity with electronic music. "Workshops Experiment in Animated Sound" is, as the name implies, an experimental film, "an inventory of divers synthetic sounds resulting from experiments conducted over the years: identical designs are engraved on picture and sound frames, a method that allows us to study the graphic equivalents of the sonorities produced" (Olivier Clouzot). It is hardly surprising that discoveries of such importance should have met with international recognition.

CONCLUSION

"La musique reflète toujours une époque, une
manière de penser et de sentir."
Norbert Dufourcq

Historical and musicological studies bear out our contention
that Canadian composition (however varied in style and eclectic
in some instances) is markedly different from music written in
other countries. That Canadian music itself is diversified in the
extreme, could no doubt be attributed to a variety of causes—
to the multi-racial composition of the population, for instance,
to inherited characteristics. Diversification should not surprise
us in a vast country like Canada, less a country than a continent, extending over more than 10 million square kilometres,
harbouring 20 million people of different origins and exposed
to every climate under the sun. It is perhaps not too important
to uncover all the reasons for disparity, for the lack of stylistic
unity; ethnical kinship, however, and geographical location
play a large role in the formation of easily distinguishable
groups.

The United States, our good neighbour to the South, influences our composers a great deal, some of them at least.
The practitioners of jazz have learned to master the idiom—its
captivating rhythms, its subtle and intricate forms, its highly
original instrumentation, its creative impulses. The sojourn of
men like Schoenberg and Krenek in the United States had great
repercussions; the fact that Copland, Hindemith, Bartok, Stravinsky, resided there also was a determining factor in the development of some Canadian composers. French-speaking
composers were in sympathy with (and reflect) the neo-modalism stemming from Fauré, Debussy and Ravel so characteristic
of French music between the two world wars. Champagne's
modalism harks back to France, Weinzweig's chromaticism is
of German provenance, his serialism is of Austrian extraction.
It is worth noting that French-Canadian composers—like their
opposite numbers in France—started to use twelve-tone techniques well after Torontonian musicians had done so (Wein-

zweig, for instance, in 1939). Studying stylistic differences, we cannot ignore such cultural contexts.

In concluding our short survey of Canadian composition and its history it should perhaps be pointed out that the present chapter was not designed to cover every detail; it fulfills the modest function of presenting a provisional outline. Violet Archer, Alexander Brott, John Beckwith, Oskar Morawetz, Udo Kasemets, Robert Fleming, deserve more than a casual mention; their works will be dealt with in a separate study.

That the young occupy such a prominent place in our narrative is easily explained: in a country where all is present and future, the rising generation is of surpassing importance. It is true, of course, that history's concern is with the past; but we shall perhaps be forgiven for not waiting until death writes *finis* under the last line of a chapter, for pointing out that even work hardly begun may be pregnant of the future. As to the *avant-garde*, it would be presumptuous to deliver a verdict here and now; we must needs wait until the period of gestation is over, until definite results are forthcoming. Novel aspects of art —giving rise to new approaches, new techniques—deserve attention, however puzzling they may seem at first: art is an integral part of life and life a never-ending creative process.

Having dealt with what we called "the second period" (that drew sustenance from earlier times), we found ourselves in the presence of a vast landscape reaching from our shores to Paris, Vienna, Munich and New York. The affinities expressed, the relationships established will influence the shape of things to come, will lead us into a Golden Age perhaps in which great writers (following in the footsteps of Canadian poets and painters) might reach that innermost depth that is accessible only to those who can penetrate beyond the patterns of the abstract play and reach into the substance.

APPENDIX

Since the foregoing chapter was written in 1966, it makes no mention of the remarkable achievements of our Centennial year. That year was certainly a vintage year for composition, in quantity as well as quality. Over 130 commissions went to composers in every nook and corner of the country. Some scores have yet to be performed; to judge the lot of them would certainly be premature. It can be said, however, that in their very diversity they are a true mirror of our country, which progresses by leaps and bounds rather than by measured step (and sometimes violently so); which happens to every young country full of creative energy. It is creative energy that characterizes the works under discussion; we must leave it to future historians to decide whether 1967 marked the beginning of a new era.

Somers' opera *Louis Riel*, Roger Matton's *Te Deum*, Otto Joachim's *Contrastes*, Clermont Pepin's *Quasars* (not to forget the latest works of Anhalt and Morel) are notable achievements, signposts in the development of each of these composers, landmarks in the evolution of Canadian composition as a whole.

Performers

GILLES POTVIN

BY ITS very nature, music is perhaps the most universal of all the performing arts. It addresses itself to all men without exception, without any distinction of race or culture. But in order to play its role to the full, music, just like a human being, needs to be alive, and it is the performer's function constantly to bring music to life, to animate as if by magic all the notes which lie dormant in a score.

One must agree that composers, by virtue of the fact that they are creators, play the fundamental role in the establishment of a national form of music in any given country. But one must grant the performer the importance which is his due, and which is not at all secondary. On the contrary, in fact, he is of vital importance, for it is necessarily to the performer that the composer has first to turn, unless he is himself a performer, if he wants to be sure that his work will reach an audience at all.

It is also the artist's mission to perpetuate, by interpretations which are as authentic as possible, the great international repertoire. It is both a privilege and a responsibility for the performer to be called upon to transmit to the public a Bach oratorio, a Beethoven sonata, a lied of Schubert or a prelude by Debussy. The performance of a work from a written score is one of the noblest professions. Although the composer is the one who opens the way, the performer is his indispensable travelling companion.

When the performer stands alone, he carries on his shoulders the responsibility of bringing the works to life, and to do so he must use all his talent and all his knowledge. It often happens that a musical performance is a collective venture, when two or more performers come together to play the same work. They are then obliged to share their knowledge and to sacrifice their personal views on a work in favour of a common ideal. When there are very many performers—as in symphonic and choral works, in opera—the presence of a conductor is indispensable. Then everyone is obliged to comply with the wishes of a single person.

Without wishing to minimize the contribution of soloists, it may be said that the real musical climate of a country can be measured most effectively by group performances, by the number and quality of the country's orchestras, its choral groups, its opera companies and its chamber music ensembles.

It is the purpose of this chapter to present a rapid survey of the performance of music in Canada at the present moment. Neither the number nor the importance of all the elements concerned can be condensed in a few pages. The reader is therefore asked to understand and excuse certain gaps and omissions which are unavoidable, considering the scope of the subject.

All aspects of the subject will be treated in turn—symphony orchestras, opera companies, solo musicians, chamber music, and music festivals, without forgetting operetta, musical comedy and choral music. The chapter will conclude with brief observations on the structure of musical societies, the participation of public bodies and individuals as well as the role of impressarios and concert agents.

As a result of the Centennial of Confederation and the holding of the World's Fair in Montreal, a host of artistic performances of an exceptional nature took place in Canada in 1967. A brief survey of these will be given at the end of the chapter.

It is no exaggeration to say that it is the symphony orchestras which form the base and nerve-centre of Canadian musical life. In this respect Canada resembles its powerful neighbour to the south whose great orchestras also play the leading role in musical life. The situation is completely different in Europe, where opera is generally of primary importance.

Montreal and Toronto each have a symphony orchestra of high calibre whose reputations today extend beyond the country's borders. The Montreal orchestra was the first to travel to Europe, on a tour to the Soviet Union, Austria and France in the spring of 1962. The Toronto Symphony however, is older, since it was originally founded in 1908, was disbanded following the outbreak of World War I and was reorganized in 1923. It is composed of about 98 instrumentalists and from 1965–66 until the end of the 1968–69 season its artistic director has been the young Japanese conductor Seiji Ozawa. He will be succeeded by Karel Ancerl, a Czechoslovakian conductor. In the 1967–68 season the TSO presented two principal series spread over thirty-five weeks, and it is expected that by 1971 the season will be forty-two weeks long. In addition to the subscription concerts for adults, there are many educational concerts for young people, concerts at moderate prices and concerts given in neighbouring cities.

In the autumn of 1965 the Toronto Symphony Orchestra represented Canada at the Commonwealth Arts Festival in London, and, on the same occasion, also appeared in Paris and Lyons. The quality of the orchestra and the dynamism of its young conductor were emphasized in enthusiastic reviews by the English and French press. "Toronto has little to fear from European rivals," sums up the opinion of the critic of the London *Daily Express*.

The Toronto Symphony has also had outstanding success in the United States in the last few years, particularly in New York and Washington. On the occasion of the Centennial of Confederation, the TS commissioned works from two Canadian composers, Otto Joachim and François Morel, as well as from the Italian composer Luigi Nono.

In the course of its regular season, the Orchestra invites the most renowned international soloists to appear with it. Among the guest conductors have been Charles Munch, Sir John Barbirolli, Joseph Krips, Pierre Monteux, Eugen Jochum, Paul Kletzki and Colin Davis, all names that show how high a standard has been reached by this Orchestra.

The Montreal Symphony Orchestra was founded in 1934 and was first called the Orchestra of the Société des Concerts Symphoniques de Montréal. Several great conductors, such as Désiré Defauw, Otto Klemperer and Igor Markevitch, guided its destiny for various lengths of time. Under the baton of Zubin Mehta, a young Indian conductor of remarkable talent, and more recently under Franz-Paul Decker's direction, the MSO has become an orchestra of the highest order, and its quality has been confirmed by two European tours. The first of these, in 1962, took the Montreal musicians to the Soviet Union, France and Austria. The second, in the autumn of 1966, was limited to the French-speaking countries of Europe: France, Switzerland and Belgium.

In Montreal, the Orchestra annually presents two subscription series in the Salle Wilfrid-Pelletier at Place des Arts, and, in addition, presents numerous concerts for school-children and university students, as well as four concerts at which admission costs one dollar, given under the auspices of the daily newspaper *The Montreal Star*.

Starting in 1938, the MSO inaugurated a series of summer concerts on the summit of Mount Royal, a site that is unique in North America. These concerts were continued for about twenty years. Now the MSO participates in an important series of summer concerts given each week at the Maurice-Richard Arena, in the east end of the City. These popular concerts were modelled on the famous Boston "Pops," where the pleasures of wine and cheese-tasting are combined with the pleasures of music.

Like the Toronto orchestra, the Montreal orchestra consists of a group of instrumentalists of high calibre, and its flexibility has been recognized by the celebrated conductors who have directed it. The MSO is now under the artistic direction of Franz-Paul Decker.

In order of importance, the country's third symphony orchestra is the Vancouver Orchestra, whose present conductor is the Englishman, Meredith Davies. The ensemble consists of about seventy-five instrumentalists and gives about seventy concerts a year. In Vancouver itself, the Orchestra's regular concert-hall is the Queen Elizabeth Theatre. Like the orchestras of Montreal and Toronto, the Vancouver Symphony Orchestra invites soloists of international reputation. It also gives many concerts in neighbouring localities.

On the occasion of the Centennial this orchestra commissioned a work from the celebrated Argentinian composer Alberto Ginastera.

It is with understandable pride that the Quebec Symphony Orchestra can claim to be the oldest in the country. It was founded by the musician and composer Joseph Vézina as far back as 1903. In spite of great difficulties, it succeeded in presenting at least a few concerts every year. It was not until much later that the QSO attained a certain stability. From 1950 to 1966, Wilfrid Pelletier was the permanent conductor and under his enthusiastic direction great progress was made. In 1960 it became a permanent orchestra and it now gives more than seventy concerts per season. Pierre Dervaux is its general director and he himself conducts most of the concerts, not only in Quebec City but also in Trois Rivières and several other cities in Quebec.

The Quebec Orchestra consists of about sixty instrumentalists and also invites outstanding conductors and soloists, several of whom, such as the renowned Roumanian conductor Sergiu Celibidache and the French conductor Jacques Pernoo, have made their North American débuts with the orchestra.

At the moment the concerts are held in the inadequate Palais-Montcalm where the orchestra will remain until the completion of the Grand Théâtre de Québec, scheduled for this year.

Like most Canadian orchestras, the Winnipeg Symphony Orchestra has developed particularly in the course of the last ten years. Its total strength is more or less equivalent to the Quebec orchestra's and it gives about the same number of concerts. Victor Feldbrill, who was the director until the end of the 1967–68 season, has been largely responsible for this expansion. The season consists of a substantial subscription series as well as numerous additional concerts, which were given in the Civic Auditorium until the opening of the new Winnipeg Concert Hall, which was completed in 1968. Mr. Feldbrill has always been a champion of Canadian music and each season's programmes have always given a considerable place to our composers. A young American conductor, George Cleve, succeeded Mr. Feldbrill.

The only important symphony orchestra east of the Province of Quebec is what was called the Halifax Orchestra, but which is now known as the Atlantic Symphony Orchestra and comprises about forty-five instrumentalists whose annual concerts number about seventy. Several conductors of European origin have in turn directed it: Thomas Mayer, Jonathan Sternberg, Leo Mueller. Recent seasons have been under the direction of John Fenwick; at the moment Klaro M. Mizerit is its official permanent conductor.

The vigour of the two principal orchestras in Alberta, those of Edmonton and Calgary, is no doubt due at least in part to the construction of the splendid auditoriums with which the Alberta government endowed the two cities in 1955, on the occasion of the province's fiftieth birthday.

The Edmonton Symphony Orchestra, comprised of about seventy musicians, was under the dynamic direction of Brian Priestman, who is an Englishman by birth but who received part of his musical education in Belgium and France. He has been succeeded by Lawrence Leonard.

In addition to its regular season, this orchestra gives educational concerts, often in far-flung localities which can only rarely expect to hear a visiting orchestra. The Chamber Orchestra founded by Mr. Priestman, which presents a different repertoire, should also be mentioned.

The Calgary Philharmonic Orchestra, consisting of about seventy instrumentalists, is now directed by José Iturbi. The Orchestra regularly invites soloists of the highest rank.

The second most important orchestra in British Columbia is that of the capital city, Victoria, and was for a few seasons directed by Otto Werner-Mueller. In the course of a single season the orchestra presents a subscription series of eleven concerts as well as matinées and special concerts. Since the fall of 1967 its new conductor has been Laszlo Gati.

Space does not permit a detailed discussion of the other symphonic groups which exist, notably in cities such as Hamilton, London, Sherbrooke, Kingston, Kitchener-Waterloo, Brantford, Lethbridge, Sarnia, Fredericton, St. Catharines, and Windsor.

Because these various orchestras have to function under difficult conditions most of the time, their work is obviously not always of the calibre that they strive to attain. But their enthusiasm and goodwill sometimes obtain astonishing results.

The orchestras in these smaller cities are especially valuable because they acquaint their audiences with the basic symphonic repertoire, and this they do while giving their members the pleasure of participating in a musical performance.

The list of Canadian symphony orchestras is, on the whole, quite impressive if one considers the population of the country and particularly if one takes into account the scattered nature of the urban centres.

OPERA AND OPERETTA

Because of its complexity and the multiplicity of the elements required for its presentation, opera is the most costly of all forms of theatre. But one cannot ignore it for such reasons. The history of opera will soon span four hundred years and its repertoire is incredibly rich and varied. In Europe, opera is a part of daily life; the opera houses are most often public institutions more than a hundred years old, and they are entirely subsidized by the state.

In the United States and Canada, opera has had to maintain itself as a private institution, at least until now. This is difficult and always problematical. It is even astonishing that the operatic situation in North America is what it is, in spite of the insecurity and danger which threaten all organizations concerned with opera.

For decades the only opera productions which Canadians could see and hear were those which came from across the border, such as the San Carlo or the Metropolitan, which had to limit its tours to the large cities.

In a short time, the situation has changed completely. The opera-loving Canadian public now has access at home to opera productions of exceptional quality, which give many Canadian singers the opportunity to distinguish themselves.

The most important opera company in Canada is unquestionably the Canadian Opera Company, founded twenty-two years ago in Toronto thanks to the vision and tenacity of Dr. Arnold Walter, director of the Faculty of Music of the University of Toronto, and of the conductor Nicholas Goldschmidt.

The first productions were modest, but as a result of the enthusiasm of both the participants and the public the company soon broke its ties with the University and became the Opera Festival, which in turn led to the formation of the Canadian Opera Company of today. On the occasion of Centennial, the company presented its most impressive season in September and October 1967: six spectacular productions, two world premières of Canadian operas, making a total of twenty-nine performances at the O'Keefe Centre and five at the Salle Wilfrid-Pelletier, within the framework of the World Festival.

The guiding force of the COC is the eminent stage director, Herman Geiger-Torel, who came to Canada in 1948 after having had a brilliant career in Europe, Latin America and the United States.

In addition to its regular autumn season in Toronto, the COC remains active throughout the year, thanks to the tours which it undertakes from one ocean to the other. These touring productions are naturally subject to particular financial conditions, yet maintain a high artistic quality. Thus the Company completely deserves being called "Canadian," since it serves the whole country.

In order to assure that the Company has the greatest possible mobility, scenery which may be easily dismantled and which can be adapted to stages of all sizes, is especially designed for the tours. As for the production, it is prepared far in advance in Toronto. Double casting permits the singers to face, without danger, a rather heavy schedule of performances and long distances. For reasons of economy, also because orchestra pits are lacking in most of the halls at its disposal, the company uses piano accompaniment only—following the example of an English group called "Opera for All" that operates in a similar way.

In the spring of 1967 Donizetti's *Don Pasquale* was presented in the western provinces, Alaska and the North-West Territories, and a few times in the United States. From January to March 1968 the same production toured Ontario, the Maritimes and Newfoundland.

All these performances are given under the auspices of various local organizations, such as concert societies or social clubs. The COC thus performs a great service in popular education by introducing a vast public to opera, and this it does throughout Canada.

Montreal, the Canadian metropolis, does not yet have a regular opera company because it does not yet have a real opera season. A private association, the Opera Guild, founded in 1940 by Madame Pauline Donalda, is nevertheless the oldest Canadian society devoted exclusively to opera.

Its activity is unfortunately limited to one production a year, presented for only two or three performances. In 1968 *The Barber of Seville* was chosen to mark the centennial of Rossini's death. But the Opera Guild has played an important role in the development of opera in Canada, since it was the first to present Canadian productions of works such as *The Magic Flute, The Abduction from the Seraglio, Fidelio, Le Coq d'Or, Otello* and *Falstaff*. Its casts always include a good number of Canadian artists.

Since the Montreal Symphony Orchestra has been housed in Place des Arts, it has added some operas, about two per season, to its purely symphonic programming. The choice of works is limited to well-known works, such as *Tosca, La Traviata, Carmen, Aïda* and *Rigoletto*. In April 1968, however, *Manon Lescaut* by Puccini was presented. Some stars come from abroad but the majority of the performers are Canadian.

It is evident that the situation in Montreal is in a period of transition, for the MSO will not be able to assume the permanent responsibility of providing a truly important opera season. Mayor Jean Drapeau cherishes the hope of establishing an opera season of the highest calibre in the city.

For its part, the Quebec Ministry of Cultural Affairs announced in July 1967 that it intended to take the first steps towards founding a company that would eventually serve the whole province. A committee headed by Léopold Simoneau drew up a long report on this subject which was submitted to the Minister's office in December 1967. This would indicate that concrete results will be forthcoming shortly.

Opera is not confined to cities like Toronto and Montreal. Since 1959 Vancouver has had its own company, which continues to make progress, presenting splendid productions with artists of the first rank, including several Canadians. The Queen Elizabeth Theatre with its 2,800 seats and vast stage has allowed the Vancouver Opera Association to become one of the principal opera societies in Canada within only a few years.

In the course of the 1966–67 season, the VOA presented *Cavalleria Rusticana* and *I Pagliacci, Lucia di Lammermoor* and *La Traviata*. The world-famous Australian soprano Joan Sutherland, who had sung the title-role of *Norma* for the first time in her career in Vancouver, returned to play the role which made her famous, that of Lucia. In July 1967, as part of the Vancouver Festival, the company presented, for the first time in Canada, *The Girl of the Golden West* by Puccini and, in October, presented *Rigoletto* again, with Louis Quilico in the title role. The 1967–68 season closed with the Canadian première of Wagner's *The Flying Dutchman* and a revival of *Tosca*.

Irving Guttman, artistic and stage director of the VOA, regularly invites the best Canadian singers. Quite recently a second company, the British Columbia Opera Ensemble, was formed in order to increase the opportunity for training young singers by presenting chamber operas on tour.

Another Canadian city where opera is making a great leap forward is Quebec, where the Théâtre Lyrique du Québec, until recently called the Théâtre Lyrique de Nouvelle-France, was founded seven years ago by Roger Gosselin. At the moment the artistic director is the baritone Gilles Lamontagne and the musical director, Jean Deslauriers.

The company started out modestly but its latest productions show what a long way it has come. Every season three or four very well prepared productions are presented in the Palais-Montcalm or in the hall of the Quebec Academy. The best local performers are brought together and are joined by Canadian singers pursuing international careers. The Quebec public is fond of the French repertoire and of French operetta, but the works of Verdi, Mozart and Puccini are also presented.

The 1966–67 season opened with *Mignon* on the occasion of the centenary of the work's creation. This was followed by Offenbach's *La Perichole* and by *La Bohême*. During the Centennial celebrations, the company was invited to give performances of *The Barber of Seville* in several cities. The 1967–68 season featured *Manon*, sung in Montreal and in Quebec City, *Monsieur Beaucaire*, *Cosi fan tutte* and *Tosca*.

The newest Canadian city to establish an opera company is Edmonton. In the autumn of 1963 *Madama Butterfly* was sung at the Jubilee Auditorium and the Edmonton Opera Association was born. *Tosca* and *Faust* were featured in 1966–67 and *The Barber of Seville* and *La Traviata* in 1967–68.

Irving Guttman, the artistic director of the Vancouver Opera Association, assumes the same responsibility in Edmonton, and a fruitful collaboration between the two cities is in the process of being established.

Just as much as opera, operetta and musical comedy find favour with the Canadian public. Occasionally, the professional opera companies follow the example of the Metropolitan Opera of New York in presenting an operetta. It would be difficult to give a complete list here of all the Canadian societies, most of them amateur, which devote themselves to operetta and musical comedy, from Gilbert and Sullivan and Offenbach to Rodgers and Hammerstein. These societies generally limit themselves to one or two annual productions and do their utmost to ensure that their shows are of the highest quality. Hundreds of amateur or semi-professional singers and instrumentalists obtain great pleasure and well-deserved satisfaction from preparing these diverting works long in advance.

SOLOISTS

Never in all its history has Canada known a blossoming of singers and solo instrumentalists equal to that of today. A complete list would be so impressive that one hesitates to draw it up, for fear of forgetting some names. Obviously, Canada has not had to wait until the twentieth century to produce artists who have made their mark in the world. Soon, a hundred years will have passed since the celebrated singer Emma Albani made her début at the Messina Opera and a young pianist-composer by the name of Calixa Lavallée launched, under adventurous circumstances, a remarkable career in the United States. It is, unfortunately, only too well known what difficulties these artists met in achieving recognition in their own country.

Happily, times have changed and the numerous singers and instrumentalists from Canada who pursue careers abroad frequently return to the country of their birth to be applauded by Canadian audiences with all the pride that their talent deserves.

Among the sopranos, one finds names such as Pierrette

Alarie, Teresa Stratas, Colette Boky, Lilian Sukis, Heather Thompson, Maria Pellegrini, Jeanette Zarou, Louise Lebrun, Micheline Tessier, Roxolana Roslak, Clarice Carson, Jean Patenaude and others who have had success in the opera houses of France, Great Britain and the United States. Lois Marshall, one of the most brilliant Canadian concert singers, is in a class by herself as is contralto Maureen Forrester. Other mezzosopranos and contraltos are also an honour to Canada, notably Gladys Kriese, Huguette Tourangeau, Fernande Chiocchio and Réjane Cardinal.

Since the time of Rodolphe Plamondon and Edward Johnson, the Canadian tenors pursuing careers on the great opera stages of the world have been amazingly numerous. To mention Raoul Jobin and Jacques Gérard, Léopold Simoneau, Jon Vickers, Richard Verreau, Pierre Duval, Emile Belcourt, Norman Harper, André Turp, Jean Bonhomme is to name only a few. Among the baritones and basses, we should name Louis Quilico, Victor Braun, Donald Bell, Robert Savoie, John Boyden, Joseph Rouleau, Napoléon Bisson, Don Garrard, Victor Godfrey, Jean-Pierre Hurteau, Norman Mittelmann, Cornelis Opthof, and Bernard Turgeon.

To sum up, Canada certainly upholds her reputation as a supplier of great operatic singers. It should be noted that while it was once considered normal for a young singer to complete his studies abroad, this is no longer so today. Many of the distinguished performers mentioned above received their entire training in Canadian institutions such as the Conservatoire de Musique et de l'Art dramatique du Québec and the Faculty of Music of the University of Toronto. In certain cases it was also in Canada that these young singers obtained their first experience of the stage and concert hall.

It is with great satisfaction and pride that we see Canadians appearing in the leading opera houses in the world, such as the Metropolitan Opera in New York, the Opera and Opéra-Comique in Paris, Covent Garden in London, la Scala in Milan and the Vienna Opera, not to mention festivals such as Bayreuth, Salzburg and Glyndebourne.

The honour roll of instrumentalists contains fewer names, perhaps, but is not less brilliant when considered as a whole. At the top of the list, and in a very special category, one must place the pianist Glenn Gould, whose breathtaking talent conquered America and Europe in a very short time, as a result of his recording of the "Goldberg Variations" for Columbia. Mr. Gould has some very personal opinions on music in general and on concerts in particular. Even if, for a few years now, his admirers have no longer been able to applaud him as a result of the premature retirement which he has imposed upon himself, they can console themselves by listening to his numerous records, by watching him on television or by reading his articles in the leading magazines.

Other Canadian pianists are gradually drawing the attention of the Canadian public as well as the public abroad, notably Ray Dudley, Ronald Turini, Richard Gresko, Marek Jablonski, Dale Bartlett, Arthur Ozolins, and Claude Savard.

Several Canadian string players also have a fine reputation, for example Betty-Jean Hagen, who won the Long-Thibaud Prize in Paris and Steven Staryk, who now pursues a career as a soloist after having been for a number of years concert-master of the Royal Philharmonic Orchestra of London, the Concertgebouw of Amsterdam and the Chicago Symphony Orchestra. Hyman Bress is pursuing a brilliant career in Europe and his many records have won critics' acclaim. Other important violinists are Albert Pratz, Andrew Dawes, Calvin Sieb, Martha Hidy, Arthur Polson, Lea Foli, Otto Armin, and Arthur Garami. The great virtuoso Ida Haendel, who was born in Europe, now lives in Montreal. Nor does the public forget Arthur Le Blanc and Noël Brunet, even if they now appear only rarely.

The most famous Canadian cellist is Zara Nelsova, who has an international career. Another eminent cellist is Walter Joachim, but he prefers teaching to a career as a soloist. He has already produced several pupils of great promise.

Like everywhere else, the harpsichord is experiencing a revival in Canada. In Toronto, Greta Kraus was one of its first adepts. In Montreal there are several very active harpsichordists such as Kenneth Gilbert, Bernard and Mireille Lagacé and Kelsey Jones.

Since the time of Lynnwood Farnam and Samuel P. Warren, Canada has produced an incredible number of organists. They cannot all be listed because of lack of space, but we might mention, as examples, Charles Peaker, Gérard Caron, Kenneth Gilbert, Mireille and Bernard Lagacé, Françoise Aubut, Claude Lavoie, Bernard Piché, André Mérineau, and Gaston Arel.

It must be understood that the names mentioned in this chapter form only a partial list of the great fraternity of soloists who are contributing to the blossoming musical life within the country and to its fame abroad. It would be necessary, in addition, to give a list of all the conductors of the principal Canadian orchestras. Their contribution as performers or as teachers is inestimable. This chapter would, however, be incomplete without noting the importance of conductors in Canadian musical life. Two great names are dominant: Sir Ernest MacMillan and Wilfrid Pelletier. Both of them have had long and brilliant careers and have made the Toronto and Montreal orchestras into professional ensembles. Canada owes a great deal to these two men and it is a joy to note that concert halls in the two cities bear their respective names: the MacMillan Theatre in Toronto and the Salle Wilfrid-Pelletier in Montreal.

Several Canadian conductors are drawing more and more attention, not only in Canada but abroad. Among these one could mention Pierre Hétu, Jacques Beaudry, Boris Brott, Mario Bernardi, Laszlo Gati, Milton Barnes, Jean Deslauriers, Otto Werner-Mueller, Sylvio Lacharité, Francoys Bernier, Roland Leduc, Jean-Marie Beaudet and Victor Feldbrill.

CHAMBER MUSIC

Even more than symphonic music or opera, chamber music demands great perfection in performance, and this means above all that the performers be of the first order. Chamber music has been enjoying ever-increasing popularity for several years not only in centres such as Montreal, Toronto and Vancouver but also in smaller cities where universities, conservatories and music schools are to be found.

Chamber orchestras, whose repertoire is rich and varied, flourish in a good number of Canadian cities. In Montreal, the McGill Chamber Orchestra, founded and directed by Alexander Brott, presents regular concerts in the Port-Royal Theatre at Place des Arts, in addition to free concerts in the Museum of Fine Arts. In Toronto the Hart House Orchestra, directed by Boyd Neel, Dean of the Royal Conservatory, brings together the best instrumentalists in the Queen City for its concerts in Toronto and on tour. These two orchestras have had the advantage of being heard in Europe where the critics have received them most favourably. It is also essential to note the excellent work accomplished by the Vancouver Chamber Orchestra under the direction of John Avison, who presents an original and varied repertoire. In Edmonton, four annual concerts are performed by a chamber orchestra whose members are recruited from the Symphony Orchestra.

In 1967, the National Arts Centre in Ottawa announced the creation of an orchestra of forty-five musicians, an ensemble between a chamber orchestra and a symphonic orchestra. The new orchestra plans to make its début in 1969. It is scheduled to present regular concerts and symphony matinées for young people during the 1969–70 season. In addition, this orchestra is to serve regions in the neighbourhood of the capital and to visit more distant places.

The highest and perhaps the most demanding form of chamber music is the string quartet, a group for which all the great composers have written. Such an ensemble cannot hope to attain a high level of performance unless its members agree to devote all their time to it. Such an enterprise is very difficult to make financially viable unless it is subsidized in some way. It is undeniable that Canada feels the need for a quartet of high standards. There have been a few fruitless efforts in this direction, but today it is possible to expect great things of the young Orford Quartet of the University of Toronto, which was formed quite recently and is a promising ensemble.

Several other ensembles, of different kinds appear more or less regularly in concert or on radio. Some of them specialize in the repertoire of one period in particular, such as the Collegium Musicum, which Greta Kraus directs in Toronto, the Manitoba Consort of Winnipeg, directed by Christine Mather, the Baroque Trio of Montreal, or the Ensemble Couperin-le-Grand of Montreal. In Toronto and Quebec one finds excellent wind quintets, while a brass quintet is very active in Montreal.

In addition, there are numerous ensembles of all kinds, some of which have acquired a national reputation thanks to radio or because of tours. Among these are the Cassenti Players of Vancouver, the Hidy Trio of Winnipeg, the Halifax Trio, the Gabora Quartet of Montreal, the Pach Duo of Fredericton, the Canadian Piano Quartet of Montreal, the Rolston Quartet of Edmonton.

Two societies deserve special mention for the effort which they have made on behalf of contemporary and Canadian music. These are Ten Centuries Concerts of Toronto and the Contemporary Music Society of Quebec. Ten Centuries Concerts (unfortunately the society ceased its activities in 1967) concentrated particularly on repertoire which has been unknown or forgotten for ten centuries, and also on presenting for the first time new works written by Canadians. The Quebec Contemporary Music Society devotes itself exclusively to the music of today, without considering the composer's country of origin. The Canadians chosen to be played generally belong to the *avant-garde*.

MUSIC FESTIVALS

Literally, "festival" means "great musical celebration." In Canada the word is used for two very distinct purposes. It can mean a series of musical manifestations of an exceptional nature or a competition whose aim it is to discover and encourage young musicians of talent.

This chapter is concerned only with festivals of a professional nature, of which several exist in Canada. The first was organized in Montreal by the Festival Society (Société des Festivals) as early as 1936, but ceased to exist in 1966. The Vancouver Festival, on the other hand, has celebrated its first twelve years of existence. The opera featured in 1967 to mark its tenth anniversary was *The Girl of the Golden West* by Puccini, presented in collaboration with the Vancouver Opera Association. Because of its geographic location, as well as the magnitude of its productions, the Vancouver Festival is one of the most important on the Pacific Coast.

Music also plays a primary role in the summer activities of the Stratford Festival, whose prestige was first acquired through its theatrical performances. For a time the Avon Theatre was host to Gilbert and Sullivan operettas produced by Sir Tyrone Guthrie. For a few years now it has been Mozart who enjoys popular favour. After *The Marriage of Figaro* and *Don Giovanni* came *Cosi fan tutte* and Britten's *Albert Herring*. The concerts and chamber music workshop take place in the Festival theatre and are organized under the direction of Victor di Bello. Many Canadian instrumentalists and singers participate in this Festival, to which distinguished guests are also invited. The summer 1967 programme included Lois Marshall, Maureen Forrester, Yehudi Menuhin, Jean-Pierre Rampal, Julian Bream and José Iturbi. The Festival orchestra and the choral group, "The Festival Singers," were conducted by Mario Bernardi and Elmer Iseler respectively.

The presence of music at Stratford has helped give a new dimension to the drama festival. One of its most important projects in 1960 was the international composers' conference which brought together creative musicians from several countries, including the late Edgard Varèse.

CHORAL MUSIC

The scope and the variety of choral activity in Canada are the result of two principal factors. The first is the intense religious life of this country which has existed since the early times of the French colonial régime. It is not astonishing, therefore, that the most modest church has its own group of choristers, most often amateurs, to meet the needs of worship. Secondly, because instrumental music has taken considerable time to become established and to develop, it was altogether natural for music lovers to come together in song.

From one ocean to the other, an incalculable number of vocal ensembles and choirs are to be found. Which town and which village does not have its choral society, not to mention all those glee clubs, university and high school choirs which present with genuine pride their annual concert every spring?

That is why the reader will easily understand that this chapter will have to content itself with mentioning a limited number of ensembles, emphasizing particularly those which distinguish themselves on a national scale.

For reasons that would take too long to enumerate, choral singing, unlike instrumental music, remained largely at an amateur level even as it evolved. In fact, there is only one entirely professional choir, the Festival Singers of Toronto. But ensembles such as the Mendelssohn Choir of Toronto, the Disciples de Massenet and the Elgar Choir of Montreal are of professional calibre or close to it. They participate regularly in the activities of the symphony orchestras, and eminent conductors pay them many well-deserved compliments.

There are other important groups across the country, such as the Bach Choir of Vancouver, the Tudor Singers of Montreal, the Winnipeg Philharmonic Choir, the Chantal Masson vocal ensemble of Quebec and the same city's symphonic Choir, not to mention an infinite number of children's choirs, women's or men's choirs affiliated with social clubs, industry and commerce.

But it is in churches, above all, that choral singing really flourishes. In most churches of all denominations one finds ensembles that cultivate the masterpieces of religious music.

ARTISTIC MANAGEMENT

Although music is an art, its development and progress, particularly in our age, cannot be fostered unless commercial aspects are also taken into consideration. The musician, whether creator or performer, plays a well-defined role in present-day society and cannot, as in the past, count on the generosity of a patron to provide his livelihood and that of his family. If one considers for a moment the scope of musical consumption in our time, one must agree that music has become a product whose consumption is determined by the laws of supply and demand, just like any other essential product. From an artistic pastime reserved for a minority, music has become almost a necessity for the majority. In our day, music has penetrated into every nook and corner. In addition to radio, television and records, one finds it in supermarkets, banks, hospitals, airplanes and buses. The practical use which is made of it forces us to conclude that it is necessary.

Since it has become a kind of industry, music can live and prosper only when it is efficiently administered, like any other enterprise. Thus, it is not surprising that artists themselves entrust the care of the management side of their careers to a third party, just as musical societies acquire impressive executive committees.

As in many other fields, Canadian musical life is influenced by the presence of our powerful neighbours to the south. How could it be otherwise when the nerve centre of musical life in North America is New York? From their enormous offices on 57th Street, the leading concert agencies and impresarios arrange the tours of the greatest performers, and Canada represents only a limited number of stops on these trans-continental tours.

To obtain the services of soloists and conductors with international reputations, our musical societies and orchestras must address themselves to New York, even though certain important concert agencies now have a subsidiary company in Canada, as does Columbia Artists Management.

In addition to managing the activities of hundreds of soloists, ensembles and conductors, Columbia is also the owner of an important circuit of local concert organisations called Community Concerts. These concerts in cities of secondary importance provide an outlet for artists of all categories and nationalities.

The administration, however, is retained by each association. For a time, severe criticism was made of Columbia because Canadian artists were not sufficiently favoured. In the last few years, Columbia has corrected this anomaly and today many Canadian artists benefit from the efficient organisation of this agency. The growing development of music has, however, led to the formation in Canada of independent agencies who, on occasion, collaborate with their American counterparts. Thus Overture Concerts, founded twelve years ago by George Zuker-man of Vancouver, is spreading throughout the Canadian west. The agency now has a circuit of 62 cities and towns. During the 1966–67 season, Overture was responsible for 250 concerts given by Canadian and foreign artists in towns which were sometimes very distant, in the Yukon or the North-West Territories.

In Montreal, Canadian Concerts and Artists, Inc. was founded a quarter of a century ago by Nicolas Koudriavtzeff. This agency devotes itself especially to the organization of tours in Canada by large international dance and variety or-ganizations. It also collaborates in sending Canadian artists abroad, particularly to the Soviet Union. In Toronto Walter Homburger has established a concert agency that organizes local productions as well as representing, on an international level, artists such as Glenn Gould, Mario Bernardi, Donald Bell and Victor Braun.

In Toronto, Montreal, Vancouver and other cities such as St. John, there are some agencies of minor importance who try, often successfully, to obtain for the Canadian musician his share in the musical life of the nation.

The task is not easy, for the public, even if it grants the Canadian artist the right to a certain priority in his own coun-try, nevertheless wants to applaud the famous foreign stars. The Canadian performer, on the other hand, needs to be ap-plauded abroad to be better appreciated at home. In this case, he needs an international agency if he wishes to be known throughout the world.

Unlike in Europe, all the musical associations in Canada—

orchestras, opera societies, chamber music ensembles—were founded and function according to the rules of private enterprise. Their legal existence is generally assured by a non-profit organization charter. The directors, executive committee or administrative committee are elected and the citizens who occupy these posts are not remunerated. The financing of the societies is provided by public and private subscription, to which are added the income from the sale of tickets and subsidies from arts councils. In addition to the Canada Council there are arts councils in Quebec, Ontario and Saskatchewan whose jurisdiction is provincial. Certain cities like Montreal also have a municipal arts council.

EXPO '67 AND THE WORLD FESTIVAL

Because the year 1967 was that of the Centennial of Canadian Confederation it gave rise to a series of musical activities which was unprecedented in number and scope. One highlight was the holding in Montreal of the international and universal Exhibition which welcomed more than 50 million visitors from April 29 until the end of October. A host of musical activities took place on the Expo grounds themselves as well as in the different halls in Montreal.

The Canadian Pavilion, one of the most impressive at Expo, welcomed a record number of Canadian musicians from all over Canada. Its auditorium of about 500 seats, graced with a Casavant organ with 18 stops and a mechanical action, was the setting for recitals and concerts given by the best soloists and ensembles. The complete list of participants is too long to be included in the present chapter. By way of example we could mention a few names: Maureen Forrester, Ronald Turini, Lois Marshall, Donald Bell, Joseph Rouleau, Victor Braun, André Turp, Betty-Jean Hagen, Pierrette Alarie, Léopold Simoneau, Kenneth Gilbert, John Boyden, and Hyman Bress. Among the ensembles one might note the Toronto Wind Quintet, the McGill Chamber Orchestra, the Hart House Orchestra, the Festival Singers, the Quebec Wind Quintet, the Pach Duo, the Hidy Trio, the Quebec Contemporary Music Society, Ten Centuries Concerts of Toronto, the Manitoba Consort, the Baroque Trio of Montreal, the Petit Ensemble vocal, the Halifax Trio and the Orford Quartet.

Every day at noon an organ recital was presented by the best organists in the country. Twenty-six of them offered varied repertoire that included many Canadian compositions. Several young Canadian artists also appeared at the Youth Pavilion as well as at the Hospitality Pavilion.

While the crowds were surging across the Expo grounds, the World Festival took place in the three halls of Place des Arts as well as at the Expo Theatre. Even if the World Festival was prestigious because of the participation of companies such as the Hamburg State Opera, the Bolshoi Theatre of Moscow, la Scala of Milan, the Vienna Opera, the Royal Opera of Stockholm and the English Opera Group of London, it also included the Canadian Opera Company and the Montreal Symphony Orchestra, which produces operas from time to time.

The Canadian Opera Company appeared in October with two works, *Louis Riel*, an opera by Harry Somers based on a libretto by Mavor Moore and Jacques Languirand, and *The Tales of Hoffman* by Offenbach. *Louis Riel* was one of two Canadian operas presented by the Toronto company on the occasion of the Centennial of Confederation; the other was *The Luck of Ginger Coffey*, libretto by Ronald Hambleton based on the novel by Brian Moore, and with music by Raymond Pannell. Only *Louis Riel* was presented in Montreal and its success was as marked as in Toronto where it had been produced for the first time a few weeks previously.

It is incontestable that the presentation of *Louis Riel* was an epoch-making event in the history of opera in Canada. The subject is one of the most controversial in Canadian history and its adaptation for opera lends it a human dimension which struck all those who heard and saw the work. Bernard Turgeon's interpretation of the title role brought great praise from the critics and the public. Leon Major's production, Victor Feldbrill's musical direction as well as Murray Laufer's sets and projections and Marie Day's costumes all made this production one of the most powerful ever to be presented in Canada. The Montreal Symphony Orchestra chose two works from the standard repertoire, Verdi's *Otello* and Gounod's *Faust*. In the first of these the public warmly received Jon Vickers (in the title role), Teresa Stratas, Fernande Chiocchio, Louis Quilico and Jean Bonhomme. The musical direction had been entrusted to Zubin Mehta and the production to Carlo Maestrini.

Faust was produced by Irving Guttman and conducted by Wilfrid Pelletier, and the cast brought together some other well-known Canadian voices—Heather Thomson, Richard Verreau, Joseph Rouleau and Robert Savoie.

In addition to these four operas, Canadian participation in the World Festival included a week of chamber music concerts organized by the CBC, a concert by the Toronto Symphony Orchestra under the direction of Seiji Ozawa featuring Lois Marshall, as well as a special concert which brought together members of the Montreal Symphony Orchestra and the Los Angeles Philharmonic Orchestra under the direction of Zubin Mehta.

But Montreal was not the only city in Canada that provided a setting for important musical activities on the occasion of the Centennial. Thanks to the Centennial Commission, the Festival Agency organized a vast programme of tours by Canadian artists and ensembles who travelled across the country from one ocean to the other.

In July and August the National Youth Orchestra directed by Brian Priestman gave eight concerts before almost twelve thousand listeners, while the New York Philharmonic, under the auspices of the American government, gave nine concerts before a public of 29,000. The Festival Agency also arranged tours for many other ensembles in the fields of theatre, dance, musical comedy and variety.

The year 1967 was thus one of abundance and rejoicing for Canadian music-lovers. It proved to the Canadian people that their artists can attain great heights and that their talent completely deserves the praise they receive from all sides.

Communications Media

JOHN ROBERTS

RADIO

In the language of Marshall McLuhan radio is a "hot" medium. One can imagine how "hot" it appeared to Canadian radio listeners when in 1936 the Canadian Broadcasting Corporation came into being. The international music world began to shrink with broadcasts from the Metropolitan Opera and the New York Philharmonic and with the music programmes which were made available to the CBC by the BBC. People everywhere who previously had only a glimmering of international standards from the relatively few gramophone recordings available started to become accustomed to hearing live music well performed. The division between amateur and professional music-making became sharply delineated as the Corporation placed more and more emphasis on professionals to satisfy audiences which were becoming increasingly discerning.

The Corporation's aims in the music field had been spelled out earlier by its precursor, the Canadian Radio Broadcasting Commission in 1933 when it stressed that the development of musical programmes of a high standard was one of its prime considerations.

However, in those pioneering days of 1933 high standards could not be set by a snap of the fingers, and the Commission drew upon the resources of choirs and embryo orchestras already available and started to search for other talent. The Commission soon ran into difficulties and in its last annual report pointed out that the extent of programme organization depended on the funds available and that the modest sums at its disposal had not permitted either the production of elaborate programmes or the engagement of the most renowned concert artists.

With the birth of the Canadian Broadcasting Corporation in 1936 a programme survey of Canada was conducted to determine the extent and character of Canadian resources and the most effective form of programme organization. At the same time another survey was conducted of programmes suitable and obtainable from other countries.

The Canadian survey revealed that there was a great variety of talent, much of which, however, required training and development. It also recommended that because of time divisions and the regional character of much of the programme material, production should be decentralized into the regions— the Maritimes, Quebec, Ontario, the Prairie Provinces and British Columbia. In trying to come to grips with Canada's music potential, the Corporation sought a great deal of expert advice, and it was therefore not surprising that both Sir Ernest MacMillan and Dr. Wilfrid Pelletier were engaged as music advisers. From south of the border the American networks made available to the CBC broadcasts by the Metropolitan Opera, the Boston, Cleveland and Chicago symphonies as well as the New York Philharmonic, and it was the success of these series, documented by the vast number of appreciative letters received, which dramatized the need for better Canadian programmes.

Five Years of Achievement, a booklet issued by the Corporation in 1941 looked back at the progress made in the first five years of its existence. One major development it records is the beginning of the CBC broadcasts of the "Proms" given by the Toronto Philharmonic Orchestra conducted by Reginald Stewart and held during the summer months in Varsity Arena: "It is an unforgettable experience to have formed part of the immense audience of six or seven thousand Torontonians, largely students of music and young people, gathered together sitting, some on seats, and some on cushions on the floor, to hear the voice of a celebrated singer or player from New York or elsewhere."

Other memorable events of those years were the broadcasts of the Summer Concerts given at the Chalet on Mount Royal in Montreal; performances of the Mendelssohn Choir conducted by Dr. H. A. Fricker, and orchestral series which went under titles such as Symphonic Strings and Melodic Strings, conducted by Alexander Chuhaldin, "who first won fame at the Russian Court in pre-revolutionary days." From Montreal Jean-Marie Beaudet directed *The Childhood of Christ* by Berlioz, Fauré's *Requiem* and Honegger's *King David*, and contributed *The Mystery of Bethlehem* by the Canadian composer Healey Willan. From Winnipeg came Dyson's *Canterbury Pilgrims*, conducted by James Robertson.

The Corporation had been broadcasting public concerts by the major orchestras in Canada since its inception, and, in addition to these, launched its own first major orchestral series in 1938, when from Montreal a symphony orchestra of seventy-two players under Jean-Marie Beaudet presented a series of broadcasts lasting for three months. Something on a smaller scale was tried in Toronto with a thirty-six piece orchestra which played under Geoffrey Waddington in a series called "CBC Music Hour." In Vancouver, portions of the newly organized Prom Orchestra were broadcast in the 1940–41 season, as well as a number of broadcasts by the Halifax Concert Orchestra.

Many of Canada's orchestral concerts at this time were heard both in Canada and in the United States. The Toronto Symphony Orchestra concerts conducted by Sir Ernest MacMillan, the summer concerts of Les Concerts Symphoniques under guest conductors, and the Montreal Symphony Orchestra conducted by Douglas Clarke were relayed to the Mutual Broadcasting System, and the National Broadcasting Company broadcast the Toronto Prom Concerts. In turn, the American Networks were continuing to play an important role in Canadian music broadcasting. Great excitement was generated in Canada by the NBC Symphony Orchestra broadcasts conducted by Arturo Toscanini, and from Britain the BBC Symphony Orchestra from Queen's Hall, London, was made available through discs sent over by the BBC.

Chamber music was not neglected. The McGill Quartet, Le Quatuor Jean Lallemand and L'Ensemble Instrumental de Montréal, all of Montreal; the Conservatory String Quartet and the Hart House String Quartet of Toronto; the Tudor String Quartet of Winnipeg; and Jean de Rimanoczy's String Ensemble of Vancouver; the Toronto Trio, the Hamburg Trio and the Griller String Quartet from England, presented a variety of chamber music broadcasts in the 1936–41 period. The CBC schedules included many recitals from major production centres across the country. There were also numerous broadcasts by choral groups such as the CBC Singers under Albert Whitehead from Toronto and the Cathedral Singers, directed by W. H. Anderson, from Winnipeg.

By the time 1941 arrived the CBC had a developing French radio network. The Director of Music, Dr. J. J. Gagnier, was mostly concerned with music in the Montreal area. Dr. Gagnier was a conductor and composer, and also Captain and director of the Canadian Grenadier Guards Band. Another distinguished Canadian musician had entered Canadian broadcasting in the person of Jean-Marie Beaudet. He joined the CBC in 1937 as Director of Programmes for the Quebec Region and in 1938 became National Music Director of both networks. His vigorous programming ideas included the encouragement of contemporary music, particularly works by Canadian composers, who before the advent of the CBC had been completely neglected. Jean-Papineau Couture puts it this way:

In 1943, upon my return from the United States, where I had gone to pursue my studies in composition, public radio seemed to suspect that perhaps it ought to do something for Canadian composers. In fact it was the International Service of the CBC which first enabled composers to write works for the public and not just compositions which were condemned to lie untouched in the bottom drawers of their desks.

Nearly all the major national music programmes for which Jean-Marie Beaudet was responsible were heard live simultaneously on both the English and French Networks, often using English and French announcers in separate booths, or employing the "voice over" technique (an English announcement superimposed over a French one or vice versa).

Those were very colourful days, and Beaudet remembers:

In the studio, I was wearing ear-phones: on one I was getting the French feed and on the other, the English, and at the same time as this, of course, I had to worry about the orchestra, soloists and chorus. How about that for bilingualism? This was done live and if any mistakes were made (and they occurred more often than we would have liked) we just had to go on. Technically, it was undoubtedly much less perfect, but it still seems to me that there was a human quality in the whole process. You also had the feeling of immediacy and a live presence. Or is this all in my imagination, since it happened so many years ago?

The French Network became a production centre in its own right and, apart from national broadcasts, produced a number of local series of its own. Of the numerous recitals designed to encourage young talent one called "Mademoiselle au Piano" ran for years. There were also *lieder* and French art-song series and organ recitals for more fully fledged professionals, as well as broadcasts devoted to French-Canadian folk songs. Special attention was paid to the works of French-Canadian composers such as Maurice Blackburn, Claude Champagne, Hector Gratton, Auguste Descarries and Gabriel Cusson. CBC Toronto was no less mindful of Canadian music. "Tribute to Young Canadians" was the title of an orchestral series conducted by Samuel Hersenhoren which included works by Robert Farnon, Barbara Pentland, Godfrey Ridout, John Weinzweig and Gerald Bales. Not content with broadcasting works already written in 1942, the CBC commissioned Healey Willan to write an opera to a libretto by the Canadian author John Coulter. *Transit Through Fire* dealt with the problems of youth in the pre-war and war periods and was part of the largest and most ambitious opera series so far undertaken by the CBC.

Apart from *Transit Through Fire*, there were operas by Purcell, Handel, Gay, Balfe, Edward German, Rutland Boughton, Vaughan Williams and Arthur Benjamin. The conductors were Eugene Goossens, Edwin MacArthur, Sir Ernest MacMillan and Arthur Benjamin, and among the singers were Rose Bampton and John Brownlee from the Metropolitan Opera. John Adaskin, Rupert Lucas and W. H. Brodie were the producers.

A highlight of 1942–43 music programming was the CBC Concert Hour which originated in Toronto and Montreal. This orchestral series included a considerable proportion of Canadian music with Sir Ernest MacMillan, Ettore Mazzoleni, César Borré, J. J. Gagnier and Jean-Marie Beaudet as conductors and Kathleen Parlow and the duo-piano team of Malcolm and Godden as soloists.

Sunday was becoming a music listeners' day with features such as a series of violin and piano sonatas performed by Albert Pratz and Gordon Kushner from Winnipeg, and a cycle of Beethoven sonatas with Zara Nelsova, Lubka Kolessa and Ross Pratt. Other distinguished recital series included "Masters of the Pianoforte" from Montreal to the French Network and the broadcasts of Max and Leila Pirani of works for violin and piano from Vancouver to the Western Network. Vancouver also contributed Healey Willan's *Chester Mysteries* to the 1942 Christmas schedule, which provided a striking contrast to Toronto's *Messiah* and Montreal's *Children's Crusade* by Pierné. Finally, a memorable series of seven broadcasts started on March 14, 1943, when the great harpsichordist Wanda Landowska was brought to Toronto by the CBC to perform concertos by Carl Philipp Emmanuel Bach. The distinguished Canadian harpsichordist Greta Kraus recalls:

Her powerful personality and stunning playing made a profound impression on everyone. During the broadcasts I was astonished to see she chewed candy for energy. Madame Landowska was conscious of her place in musical history—in fact, she always asked me to write down every word she said.

In 1943 the CBC made another statement concerning the manner in which professional Canadian musical life should be consolidated to achieve the highest possible broadcast standards:

. . . a high standard of excellence must be maintained, particularly if a worthy appearance alongside the enormous artistic resources of the American networks is to be made. For this purpose it is necessary to have groups of professional musicians at relatively few centres in fairly constant employment. If the amount of employment is spread too thinly over the whole of Canada, only a very mediocre result all round may be produced.

Notwithstanding World War II and difficulties relating to it, there were a surprising number of high quality music broadcasts at this time. The Dominion Network came into existence in 1944 and provided a further outlet for music programmes. A series of operettas was broadcast on Sundays on the French Network and, also from Montreal, there was the "Summer Opera Series," which presented such works as *Carmen, La Traviata* and *Samson and Delilah*. Arthur Benjamin conducted six orchestral programmes on the Western Network and prize-winning compositions, selected by the Canadian Performing Rights Society, were heard on the CBC Concert Hour.

The Life and Death of Jean de Brébeuf by E. J. Pratt with special music written by Healey Willan was broadcast in 1943 and again in 1944. Another special project was a series of eleven Handel oratorios from Toronto conducted by Sir Ernest MacMillan which were balanced by a variety of other choral broadcasts from Montreal, including *Rédemption* by César

Franck and the *L'Enfance du Christ* by Berlioz. The complete works of Chopin were performed by the best Canadian pianists, and a Bach Organ Cycle from Winnipeg, Halifax, Toronto, Quebec and Montreal provided an outlet for leading Canadian organists. From Winnipeg there was a further organ recital series with Hugh Bancroft, and Greta Kraus was heard in a series entitled "The Harpsichord at Home."

During 1944, NBC asked the CBC to contribute eight programmes called "Canadian Music in Wartime" to its Inter-American University of the Air summer series, "Music of the New World." These were prepared and conducted, with one exception, by Jean-Marie Beaudet. All the works included were receiving their first performance. Arnold Walter's *Symphony in G Minor* was on the first broadcast, followed by the *Piano Concerto* by Healey Willan. John Weinzweig's *Interlude in an Artist's Life* was also included, together with works by Alexander Brott, Robert Fleming, Jean Coulthard, Paul de Marky, Robert Farnon and Maurice Blackburn. Vancouver contributed one programme conducted by Arthur Benjamin which, besides one of Benjamin's own works, included *Evocation* by Claude Champagne and *The Wind in the Leafless Maple* by Dr. J. J. Gagnier. The Handel oratorios of 1943 were balanced by a series of ten Bach cantatas. Six programmes devoted to performances of the Bach *Brandenburg Concertos* preceded the cantatas, and both series were conducted by Ettore Mazzoleni, from Toronto.

In the 1945–46 concert season the CBC increased the number of public concerts broadcast by Canadian symphony orchestras and presented a variety of other studio orchestral broadcasts from the principal production centres. In Vancouver the distinguished musician Arthur Benjamin was conducting the CBX Symphony Orchestra. Benjamin, who was born in Australia, had moved to Vancouver in 1941 after having a major career in England as a pianist, teacher and composer.

Other broadcasts focused attention on such groups as the Parlow String Quartet and the Sumberg Trio, and on artists such as Lubka Kolessa and the singers Frances James and

Ernesto Vinci. From Winnipeg, apart from W. H. Anderson's choir The Choristers, many broadcasts were given by ethnic choral groups. A highlight of the 1945 choral broadcasts was a special performance of Berlioz's *Te Deum* from the church of Notre Dame in Montreal, celebrating Victory Day under the auspices of the Montreal Festivals.

As soon as the war was over, CBC radio music broadcasts entered into a spectacular era of growth and development which reached a climax in the formation of the CBC Symphony Orchestra in 1952. Largely through the opportunities provided by CBC broadcasting, Canadian professional music life had developed to a tremendous extent, and CBC schedules contained an increasing number of programmes of the highest quality.

In the spring of 1946 the Corporation presented *Deirdre of the Sorrows*, the first full-length Canadian opera by Healey Willan with a libretto by John Coulter, which the CBC had commissioned two years previously. The broadcast featured Frances James, soprano, William Morton, tenor, and Lionel Daunais, baritone, in the leading roles. A complete performance of *Les Enfants à Bethléem* by Pierné was broadcast from Montreal to the French Network on Christmas Eve, with Jeanne Desjardins, Simone Flibotte, David Rochette, and Paul Demeules as soloists, and the Cantoria Choir under the direction of Jean-Marie Beaudet.

Professor (now Sir Bernard) Heinze, the well-known Australian conductor, came to conduct a number of concerts in the 1946–47 season as a reciprocal gesture following Sir Ernest MacMillan's visit to Australia the year before. Other developments were the arrival in Winnipeg of the conductor Eric Wild to form the CBC Winnipeg Orchestra and the appointment of Geoffrey Waddington in 1947 as Music Adviser. Mr. Waddington had been associated with the Canadian Radio Broadcasting Commission in the early days of broadcasting, and between 1936 and 1947 had worked independently as a conductor in Toronto and Winnipeg, in addition to serving in the Canadian Army's special services as conductor of The Army Show.

The now well-known recital series "Distinguished Artists" came into existence in the 1945–46 season and presented such artists as Nicholas Fiore, flutist, Jean de Rimanoczy and Hyman Goodman, violinists, Zara Nelsova, cellist, Lina Pizzolongo, Alberto Guerrero and Helmut Blume, pianists, Anna Malenfant, contralto, and Gérald Desmarais, bass.

The year 1947 will long be remembered as the year in which "CBC Wednesday Night" was started. It had long been felt that many listeners would welcome such a development and that by moving in this direction the wider possibilities of radio as a vehicle for the arts would be realized. A memorable CBC Wednesday Night broadcast of 1948 was a performance of the *Saint Matthew Passion* by Bach with the Mendelssohn Choir and a Toronto Orchestra conducted by Sir Ernest MacMillan. This and other distinguished broadcasts drew considerable mail from audiences and a great deal of favourable comment in the press. The CBC pointed out that listeners not interested in "CBC Wednesday Night" would probably find something to their taste on the Dominion Network.

In 1947–48 the CBC annual report touched on what was to become an increasingly serious problem over the years, namely the financing of the Corporation in relation to rising costs:

In spite of rising prices everywhere, the cost of the national radio system to the listener has remained the same. The resulting financial pressure has been met in part by the Government's absorbing the cost of collecting licence fees and also by revenue from an increased number of commercial programmes. By careful budgeting, the Corporation is able this year to show a net operating surplus, but it is concerned about the future in view of continually rising costs.

This concern was not unfounded because over the years the struggle to combat rising costs and maintain quality broadcasts at the same time has become a major problem to those responsible for guiding the destiny of the Corporation.

In the summer of 1948 the CBC formed the CBC Opera Company following the success of an earlier series of five broadcasts prepared by the Opera School of the Royal Conservatory of Music in Toronto. The CBC, recognizing the work of the Royal Conservatory of Music in Toronto in the development of Canadian singers, and realizing the limitations imposed on their futures by the fact that there was no permanent opera company in Canada, broadcast a limited number of opera productions of its own to help the music profession and enrich Canadian music life at the same time. Conductors Geoffrey Waddington, Nicholas Goldschmidt, Ettore Mazzoleni and Ernesto Barbini, producer Terence Gibbs, director Herman Geiger-Torel and singers such as Lois Marshall, Elizabeth Benson-Guy, Nellie Smith, Marguerite Gignac, James Milligan, James Shields, Andrew MacMillan and many others were all very much associated with the success of the Company.

Other highlights of the 1947–48 broadcasting year were the *Missa Papae Marcelli* by Palestrina performed by the Leslie Bell singers and a CBC Wednesday Night project consisting of two, two-and-a-half hour programmes called "A Layman's History of Music." The response now to "CBC Wednesday Night" programmes was overwhelming and this pocket of English Network scheduling was satisfying what one person called "a nutritional deficiency in radio programming."

The French Network did not have an exact parallel to "CBC Wednesday Night," but its Sunday programmes were of a very high order. In 1948 it started "Les Petites Symphonies," a chamber orchestra series with an enviable history of outstanding broadcasts, which ended recently when the orchestra was expanded to become the CBC Montreal Orchestra. Roland Leduc the conductor and producer Jacques Bertrand were closely associated with "Les Petites Symphonies." French Network recital periods included such artists as Anna Malenfant, Denis Harbour, Gérald Desmarais, Jean Beaudet, Steven Kondaks and John Newmark.

CBC music in western Canada was experiencing an upward swing in 1949. The Choristers had developed a large, appreciative audience and the CBC Winnipeg Orchestra had brought about a stabilization of Winnipeg's professional music life. A chamber music series on Saturday nights in Vancouver had begun as a result of complaints about the lack of good music on that evening, and the audience response was so great that the seating capacity of the studio concerned was severely taxed. All across Canada there was an increasing demand for fine music and this had no doubt been precipitated by a generally higher level of programme content and performance in CBC schedules.

Special attention was paid to the English composer Benjamin Britten in the 1949–50 year with a performance of his opera *Peter Grimes*, conducted by Geoffrey Waddington, and the *Saint Nicholas* cantata, conducted by the composer. Among the soloists in *Peter Grimes* were Frances James, William Morton, Edmund Hockridge and Doreen Hulme. This programme received the first award for music in the Canadian Radio Awards with a citation that said: "A stupendous effort was required and enormous preparations were made. The result was a superb achievement. This opera, although undoubtedly the best single broadcast, is at the same time representative of the high standards maintained throughout the series." Of course, this was a feather in the cap of the CBC Opera Company, and when Britten, after listening to the recording of the broadcast, wrote a glowing article in the British magazine *Opera*, everyone was walking on air. The other operas presented by the CBC Opera Company that season were *Don Giovanni*, *Madama Butterfly*, *Fidelio* and *Carmen*.

Among the Canadian composers to have works performed by the CBC in 1949–50 were Oskar Morawetz, Murray Adaskin, John Beckwith and Sylvio Lacharité; included in the galaxy of recitalists were violinist Elie Spivak, bass Jan Rubes and tenor Peter Pears, accompanied by Benjamin Britten.

A festival of special events to mark the bicentenary of the death of Bach took place in 1950. All the orchestral works were performed and there was a series of Bach organ works presented by organists from various parts of the country. An interesting experiment was the inclusion of a number of programmes by Sir Thomas Beecham in which the famous conductor played his favourite recordings, with comments about the music and anecdotes from his long career. The Toronto

Symphony Pops Concerts were most popular on the Trans-Canada and French Networks and, in addition, the Vancouver Symphony Pops Concerts were available to listeners in western Canada. In contrast, Vancouver, also in 1950–51, contributed fourteen half-hour programmes presenting thirty-five compositions by twenty-two Canadian composers, and in June 1951 the CBC invited the French composer Darius Milhaud to come to Canada to conduct a concert of his own music.

In 1952 Geoffrey Waddington was appointed Director of Music, and in the same year the orchestra which became the focal point of his work with the CBC over the next twelve years was born. When the CBC established the CBC Symphony Orchestra it gave Canadian artists an opportunity to play with a major symphony orchestra, and to gain experience with outstanding conductors. In the first season, twelve Canadian conductors were invited to lead the orchestra and an equal number of Canadians appeared as soloists.

Over a period of years, many of the world's greatest foreign musicians have either directed the orchestra or were soloists with it. In addition, a number of the greatest composers of our time were engaged as conductors, culminating with the visit to Toronto in 1962 of Igor Stravinsky, who, together with his associate, Robert Craft, precipitated the orchestra's international reputation through the release of numerous commercial recordings under the Columbia label.

The CBC Symphony Orchestra also provided a stimulus to Canadian composers because it offered an outlet for their orchestral works. In fact, as a result of the Orchestra, Canadian orchestral music underwent a major development as more and more Canadian works were broadcast under the direction of Canadian conductors. Geoffrey Waddington, in particular, is identified with very many first performances of Canadian works. Other orchestral broadcasts in 1952 and 1953 were provided as in previous years by the Toronto Symphony Orchestra, Les Concerts Symphoniques de Montréal, the Winnipeg and Vancouver Symphony Orchestras, Les Petites Symphonies, the CBC orchestras in Winnipeg and Vancouver and the Halifax Symphonette which broadcast to the Maritime Network.

These and scores of other programmes augured well for the future, and new talent kept coming to light as a result of auditions and the "Opportunity Knocks" series run by John Adaskin. But what exactly did the future hold? In those days relatively few people grasped clearly how dramatically the coming of Canadian television would change the lives of vast numbers of people. With the establishment of CBC television in 1952, and the massive exposure of the population to Canadian and American commercial television, the role of radio changed and entered a new epoch.

CBC RADIO MUSIC PROGRAMMING SINCE THE ARRIVAL OF TELEVISION

In the years following 1952, CBC radio adjusted to changed listening habits brought about by television viewing. Radio became more personal. The great increase in the sale of sets indicated that instead of the family gathering around a single set as it had in the old days, numerous receivers within a single household provided individual companionship. This in turn led to broadcasting to segments of the population with specialized interests. In fact, in commercial broadcasting a great many stations concentrated on addressing themselves to particular audiences and developing a certain station sound. A good example of this are the Toronto private stations CHUM-AM, which caters to a certain part of the popular audience, and CHUM-FM, which broadcasts serious music to the so-called "minority" audience. CBC radio had a tough time coming to grips with this situation, because, with the eventual demise of the Dominion Network, it was restricted to a single radio network in each language, and within a single broadcasting week had to address itself to a great many audiences.

Nowadays, in certain cities where the CBC-FM Network exists, it is possible to offer the listener alternative programming, but in general CBC-AM has remained viable through the use of block programming in its schedules. In music, this has meant grouping programmes together to provide continuous listening throughout a specific part of the day. However, this development was an evolution rather than a revolution, and its unfolding is fascinating in retrospect.

During the 1952–53 year the CBC Opera Company presented a series which included Verdi's *Falstaff*, Wolf-Ferrari's *The School for Fathers*, and the Canadian première of Dallapiccola's *The Prisoner*, and performances were given of Canadian works such as Godfrey Ridout's cantata *Esther* and Violet Archer's *The Bell*. In the next CBC year, from April 1953 to March 1954, more than sixty Canadian compositions, ranging from solo pieces to symphonic works, were performed. An important concert of Canadian music presented in New York's Carnegie Hall and conducted by Leopold Stokowski was broadcast in October of 1953. An hour-long portion of the Montreal concert of the Canadian League of Composers was also heard.

The CBC Symphony Orchestra had gained a great deal of support during the first year of its operation, and in its second season continued to play a unique role in Canadian broadcasting. Some of the conductors at that time were Victor Feldbrill, Jean Beaudet, Alexander Brott, Jean de Rimanoczy and John Avison. Heinz Unger conducted the first Canadian performance of the *Symphony No. 4* by Carl Nielsen and Ettore Mazzoleni conducted the *Symphony No. 1* by Richard Johnston. In addition, Sir Ernest MacMillan directed the Orchestra in a programme in honour of Sibelius' birthday, and conducted the *Symphony No. 2* by Healey Willan.

Numerous programmes in 1953 were related to celebrating the coronation of Queen Elizabeth II. "CBC Wednesday Night" presented a series of programmes of Elizabethan music from Toronto, and there were performances of specially commissioned works by Canadian composers such as William Keith Rogers, Jean Papineau-Couture, Jean Coulthard, Alexander Brott and others. "CBC Wednesday Night" again presented the CBC Opera Company in a series which included *The Rake's Progress* by Stravinsky, *Turandot* by Puccini and *Cosi fan*

Tutte by Mozart. These were supplemented by other operas from Vancouver and Montreal. As in past years, a steady stream of national recitals and chamber music broadcasts continued to feature well-known artists and chamber music groups in all the principal production centres across the country.

In the year 1954–55 the CBC Symphony Orchestra was gaining a reputation as "one of the world's great orchestras" and presented a longer series. The distinguished line of soloists included the pianists Neil Chotem, Ray Dudley, Glenn Gould, Pierre Souvairan and Patricia Grant Lewis, and the singers Irene Jessner, Jon Vickers, James Milligan and Elizabeth Benson-Guy. In October of 1954 forty-five members of the Orchestra journeyed to Ottawa to give a special performance and broadcast of a programme of Canadian works for the delegates of the Colombo Plan Conference.

Les Petites Symphonies from Montreal was broadcast on the French and English Networks and also carried by the Mutual Broadcasting System in the United States. The French Network also broadcast a new series, "Premières," devoted to works by Canadian composers. These programmes provided an outlet for composers such as Jean Papineau-Couture, François Morel, Kelsey Jones, Serge Garant, Roger Matton and Gabriel Charpentier.

Also in October 1954, the newly organized Hart House Orchestra, under the direction of Boyd Neel, made its first appearance on the Trans-Canada Network. Other noteworthy events were Haydn's *Seven Last Words* from Vancouver, the performance of Brahms' *Requiem* by the Mendelssohn Choir, and the Toronto Symphony Orchestra, the music competitions, "Nos Futures Etoiles" on the French Network and "Singing Stars of Tomorrow" on the Trans-Canada Network. The CBC Opera Company presented six full-length productions, including *A Tale of Two Cities* by Arthur Benjamin, *Eugene Onegin*, *Tales of Hoffmann*, and *Pelléas et Mélisande*.

Costs were rising, however, and the demands of an expanding television system were seriously straining the financial resources of the Corporation. The CBC annual report of 1955–

56 notes a fantastic rate of growth in the expansion of CBC television coverage unmatched in any other country. Three radio networks had to be maintained, which meant that "the CBC found itself responsible for one of the largest and perhaps of necessity, the most complex broadcasting systems in the world, with diminishing financial means in sight." The report continued: "But in the year ahead the Corporation faced a considerable increase in expenditures for television just to maintain the service in the two languages for a full twelve months on the scale as at March 1956." In spite of this anxiety, CBC radio presented an impressive array of programmes during 1955 and 1956.

The CBC Symphony made its first public appearance with a concert in Massey Hall, Toronto in May 1955 and appeared in Montreal in August in connection with the Montreal Festival and Les Jeunesses Musicales. In the programming there was an emphasis on Bruckner, Berlioz and Mahler, while Sibelius and Mozart received prominence by reason of anniversaries. Les Petites Symphonies from Montreal specialized in Mozart performances in 1956 to commemorate the two-hundreth anniversary of his birth. Special Mozart broadcasts came from all the major production centres, including a performance of *The Marriage of Figaro* by the CBC Opera Company.

"Premières" from Montreal again broadcast works by Canadian composers including Roger Matton, Jean Vallerand, John Beckwith and Clermont Pépin. From Winnipeg there was a broadcast of Vaughan Williams' *Sea Symphony* and a special concert during which a choir in Calgary sang with a CBC orchestra hundreds of miles away in Winnipeg, to mark the Jubilee celebrations of Alberta and Saskatchewan. In the summer, numerous broadcasts brought the riches of the Stratford Music Festival to the whole country and, in addition, an imported music series, "World Music Festivals," was carried from New York on Sunday afternoons. The CBC itself was giving greater prominence to European music festivals, and, through the CBC International Service, obtained programmes from Strasbourg, Bordeaux, Aix-en-Provence, Florence, Lucerne,

Ansbach and Munich, and, of course, special Mozart concerts from Salzburg as well.

During the next year the French Network carried concerts by the Orchestra of Radiodiffusion-Télévision Française, and the English Network featured a substantial amount of material supplied by the BBC Transcription Service. The CBC Symphony Orchestra, during its fifth year of operation, performed at the Stratford Festival and gave many other distinguished broadcasts. Numerous Canadian works were performed, including *Five Songs for Dark Voice* by Harry Somers, John Weinzweig's *Rhapsody for Orchestra* and Norman Symonds' *Concerto Grosso for Jazz Quintet and Symphony Orchestra*. To mark the retirement of Sir Ernest MacMillan after twenty-five years as conductor of the Toronto Symphony Orchestra, the CBC invited him to conduct the CBC Symphony in the season's final broadcast— a public performance from Massey Hall, Toronto. A performance of MacMillan's compositions was presented on "CBC Concert Hall," a Dominion Network series.

During the 1956–57 year there was a greater co-ordination of actual programme content and scheduling of the various orchestral series. The Winnipeg Pops Concerts conducted by Eric Wild were bringing pleasure to a substantial audience and the well-chosen programmes of the new Halifax Symphony Orchestra under Thomas Mayer were also an encouraging sign. Both the Toronto and Montreal Symphony Orchestras did much to enhance programming on the Dominion Network, and, of course, the other orchestras on the French and Trans-Canada Networks completed the spectrum of orchestral music. The CBC Opera Company's production of *Troilus and Cressida* by Walton, with Mary Simmons, Jon Vickers and Harry Moss-field in leading roles, was an exciting event. From Montreal came *Hippolyte et Aricie* by Rameau, with such singers as André Turp, Louis Quilico, Robert Savoie and Elizabeth Benson-Guy. There were also many other interesting events, such as *Janufa* by Janáček, Haydn's *Lord Nelson Mass*, *Oedipus Rex* by Stravinsky and *Prima Donna* by Benjamin. Further musical highlights on the French Network included "Les Festivals du Dimanche," with broadcasts from the Prades Festival. The French Network also carried most of the musical presentations on "CBC Wednesday Night" and featured Canadian compositions by Clermont Pépin, François Morel, and Serge Garant. Benjamin Britten's opera, *The Rape of Lucretia*, was one of fifteen broadcasts carried from the Stratford Music Festival, and there were many other distinguished broadcasts presented by leading artists such as the pianist Glenn Gould. Now one of the world's greatest pianists, Mr. Gould explains how the CBC influenced his career:

In January 1950, I took part for the first time in a CBC broadcast and made a discovery that influenced in a most profound way my development as a musician. I discovered that in the privacy, the solitude, the womb-like security (Freudians, stand clear!) of the studio, it was possible to make music in a more direct, more personal manner than any concert hall would ever permit. I fell in love with broadcasting that day, and I have not since been able to think of the potential of music (or for that matter of my own potential as a musician) without some reference to the limitless possibilities of the broadcasting and/or recording medium. For me, the microphone has never been that hostile, clinical, inspiration-sapping analyst some critics, fearing it, complain about. That day in 1950, it became, and has remained, a friend.

During the 1957–58 year CBC radio undertook a major reassessment of its programme responsibilities in all main areas, including music. Because of evening television viewing, it was considered realistic to schedule numerous live radio-music broadcasts in afternoon periods. A policy of double exposing certain evening broadcasts during the day-time schedule was also tried, but only in a limited way with music programmes, because of difficulties related to union agreements.

On February 2, 1958, Les Petites Symphonies celebrated its tenth anniversary and in the course of the year it presented works commissioned from Canadian composers. The CBC Symphony Orchestra broadcast some interesting programmes of contemporary music, including two in which the composers Aaron Copland and Heitor Villa-Lobos conducted their own works. Some of the other conductors were Walter Susskind, Sir Malcolm Sargent, Charles Mackerras and Edouard van Remoortel. Apart from these visiting musicians, most of the concerts were conducted as usual by Canadians, and numerous Canadian works were performed, such as the *Concerto for Orchestra* by Arnold Walter.

Outstanding "CBC Wednesday Night" programmes of this period were the performance of Brahms' *Piano Quintet* played by Glenn Gould and the Montreal String Quartet, and "An Evening with Nadia Boulanger" from Montreal, in which the great teacher-conductor was interviewed in French and English and directed performances of Jean Papineau-Couture's *Psalm 150* and Stravinsky's *Mass*. There was also a production of Mozart's *Cosi fan Tutte* by the CBC Opera Company and "A Portrait of Kathleen Ferrier" by her sister Winifred. A full evening devoted to a documentary, "Music and Western Man," was devised as a result of the fifty one-hour broadcasts under this title arranged by Peter Garvie in Vancouver, which had previously been broadcast to the Western Network. These programmes created so much public interest that they were eventually released internationally in book form. Peter Garvie also instituted a very valuable series called "Music Diary," which today is still an important part of the CBC's music schedule. Other broadcasts which had faithful audiences were Allan Sangster's "The Music of Beethoven" and Leslie Bell's "Speaking of Music" on the Dominion Network, and a new twenty-week series given by the Ottawa Philharmonic Orchestra under the direction of Thomas Mayer. Broadcasts by Le Petit Ensemble Vocal and such series as "Festival du Dimanche," "Les Artistes de Renom" and "Concert International" all added lustre to the French Network.

Broadcasting schedules in the 1958–59 season revealed that while television was for commercial reasons dependent upon importing a substantial number of American programmes, the Canadian content of CBC radio programming had risen to ninety-five per cent. Surveys showed that the average family watched television or listened to radio for a total of about six hours a day. It was therefore not surprising to find the use of ratings being debated at the time. The CBC annual report commented: "It is generally agreed that while ratings are a useful guide to trends in listening and viewing, they may give little useful indication of the relative importance of a programme to Canada as a whole." Another point the report stressed was that while television had completely changed the patterns of listening, radio had maintained a strong position in the Canadian home. This was evident because since 1952, more radios had been purchased than television sets. In fact a total of four million four hundred and thirteen thousand radio receivers had been bought. On both English and French radio networks, programming had been geared to meet the changing needs of audiences through an increased emphasis on daytime programming, a concentration on programmes best suited to radio and a greater use of the medium to meet specialized tastes.

An interesting development at this time was the introduction of more live performances of radio-music broadcasts. The CBC Symphony Orchestra gave a series of concerts before audiences in the CBC's Carlton Theatre in Toronto. In the course of the year the now-famous young conductors Colin Davis and Zubin Mehta made their North American débuts directing the Orchestra. Sir Thomas Beecham and Josef Krips were also engaged and many soloists of note appeared. The performances of the *Violin Concerto* by Berg, played by Hyman Bress, and Violet Archer's *Piano Concerto*, played by William Stevens, come quickly to mind. Another event of great interest was the concert in which Geoffrey Waddington conducted the première of *Horoscope* by the Quebec composer Roger Matton. To complement the full-length operas being presented on CBC television, the Music Department decided to broadcast on "CBC Wednesday Night" a series of intimate chamber operas. One of the most interesting broadcasts was the première of the CBC-commissioned opera by John Beckwith and James Reaney, "Night Blooming Cereus," in 1959. "CBC Wednesday Night" also presented a broadcast of Heinz Unger conducting the *Symphony No. 5* by Mahler. (Over a number of years the CBC broadcast many of Heinz Unger's distinguished Mahler performances presented by the York Concert Society of Toronto.) Again on "CBC Wednesday Night," a new series was started called "CBC Celebrity Series," in which artists like Ruggiero Ricci, Benno Moiseivitch and Maureen Forrester gave CBC recitals before an invited audience at the University of Toronto. Other broadcasting periods featured such artists as the baritone James Milligan and chamber music groups like the Toronto Woodwind Quintet, the Cassenti Players of Vancouver, the Dirk Keetbaas Players of Winnipeg, the Halifax Trio and the Montreal Bach Choir conducted by George Little in the première of Violet Archer's *Apocalypse*. The CBC Vancouver Chamber Orchestra was also playing a major part in Canadian music life and gave public performances at the Vancouver Festival. It had grown out of the old CBR Concert Orchestra and was formed in 1938 by Ira Dilworth, then CBC Regional Director for British Columbia, to fill a need both of the radio audience and of musicians in Vancouver. One of Canada's leading conductors, John Avison, has directed the Orchestra through the greatest part of its life, and in 1952 the Canadian composer Robert Turner became responsible for the production of the broadcasts. Contemporary music became a feature of the CBC Vancouver Chamber Orchestra's programming and all major Canadian composers have had their works performed by it.

Broadcasts from Canadian festivals greatly enriched CBC schedules. From the Vancouver Festival, apart from the CBC Vancouver Chamber Orchestra concerts, there was a production of Mozart's *Don Giovanni* conducted by Nicholas Goldschmidt, with Canadian singers such as Léopold Simoneau and Pierrette Alarie, and Joan Sutherland making her North American début as Donna Anna. From Stratford there was a broadcast of *The Beggar's Opera* with Robert Goulet, from Vancouver a performance of the prize-winning cantata *Judith* by Paul McIntyre, and the Montreal Festival contributed other events. The "Distinguished Artists" series presented artists like Joan Sutherland, Ronald Turini, William Primrose and Dietrich

Fischer-Dieskau; yet another unusual feature was the talk by the eighty-six-year-old pianist Adelina de Lara, who described her studies with Clara Schumann and her friendships with Brahms, Dvořák and Grieg.

During the following year the CBC Symphony Orchestra broadcast the nine symphonies of Beethoven conducted by Efrem Kurtz. Other events in this year were programmes from festivals in Stratford, Saskatoon, Montreal and Vancouver, and the French Network broadcasts of Les Jeunesses Musicales concerts. The distinguished musician and broadcaster Helmut Blume presented a number of programmes called "Form in Music" in the "University of the Air" series which were later released as two long-playing records. Another outstanding broadcaster, composer John Beckwith, played a valuable role in introducing the public to everything from electronic music to little known works of the past in "The World of Music." The concern with developing programmes which radio could do best led to the broadcasting of special documentaries such as "Music by Royal Composers," which won an Ohio First Award. Apart from these programmes, there was the world première of the opera *Diary of a Madman* by Humphrey Searle and the radio première of *Une Mesure de Silence* by Maurice Blackburn from Montreal, as well as the Montreal String Quartet's performances of the last quartets by Beethoven.

On April 1, 1960 the CBC began an experimental bilingual FM Network which consisted of three cities only—Montreal, Ottawa and Toronto. The Network operated on a shoe-string budget and contained live programmes double-exposed from the Trans-Canada and French Networks, but most of the broadcasts drew upon recorded music and music supplied by broadcasting organizations overseas and imported through the CBC's International Service. One of the most attractive aspects of the FM Network was that it devoted substantial blocks of time to music, and an innovation was the inclusion of serious music items in three-hour blocks of programming on Saturday and Sunday afternoons which were devised by the ORTF and BBC respectively. The rich resources of the BBC Transcription Service did much to enhance the schedule, and the broadcasting organizations of many other countries, such as the Soviet Union, Germany, Sweden and Italy, provided music of exceptional interest. As there were so few Canadian commercial recordings available, Canadian content was boosted through the use of the music transcriptions of CBC International Service. Other programmes were "Les Jeunesses Musicales," "European Festivals" presented by Maryvonne Kendergi, "Aspects de la Chanson Canadienne," and the Petit Ensemble Vocal's "A Musical History of France." On March 31st, 1962, the network fell victim to the austerity measures prescribed by the government and ceased to operate.

In the summer of 1960, as one of the sponsors of an International Conference of Composers at Stratford, the CBC played an important part by broadcasting many of the events and making them available to countries abroad through the CBC International Service. At one of the concerts given by the Festival Orchestra, conducted by Victor Feldbrill and Frederick Prausnitz, *Déserts* by Edgar Varèse was performed in the presence of the composer. A concert of electronic music with works by Berio, Moderna, Cage, Luening and Ussachevsky was broadcast, and the CBC Symphony Orchestra, conducted principally by Walter Susskind, presented a concert which included John Weinzweig's CBC-commissioned *Wine of Peace* sung by soprano Mary Simmons, *Mtsyri* by Taktakishvili (conducted by the composer) and the *Symphony* by Istvan Anhalt. Also from Stratford there were outstanding concerts by Glenn Gould, Leonard Rose and Oskar Shumsky, and a broadcast of Gilbert and Sullivan's *H.M.S. Pinafore.* From Vancouver came performances of *Madama Butterfly* with Canadian soprano Teresa Stratas in the title role, and from Montreal there were two programmes on "The Music of India" prepared by Rosette Renshaw.

To open the 1960–61 season of the CBC Symphony Orchestra, Geoffrey Waddington conducted a concert of music by Healey Willan as a salute to the composer on his eightieth birthday. During the course of the season, Pierre Monteux was one of the guest conductors and Glenn Gould gave an illuminating performance of the *Piano Concerto* by Arnold Schoenberg conducted by Robert Craft. That year also saw the Orchestra make two visits to the United States. In April it gave a concert conducted by Geoffrey Waddington, at the Inter-American Music Festival in Washington, at which Canadian works were performed including the première of Harry Freedman's *Symphony*. Later, in the fall, it returned to give two concerts to commemorate the sixteenth anniversary of the United Nations. The first of these, conducted by Geoffrey Waddington, took place in Washington and the second on United Nations' Day, was given in the General Assembly of the United Nations and was conducted by Sir Ernest MacMillan. Godfrey Ridout's CBC-commissioned *Fall Fair* had its première on this occasion and the programme was carried across the world by the United Nations' shortwave service.

These highlights were not the only riches this period had to offer. Sunday concerts presented everything from the songs and dances of the thirteenth to the fifteenth centuries, performed by the Rowland Pack Singers and Players, to unfinished songs by Schubert and Canadian music. Heather Thompson, soprano, and Michel Dussault, pianist, won the CBC Talent Festival awards. In the following year the winners were William Aide, pianist, and Claude Corbeil, baritone, and it was in this season that the newly formed Canadian String Quartet gave frequent broadcasts; the McGill Chamber Orchestra, conducted by Alexander Brott, was heard and Joan Sutherland, in spite of a blinding snowstorm, drew a capacity audience at her Toronto début—a CBC Celebrity Recital at Hart House. In the summer the many festival broadcasts included *The Pirates of Penzance* from Stratford, *Elegy for Young Lovers* by H. W. Henze from Glyndebourne, the Italia Prize-winning work, *Ondine*, by Akira Miyoshi of Japan and, from the Soviet Union, a concert devoted to the music of Shostakovich. The French Network also presented many series, including "Les Grandes Pages de l'Oratorio," "Musique Canadienne" from Montreal and, from Quebec City, broadcasts by the Quebec Symphony Orchestra and a special Christmas performance of *L'Enfance du Christ* from the Basilica.

The most important CBC music events of 1962 centred on Igor Stravinsky, who came to Toronto twice that year to record radio and television programmes, in honour of his eightieth birthday. Stravinsky arrived in January with his associate Robert Craft (in the wake of one of the worst ice storms in years) and, after recovering from the non-arrival of luggage and scores, was kept very busy working on a radio documentary, "Igor Stravinsky, Inventor of Music," and a major television project, "Stravinsky at 80." He was so delighted with the CBC Symphony Orchestra and the Festival Singers of Toronto, and their director, Elmer Iseler, that he agreed to return for a public concert in Massey Hall on April 29. The concert was broadcast on "CBC Wednesday Night," and also on the French Network. It included the North American première of *A Sermon, a Narrative and a Prayer*, the world première of *Eight Instrumental Miniatures*, and the world broadcast-première of the anthem *The Dove Descending Breaks the Air*. In the first half of the programme Robert Craft conducted the Canadian premières of three Schoenberg works, *Prelude to a Genesis Suite*, *A Survivor from Warsaw*, and the *Violin Concerto*, with Israel Baker as the soloist. As he left the stage, Stravinsky was overcome by the standing, cheering audience and, commenting on the excellence of the performances, said he looked forward to returning to Toronto. Columbia Records was on hand, and in the next few days taped the whole programme with the help of the CBC, which asked the Mayor of Toronto, Nathan Phillips, to divert traffic away from unsoundproof Massey Hall. The three policemen concerned were incredulous on learning of their assignment and the incident created a "party story" in New York music circles.

"Igor Stravinsky, Inventor of Music" was not broadcast until June, in order to coincide with the composer's birthday. Stravinsky spoke at length. There were also comments by Robert Craft, Nadia Boulanger, Hans Werner Henze, W. H. Auden and many other distinguished people; the whole project was given coherence with a commentary by Harry Somers. The International Service of the CBC made these Stravinsky radio programmes available overseas and they were broadcast more than two hundred times in Europe, the United States, and other parts of the world.

In the fall the CBC Symphony Orchestra presented the first of another series of contemporary music broadcasts in which Canadian works such as John Weinzweig's *Divertimento No. 5*, John Beckwith's *Fantasy Concerto for Piano and Orchestra*, played by Mario Bernardi, Godfrey Ridout's *The Ascension*, sung by Mary Morrison, Murray Adaskin's *Capriccio for Piano and Orchestra*, played by Kendall Taylor, the *Symphony No. 1* by Jean Papineau-Couture and many others were presented. These CBC Symphony broadcasts alternated with the broadcasts of the CBC Vancouver Chamber Orchestra in a single Sunday afternoon period. This was a new departure, brought about partly as a result of the welding of two schedules through the merging of the Trans-Canada and Dominion Networks into a single more extensive English national network called the CBC Radio Network.

In the 1962–63 year the French Network presented the internationally renowned Quebec duo-pianists Renée Morisset and Victor Bouchard in thirteen recitals, and also broadcast for the first time a radiophonic cantata *Psaumes pour Abri*, commissioned from Pierre Mercure. Also from Montreal came the opening concert of the magnificent Place des Arts and a "Tribute to Kurt Weill." An unusual contribution from Toronto was a special concert of Commonwealth Music in honour of the delegates to the Commonwealth Broadcasting Conference which was taking place in Canada at that time.

During the 1963–64 year the CBC Symphony Orchestra again alternated with the CBC Vancouver Chamber Orchestra, and its last public concert was one of the official opening events of the Edward Johnson Building in the University of Toronto. It was jointly announced by the CBC and the Toronto Symphony Orchestra Association that the Corporation would suspend the activities of the CBC Symphony Orchestra and use the Toronto Symphony instead. There were several reasons for making this change, but the announcement stressed "the primary advantage should be the concentration of the best orchestral players in Toronto into one unit." There was considerable controversy over the Orchestra's disbandment. The Toronto *Globe and Mail* declared that "The CBC will hire the members of the Toronto Symphony Orchestra just as it hired the members of its own Orchestra, and they are justified in their argument that the taxpayer should be given the best possible for his money. This best was provided by the CBC Symphony Orchestra. And one wonders what would happen if the BBC decided to disband its orchestra because, for example, the London Symphony Orchestra wanted an orchestral monopoly in London." In spite of these fears, most of the aspirations of the CBC Symphony have lived on in the "Concerts from Two Worlds" series.

Mediæval, Renaissance and Baroque music came to the fore in the 1963–64 season. The Montreal Consort of Viols, directed by Otto Joachim, presented "From Charlemagne to Elizabeth I," Shakespeare's quadri-centenary was celebrated in all the main production centres and the Festival Singers devoted an evening to Don Carlo Gesualdo, Prince of Venosa, including his *Tenebrae for Holy Saturday* which had not been performed for several hundred years. Bach dominated the scene at Easter with the *B Minor Mass, St. Matthew Passion* and *St. John Passion*. The colour of the romantic period was captured in a documentary called "The Vogue of the Virtuoso." A programme called "Summer is Icumen In" was dedicated to the memory of the young Toronto musician Rowland Pack. It consisted of thirteen variations on the mediæval tune by as many Canadian composers. CBC Vancouver broadcast documentaries on Strauss and Klemperer, as well as Britten's *The Rape of Lucretia*. A memorial programme, "The Legacy of Paul Hindemith," was presented in honour of the composer's death. New Canadian music raised its voice in two programmes of works by Serge Garant, Murray Schaefer, Gilles Tremblay and Udo Kasemets, and there was another Canadian series lasting two months which presented premières of CBC-commissioned chamber works. From Montreal came a broadcast of "Jean le Précurseur" by the French-Canadian composer Guillaume Couture. CBC Toronto was continuing its "love affair" with Stravinsky when the composer arrived to supervise broadcasts and recordings of Mavra and other works. At the same time the Festival Singers broadcast and recorded works by Schoenberg.

A major development during the 1964–65 year was the establishment of an FM Network, consisting of Toronto, Ottawa, Montreal and Vancouver. Apart from the addition of Vancouver, the new Network differs from the old in that it is not bilingual. As in the past, it is broadcasting all major music series from the AM schedule, including the CBC Montreal Orchestra from the French Network, and is very dependent on programmes of recorded music, CBC transcriptions and programmes imported from abroad. The FM Network is playing a vital role in CBC broadcasting by providing alternative programming to CBC AM stations in the cities in which it exists. It caters to a variety of music audiences ranging from jazz buffs to those interested in the *avant-garde*. Some of the series so far heard have included "Music of Today," with Harry Somers as host, "The Age of Elegance," devoted to music of the Baroque era, "Pianists of Today," "New Records," in which new releases are reviewed, "R.S.V.P.," a two-hour listeners' choice period, in which records are given away, "Jazz Club," "Opera Theatre," and "Great Conductors of Our Time." In addition, there are afternoon concerts of exceptional interest and series devoted to specific composers such as Michael Tippett, Tchaikovsky, Haydn and Monteverdi, as well as Canadian music of all kinds. There are also projects such as "Music and Mythology," "Composers of Latin America," "The Art of Glenn Gould," and "The Perfect Anti-Wagnerite."

The French Network has one FM station in Montreal which, apart from exposing major music series taken from its AM service, provides a great deal of alternative programming, consisting of recordings, transcriptions and some programmes which it obtains as a member of La Communauté Radiophonique des Programmes de Langue Française. If, in the future, further CBC FM French stations develop in Ottawa and Quebec City, a CBC FM French Network might come into being, and a French Network FM station has recently opened in Vancouver to provide an outlet for its AM service. (A major expansion of the French Network's AM service occurred in 1954 when CJBC Toronto became almost exclusively a French station.) Again, looking ahead, the day will come in which the English Network will have a much more comprehensive FM or second network than at the moment, and there is a strong possibility this will provide a complete music service in the near future.

In October of 1964 "Concerts from Two Worlds" was first presented. This series has concentrated on music by Canadian composers and other interesting orchestral works from both the past and present which are not well represented in other orchestral series. It included many Canadian premières performed by the Toronto Symphony Orchestra, such as the *Turangalila Symphony* by Messiaen, conducted by Jean-Marie Beaudet, the *Symphony No. 6* by Mahler, conducted by Heinz Unger and Franz Bauer, the *Symphony No. 7* by Mahler, conducted by Herman Scherchen, the world première of *Five Shakespeare Songs* by Gunther Schuller, conducted by the composer, *In Memoriam Anne Frank* by Godfrey Ridout, sung by Mary Morrison and conducted by Victor Feldbrill, and North American premières of Schoenberg's *Six Songs*, Opus 8, sung by Mary Simmons, and *Abraham and Isaac* by Stravinsky, conducted by Robert Craft. Canadian composers represented were Claude Champagne, Sir Ernest MacMillan, Harry Somers, Irving Glick, John Weinzweig, Pierre Mercure, Murray Schaefer and Bruce Mather. A significant broadcast was the one in which Pierre Boulez, making his Toronto début, directed the orchestra in a programme of French music. From Europe came two programmes devoted to the music of Janaček, Sibelius, Nielsen and a number of composers little known in Canada.

In 1964 the CBC increased the number of commissions to Canadian composers and there was an increase in the amount of Canadian music in CBC schedules. "CBC Sunday Night" programming was enhanced by performances of important new Canadian choral works, such as *Jonah* by John Beckwith and the same composer's CBC-commissioned *Trumpets of Summer*, Harry Freedman's *Tokaido*, Kelsey Jones' *Prophecy of Micah*, and Violet Archer's *Sing the Muse*. These works were balanced by others ranging from *La Messe de Notre Dame*, by Guillaume de Machaut, to Britten's *War Requiem*. In the "CBC Celebrity Series," broadcast from major universities in Canada, there were recitals by pianist Ronald Turini from Memorial University in St. John's, Newfoundland, Victoria de los Angeles, soprano, from Laval University in Quebec City, and Yi Kwei Sze, bass, from the University of Alberta in Edmonton.

Other broadcasts of interest were a recital of Indian music by the *sarode* player Ali Akbar Khan and a programme from Vancouver concerned with the "Music and Letters of Mozart," Ruby Mercer's "Opera Time," "Gilmour's Albums," Allan Sangster's "Music of Handel," Britten's opera *Curlew River* and a documentary presented by Glenn Gould called "Dialogues on the Prospect of Recording."

"Music in Canada," a joint English-French Network series of unusual interest started in July 1965. These thirteen broadcasts were based on Helmut Kallmann's book, *A History of Music in Canada 1534 to 1914*, and traced the growth of Canadian music from the arrival of the first French settlers to the present day. Earlier in the year, also as a joint English-French Network production, there had been a broadcast of the first Canadian opera, written in the eighteenth century, *Colas et Colinette* or *The Bailiff Duped*, by Joseph Quesnel. In addition to the earliest Canadian music, the very latest was also heard, such as the CBC-commissioned *Variations for Flute, Oboe and Harpsichord* by Harry Freedman and John Beckwith's *Canada Dash, Canada Dot—The Line Across*, with a text by James Reaney. From the Stratford Festival, "CBC Sunday Night" broadcast Handel's *Solomon*, and other events, such as Kurt Weill's *The Rise and Fall of the City of Mahagonny*. Other Canadian festival broadcasts, including those of Les Jeunesses Musicales at Mount Orford, Quebec, were recorded by the French Network. CBC Winnipeg broadcast a concert of music by Bernard Naylor, conducted by the composer, and a complete evening on "CBC Sunday Night" from Vancouver was devoted to the Sibelius and Nielsen anniversaries. Some of the "CBC Celebrity Series" recitalists were Andrés Segovia and Lois Marshall in eastern Canada, and Paul Badura Skoda in the west. Paul Badura Skoda's concert was part of a festival called "CBC—Music on Campus," held at the University of Manitoba under CBC auspices. The CBC Winnipeg Orchestra performed, and there were numerous chamber music concerts and recitals with local artists, such as the singer Gladys Kreise of the Metropolitan Opera who flew home from New York to add lustre to the occasion. All the concerts were jammed to the doors and the *Winnipeg Free Press*, commenting facetiously on "the dense patient groups of 'standees,' " thought that perhaps an "interplanetary take-over" had taken place.

In November 1965, "CBC Sunday Night" became "CBC Tuesday Night," but the context remained unchanged. Vancouver contributed a memorial programme to the composer Varèse and the broadcast-première of Harry Somers' opera *The Fool*. From Toronto and Montreal came a series of youth concerts specially arranged for school children, with the Hart House and the McGill Chamber Orchestras. Vancouver, Toronto and Montreal all contributed a number of programmes devoted to the music of Bruckner. A documentary of great interest was "The Boulez View," a study of the controversial French composer Pierre Boulez. Broadcasts from "Ten Centuries Concerts" in Toronto of works by contemporary Canadian and foreign composers added zest to "CBC Tuesday Night"; broadcasts from Montreal concerned with the Busoni Centenary were also of particular interest. "Illumination I," a CBC commission from Otto Joachim, met with a lively reception. The *Montreal Star* commented:

A dark studio of charts, a composer-producer who pushed light buttons to control whether the musicians could see what they were doing or not; a pianist who dumped a bit of chain into the piano and thumped on it with a mallet—what sort of music was this? . . . It was fascinating music. . . . The music of this Joachim work gave ears a new reach. He caught the sense of today, of space, and confusion, and a mystery that is at once of planets and the soul. A strange work, but gripping. We must hear it again.

In the fall of 1964 the Director of Music of the French Network, Roy Royal, retired and was succeeded by the distinguished composer and critic, Jean Vallerand, an appointment he held until the summer of 1966, when he was succeeded by Jacques Bertrand. One of the first things Jean Vallerand did was to develop the French Network's Les Petites Symphonies into the more substantial CBC Montreal Orchestra series, and in the fall of 1965 a policy of using guest conductors was established. In the course of the 1965–66 season, the Orchestra was directed by visiting conductors such as Aaron Copland, Josef Krips, Vladimir Golschmann, Hans Swarowsky and Canadians such as Wilfrid Pelletier, Pierre Hétu, Hans Bauer, Jean-Marie Beaudet, Jean Deslauriers and Michel Perrault. Some of the soloists were Witold Malcuzynski, Christian Ferras and Canadians Lise Boucher and Jacques Simard. The French Network also gave the première of Gilles Tremblay's *Kekobah* for voice and instrumental ensemble and taped Jean Papineau-Couture's *Psaume 150*. Both these Canadian works were broadcast on the Belgian, French and Swiss radio systems as part of an exchange programme through La Communauté Radiophonique des Programmes de Langue Française. Among the many other French Network broadcasts were programmes presented by the Quintette à Vents de Québec and "Musique de Clavecin," which provided an opportunity for harpsichordists in the Province of Quebec to be heard.

During the following season of "Concerts from Two Worlds," an ever increasing number of Canadian works was performed, including the CBC commissions *Centennial Colloquy* by Alexander Brott and the *Piano Concerto* by Jean Papineau-Couture, as well as *From Dreams of Brass* for narrator, soprano, choir, orchestra and electronic music by Norma Beecroft. The English composer Michael Tippett conducted a concert of his own music, including the North American broadcast-première of his *Concerto for Orchestra*. Hermann Scherchen directed a concert including works as far apart as the "Adagio for Winds" from *The Seven Last Words* by Haydn and *Polla-Tadina* by Xenakis. Robert Craft conducted a programme encompassing Stravinsky's entire career from the *Symphony Opus 1* to his latest piece, *Canon on an Old Russian Folk Song*, and Seiji Ozawa, Walter Susskind's successor as the permanent conductor of the Toronto Symphony, directed the Canadian première of Charles Ives' *Symphony No. 4*.

In March, the CBC Music Department in Toronto organized twenty-two transcription projects for unlimited use in its programming. These included *Evocations*, a CBC commission from Harry Somers, the *Symphony No. 2* by Oskar Morawetz and *Guernica* by Clermont Pépin. The CBC Vancouver Chamber Orchestra and the Hugh McLean Consort of Vancouver contributed programmes, and, in Winnipeg, apart from Canadian compositions conducted by Victor Feldbrill, numerous works of the Mannheim School were recorded. Many individual artists taped recitals, including the singers Joan Maxwell and Lois Marshall. Other useful transcriptions came about through recording sessions with the Halifax Trio and the McGill Chamber Orchestra of Montreal.

Two other developments of this period must be mentioned. The fall of 1965 saw the opening of the CBC's first stereo station in Winnipeg. (Another has opened in Vancouver since then and in time there will be a chain of them.) The "CBC Talent Festival" was expanded into a competition with four first prizes of one thousand dollars for each of the following categories: singers, pianists, string players and woodwind and brass instrumentalists. In addition to the first prize, winners were offered a further five hundred dollars each for tuition fees and given CBC radio and television engagements. The second prize-winners were awarded five hundred dollars and also invited to appear on CBC programmes. In recent years "CBC Talent Festival" has become a joint project of the English and French Radio Networks, and representatives from both networks have undertaken auditioning tours from coast to coast. Sir Ernest MacMillan has played an important part as conductor and adjudicator since the competition began. Apart from "CBC Talent Festival," both the English and the French Networks have broadcast competitions sponsored by Les Jeunesses Musicales and the Institut International de Musique du Canada.

There were so many major radio music programmes in 1966 that it would be impossible to give a detailed picture of them. However, many will be in recent memory. Apart from documentaries on Ives and Bartok and a special concert of music by Kodaly in the presence of the composer, a wide variety of other programmes included series aimed at those interested in sharpening their knowledge of music. Such series were "The Language of Music," "Contemporary Music without Tears," and the FM Network quiz "Who's the Composer?". Very little needs to be said about the musical riches of 1967. The CBC commissioned many works, including four operas on Canadian subjects of which three have been broadcast: *Grant Warden of the Plains* by Murray Adaskin, *Sam Slick* by Kelsey Jones and *The Brideship* by Robert Turner. *Louis Riel*, by Harry Somers and commissioned by the Floyd Chalmers Foundation for the Canadian Opera Company, was exposed to the whole country through CBC radio. Major events at Expo's "The World Music Festival" in Montreal's Place des Arts, special talent competitions, many outstanding concerts in the theatre at the Canadian Government's Pavilion, Britten's *War Requiem* in Vancouver, and the Canadian Government's Concert of Canadian Music in Montreal on July 1—all were made national, instead of local, events through the CBC's English and French Radio Networks.

The Corporation itself organized major music festivals in Vancouver, Winnipeg, Toronto, Ottawa, Montreal and Halifax which developed into the biggest project of this kind ever undertaken by a broadcasting organization. At the invitation of the CBC, Stravinsky came to Toronto to conduct part of a programme of his music. This public concert in Massey Hall was held in honour of the great man's eighty-fifth birthday and, as a special tribute, the Canada Council presented him with its Medal. (Stravinsky was the first non-Canadian to have received it.) The "CBC Celebrity Series" provided special events for young people in numerous other cities, such as St. John's, Charlottetown, Windsor, and Regina, and in Toronto there was a series of concerts for school children called "Mods Make Music." A series organized by the French Network covered the whole output of piano music by Canadian composers. As the year drew to a close, the Music Department in Toronto made nearly sixty transcriptions of Canadian artists and composers for the CBC Transcription Service. These recordings, together with the CBC International Service's transcriptions and the limited number of commercial recordings of Canadian artists available, are being widely used in CBC recorded music pro- grammes in an effort to make Canadians more aware of the rich musical resources of their own country. Last but not least, many local or regional music broadcasts added to the richness of CBC schedules, quite apart from programmes heard on the national radio networks. Regional broadcasting is, of course, an important part of the CBC's operations, and in Vancouver, for instance, where the difference in time zones between east- ern and western Canada makes possible extended periods of time outside network broadcasting, "CBC Saturday Evening," a block of enterprising regional programming something like "CBC Tuesday Night," has been developed. In the prairies, which are so rich in ethnic choirs, there have been many choral broadcasts, while in Ottawa public concerts have been a regular feature each year at the National Gallery. In Halifax there have been music broadcasts from the Neptune Theatre. If one adds to this many recitals and chamber music broadcasts, together with other balancing music programmes, the important contri- bution being made to the overall CBC music picture by local and regional programming is revealed.

TELEVISION

Music has played an important part in CBC Television since the CBC started transmitting the "new medium" in 1952. It is sometimes forgotten just how much music has been broadcast by the English and French Television Networks since those early days. As the records are surveyed, a phantasmagoria of distinguished opera singers, ballet dancers, conductors and concert artists is conjured up. One is reminded of the tremendous diversity of music telecasts seen in Canada in the last fifteen years and also of the trail blazing that has been done by CBC producers.

Unlike some other countries, Canada quickly understood that television, while useful for relaying music events, could not lean sycophantically on the concert hall and the opera house, but would have to find its own way of translating music into the frame of the twenty-one-inch window. Of course, the concept of a music television art form, like anything new, was violently contested, especially initially, and a great deal of ink has been spilled concerning the viability of music on television. Nowadays, while some productions may be less compelling than others, it is generally accepted that music in television is here to stay. Certainly, without it, thousands of people in Canada would never have seen either an opera or a ballet; and, in fact, it is true to say that through television, music is being brought to many people for the first time.

On May 14, 1953, the CBC broadcast from Toronto its most ambitious production to date—the first full-length opera to be televised in Canada. Mozart's *Don Giovanni* was sung in English with Don Garrard in the title role. Herman Geiger-Torel was the stage director; the producer was Franz Kraemer, who stated at the time:

I believe television can bring a new and penetrating interpretation to this classic opera. There have been revisions in some scenes, so that the fullest use can be made of television techniques. On the stage, Don Giovanni often seems to move slowly. In the television production, a swifter pace will be possible as the cameras in Studio A in Toronto move backwards and forwards among five major and numerous smaller sets which have been prepared under the supervision of Rudi Nicoletti.

Later in 1953, after seventy hours of full-scale rehearsals,

CBFT Montreal presented Gounod's *Faust*, produced by Pierre Mercure, with Pierre Boutet as Faust, Irene Salemka as Marguerite, and Yoland Guerard as Mephisto. Irving Guttman was the stage director. In the summer of 1953, the "Toronto Promenade Concerts" from Varsity Arena were relayed as a simulcast live on CBC radio and television using an English announcer in Toronto and a French one in Montreal.

A major event in 1954 was the telecast of *The Barber of Seville* from Montreal, conducted by Jean Deslauriers. In an article printed in the *CBC Times*, the producer, Pierre Mercure, said:

One of the biggest problems is the co-ordinating of the sound perspectives with the visual. It is a bit disconcerting to the viewer sometimes not to hear what he sees. We have been told we came off pretty well in this respect in *Faust* and yet we learned a good many lessons. We hope to take full advantage of them in *The Barber*, although the atmosphere is entirely different. The comic effects will dominate and their successful reproduction will depend largely on lighting and sharp camera cutting.

Conducted by Nicholas Goldschmidt, Menotti's opera *The Consul* was produced at CBLT Toronto in January 1954 by Franz Kraemer under the general direction of Sydney Newman (now head of the BBC Television Drama Department). A further dimension was added through the use of special film sequences which were pre-shot and incorporated into the production.

Of course, apart from the CBC's productions, Canadian viewers were able to watch operas from the NBC-TV "Opera Theatre," which were carried by CBC Television. One of the king-pins of this concern was Samuel Chotzinoff, who in an interview with the *New York Herald Tribune*, prior to a production of *The Marriage of Figaro*, said the NBC Opera Company was trying to take the grand out of "grand opera" and make it more immediate on television. He felt that stage opera "as it is usually done is a recital in costume rather than a music drama." This, of course, was an extreme view, but it is undoubtedly true to say that developments in television and film operas added new dimensions to many productions seen today in the progressive opera houses of the world.

In January 1954 a dramatic development in CBC television music programming took place with the birth of the CBFT series "L'Heure du Concert." In the period from January 14, 1954, to June 23, 1955, there were sixty-three programmes. "L'Heure du Concert" consisted mostly of carefully constructed combinations of extracts from operas and ballets, concertos or orchestral works, and solo recital material.

The producers, Pierre Mercure and Noël Gauvin, were able to do a great deal of experimenting in the operatic field by presenting excerpts from operas as diverse as *Fidelio* and *Pelléas et Mélisande*. This in turn provided a valuable outlet for Canadian singers. In fact "L'Heure du Concert" became a marvellous vehicle for developing promising Canadian artists of all kinds, as well as presenting Canadian and foreign celebrities to the rapidly expanding television audience. By June 1957 many ballet items had been seen, including everything from excerpts of *The Nutcracker*, danced by the Ballets Chiriaeff of Montreal, and *Prélude à l'Après-midi d'un Faune*, danced by the National Ballet from Toronto, to Canadian ballets such as *Le Diable dans le Beffroi* by Jean Vallerand and *Kaleidoscope* by Pierre Mercure, danced by the Ballets Chiriaeff. Apart from employing many outstanding Canadian dancers, such as Irene Alpiné and Jury Gotshalks, television ballet was providing a challenge to choreographers such as Eric Hyrst, Celia Franca, Ludmilla Chiriaeff and Brian MacDonald.

No less important than the dancers and opera singers were the solo artists seen on "L'Heure du Concert." Among the Canadians were Ellen Ballon, Glenn Gould, Zara Nelsova, Maureen Forrester and Hyman Bress; foreign celebrities included Andres Segovia and Paul Tortelier. The final programme of "L'Heure du Concert" in the 1954–55 season consisted of music by French Canadians. Apart from the ballets by Jean Vallerand and Pierre Mercure already mentioned, there were works by Michel Perrault, Gabriel Cusson and Jean Papineau-Couture.

It had been a remarkable year. Toronto had produced Johann Strauss' *Die Fledermaus*. There was also a series of three chamber operas, *Le Pauvre Matelot* by Milhaud from Montreal, *Down in The Valley* by Kurt Weill and *The Telephone* by Menotti from Toronto. A Montreal series called "At Home with John Newmark" had experimented with presenting chamber music on television. A replica of the distinguished pianist-accompanist's living-room was the set, and Mr. Newmark talked informally about the music to be performed with his colleagues.

The ever increasing comments from viewers were a reminder that the television audience in Canada was now expanding faster than in any other country. By the end of the 1955–56 year, CBC television, in less than four years, and in spite of Canadian geography and two languages, had been made available to eighty per cent of the population.

When "L'Heure du Concert" returned to the air in September 1955, ballet was strongly represented with Jerome Robbins' choreography of *Prélude à l'Après-midi d'un Faune* danced by Tanaquil Leclercq and Jacques d'Amboise from the New York City Ballet. Also on the programme were the *Symphony in C* by Bizet, conducted by the late Désiré Defauw, and songs by Debussy sung by the mezzo-soprano Anna Malenfant, who was accompanied by Charles Reiner. The regular host, Henri Bergeron, tied the various components together with great aplomb.

In October, the same series presented the first Canadian performance of Ibert's *Angélique*; Wilfrid Pelletier was the conductor. Also from Montreal came Françoys Bernier's production of *L'Histoire du Soldat* by Stravinsky, with Marcel Marceau as the devil, *The Secret of Suzanne* by Wolf-Ferrari, and a full-length performance of *La Bohème*, produced by Pierre Mercure with Claire Gagnier as a touching Mimi.

In contrast to *La Bohème*, "L'Heure du Concert" introduced to Canadian viewers two further operas. Leonard Bernstein's *Trouble in Tahiti* was broadcast in December, and shortly afterwards New York soprano Rosemary Kuhlmann sang the lead in Rossini's *La Cenerentola* (*Cinderella*). Another visitor from New York was the famous choreographer, Georges Balanchine, who directed the New York City Ballet in the television première of *Concerto Barocco*, danced to Bach's *Double Violin Concerto* played by Henryck Szeryng and Noël Brunet.

As part of the Mozart Bicentennial Celebrations in 1956, "L'Heure du Concert" presented the first half of *Cosi fan Tutte* before the end of January. (The second half followed a week later.) Roland Leduc conducted; Jean Gascon was responsible for the staging and the production was in the hands of Noël Gauvin.

The world television première of Stravinsky's *Les Noces* was another outstanding Montreal telecast during this period. Françoys Bernier devised a shooting script for Ludmilla Chiriaeff's choreography. This placed the main emphasis on the dancing and *Les Noces* emerged as a full-fledged ballet, rather than a cantata with dances. While Montreal's "L'Heure du Concert" continued to be the mainstay of CBC music television, several Toronto series paid attention to music. In April 1955 "Scope" presented the National Ballet in a performance of Louis Applebaum's *Barbara Allen* and also the Canadian television-première of *L'Heure Espagnol* by Ravel. Towards the end of the year "Folio" presented a French ballet-night, consisting of *Lilac Garden* and *Offenbach in the Underworld*. Both were danced by the National Ballet of Canada, which was fast building a national and international reputation under its artistic director, Celia Franca, through tours across Canada and a recent visit to the United States. *Lilac Garden*, a ballet set in the Edwardian era, was choreographed to Ernest Chausson's *Poème*, and involved four protagonists, danced by Lois Smith, James Ronaldson, David Adams and Celia Franca, while the effervescent divertissement *Offenbach in the Underworld* was both frivolous and brilliant.

The following evening of December 12, CBC television carried NBC's production of Tchaikovsky's *The Sleeping Beauty*, danced by the Sadler's Wells Company visiting from England. It was an historic occasion for it was the first time the Company had presented a full-length ballet on television.

In the course of Mozart Bi-centennial celebrations "Folio" presented *The Marriage of Figaro*, produced by Franz Kraemer, with Herman Geiger-Torel as the stage director (this production was also broadcast on CBC Radio); Geoffrey Waddington conducted. "Folio" added significantly to the summer season with Norman Campbell's production of *The Pirates of Penzance*, conducted by Godfrey Ridout, and a second telecast—this time from Vancouver of Weill's *Down in the Valley*—was produced by Gene Lawrence.

That the standards being achieved by CBC television music productions compared more than favourably with those of foreign broadcasting organizations was undoubtedly a result of the amount of music being shown and the opportunities provided by these programmes for producers to experiment and bend the medium to the very special demands of music presentations.

The CBC made a statement about standards in the 1956–57 year:

While taking pride in its achievements in the past twenty years, the CBC is aware of its constant duty not only to maintain recognized standards, but to create new ones in keeping with the nation's growth and with scientific, artistic and social advances. . . . In the furtherance of the Arts—music, drama, ballet, design—CBC has set its sights at the international level, and national standards, like good currency, should be freely exchangeable among civilized people.

(It is interesting to notice that over the years, many of the CBC's music programmes have been shown in countries as disparate as Australia, Japan and Yugoslavia.)

With the beginning of the 1956–57 "L'Heure du Concert" season in October, the opening programme was devoted to a performance of the first act of *The Tales of Hoffmann* by Offenbach, conducted by Wilfrid Pelletier. This was followed by Menotti's *The Old Maid and the Thief*, and an abbreviated version of *La Traviata,* with Janine Michaud of the Paris Opera and a supporting cast of Canadian singers.

During November, "L'Heure du Concert" presented a ballet-evening with Les Ballets Canadiens (known previously as Les Ballets Chiriaeff), with Marjorie Tallchief and George Skibine as guest stars in a programme which ranged from *Les Sylphides* to two contemporary ballets. Later in the same month there was an ambitious production of Stravinsky's *Oedipus Rex* by Pierre Mercure, with Léopold Simoneau as Oedipus and Elena Niko-laidi as Jocasta. This was the one hundredth programme in the "L'Heure du Concert" series.

With the introduction of videotape and the first installation of videotape recording units in Winnipeg, viewers outside the principal production centres could begin to look forward to a picture quality greatly improved over the old kinescope re-cordings.

In December of 1956 Norman Campbell produced a ninety-minute presentation of *Swan Lake,* with the National Ballet Company of Canada. Lois Smith danced the double role of Odette-Odile and David Adams was Siegfried. Closer to Christmas, the Festival Singers of Toronto, conducted by Elmer Iseler, performed Britten's *Ceremony of Carols* on "L'Heure du Concert" with harpist Marie Iosch, and on Christmas Day from Montreal there was an original ballet by Brian MacDonald called *Under the Christmas Tree.* "L'Heure du Concert"'s last December production was *L'Enfant et les Sortilèges* by Ravel, with Claire Gagnier and other leading Montreal singers per-forming. This was such a success with the public that the pro-duction was repeated the following year. Just before the old year ended, "Folio" brought Puccini's *Gianni Schicchi* to Cana-dian viewers in a production by Mario Prizek.

In the first few months of 1957, "L'Heure du Concert" con-tinued to be the mainstay of CBC music television. Jean-Marie Beaudet conducted Gounod's *Mireille* and Ettore Mazzoleni *Lord Byron's Love Letter* by Raffaello de Banfield. The McGill Chamber Orchestra, directed by Alexander Brott, brought music of the Baroque era into view with a performance of the *Four Seasons* by Vivaldi.

Later in the same year, Maureen Forrester was the soloist in an all-Brahms concert conducted by Igor Markevitch, and there was a programme on the music of India starring Ravi Shankar and introduced by Rosette Renshaw. Still another departure was an abridged version of Alban Berg's opera *Wozzeck*, with baritone Louis Quilico in the title role. More standard fare was provided by performances of Act I of *The Barber of Seville* and an abridged version of Gounod's *Roméo et Juliette*. In September a television concert was presented in honour of the Queen's visit to Canada. Many leading Canadian artists appeared, including Glenn Gould and Richard Verreau, and works by Canadian composers such as Clermont Pépin, Roger Matton and Michel Perrault were performed.

"Folio" 's first music production in the 1957–58 year was Gilbert and Sullivan's *Patience*. In November an evening was given over to two important modern ballets: *Games*, danced by the Donald McKayle Company, and *Rites*, by the Pearl Lang Company. *Games* dealt with the street games of slum children. *Rites*, set to music from Bartok's *4th and 5th String Quartets*, was in its overall concept a ritualized birth-growth-death cycle. The producer was Harvey Hart, who had established a reputation as an experimenter in this field. Norman Campbell, following the success of his *Swan Lake* production, produced *Coppelia* by Delibes for "Festival" in December, with Betty Pope and Earl Kraul of the National Ballet Company of Canada. In January 1958, Franz Kraemer produced *Tosca* with Giussepe Campora of the Metropolitan Opera singing Cavaradossi, Illona Kombrink, Tosca, and James Milligan, Scarpia.

Other operas chosen during the season were Cimarosa's *The Secret Marriage* and *Madama Butterfly*. In the latter opera, Françoys Bernier strove for a production which looked authentically Japanese and, to this end, he engaged a Japanese adviser and sent the designer Gilles-André Vaillancourt to New York to collect Japanese costumes and properties. The cast was all

Canadian. Later in the season, Raoul Jobin, one of Canada's greatest operatic stars, sang Canio in a performance of *I Pagliacci*, staged by Jan Doat. Among the ballets on "L'Heure du Concert" were *Petrouchka* by Stravinsky, which was danced in honour of the composer's seventy-fifth birthday by Les Grands Ballets Canadiens and *Le Porte-rêve* ("Dream Charm"), composed especially for "L'Heure du Concert" by Clermont Pépin with a scenario devised by the French-Canadian poet and playwright Eloi de Grandmont.

In the five years "L'Heure du Concert" had been on the air 128 programmes had been produced. These had included 88 operas or operatic excerpts and 82 ballets, and a wide variety of other music. All this required a total of 7,239 engagements of artists of all kinds, many of whom were, of course, used on more than one programme. Of the total, all but 244 were drawn from Canadian talent.

A highlight of the spring of 1958 was the world television-première of Benjamin Britten's *The Turn of the Screw*, produced for "Folio" by Franz Kraemer, with sets by Nikolai Soloviov and costumes by Suzanne Mess. Charles Mackerras, a conductor of Britten's English Opera Group, flew to Toronto to conduct.

A momentous occasion in the life of the country was the opening of the coast-to-coast microwave network on July 1, 1958. This, of course, represented a great leap forward, but as television was developing at such a rapid rate it was impossible to maintain a corresponding development in the expansion of facilities (e.g., studios); on many occasions CBC music productions represented a triumph over problems of restricted space and other difficulties. Even after the opening of larger studios in Montreal and Toronto, as many as three studios were still employed for major productions to accommodate orchestras, an army of singers and performers, not to mention the necessary CBC personnel!

In December 1958, CBC presented Tchaikovsky's *Eugene Onegin* in English in a remarkable production by Franz Kraemer; Walter Susskind conducted. The celebrated actor-playwright, Peter Ustinov, introduced the programme to viewers and read passages from the poem by Pushkin which had inspired Tchaikovsky's music, immediately before and after each of the scenes of the opera. By doing this, and through the use of mime in appropriate places, Kraemer endeavoured to remove the blocks which often limit the opera's success in the theatre. Franz Kraemer said: "As viewers watch *Eugene Onegin* singly or in groups in the privacy of their own homes, they will be experiencing it in circumstances close to those considered by the composer to be ideal. . . . Tchaikovsky preferred to think of the opera as a sequence of lyric scenes from Pushkin's poem."

Among the many letters to the CBC following the telecast was this one:

Eugene Onegin was to take up most of the evening. The prospect did not please me at all and my wife even less. The show began and within ten minutes my wife was off to bed. I would have too, except that I had to finish a cigarette. So I stuck with it. As the story unfolded, so did the music and the dancing, and the first thing I knew, I was on the third cigarette. At exactly 11.00 p.m. I called my wife to tell her she was missing the finest television programme ever to be seen in our home.

"Folio" 's Christmas presentation in 1958 was a production of *The Nutcracker*, danced by the National Ballet of Canada; another *Nutcracker* production, this time from New York, was presented by NBC two days after the "Folio" production.

A great deal of excitement surrounded the world television-première of Benjamin Britten's *Peter Grimes* on "Folio" on January 13, 1959. There was an "on-camera" chorus, and the Festival Singers provided the "off-camera" group. Lois Marshall made her first appearance in a full-length operatic role as Ellen Orford, and Richard Cassily of the New York City Centre Opera sang Peter Grimes. Franz Kraemer and Eric Till were responsible for the production, and Mario Bernardi (now the chief conductor of Sadler's Wells First Opera Company in England) played an important role in coaching the cast.

Offenbach's *La Grande-Duchesse de Gérolstein* was a highlight of the 1958–59 "L'Heure du Concert" season. Maurice Sarrazin, director of Le Grenier de Toulouse, one of France's leading theatrical groups, came to Montreal to stage the performance. The all-Canadian cast of Françoys Bernier's glittering production included Pierrette Alarie as the Grande-Duchesse.

Important "L'Heure du Concert" productions were: Honegger's *Jeanne d'Arc au Bûcher*, presented by Pierre Mercure, and Roger Matton's *Horoscope*, performed by Les Grands Ballets Canadiens with choreography by Eric Hyrst. In May 1959 "Folio" presented *The Merry Widow* by Lehar in an English translation by Christopher Hassall, produced by Norman Campbell, and in July a series of concerts called "Classical Parade."

From Toronto "Ford Startime" in December 1959 brought to Canadians the North American television première of the ballet *Pineapple Poll* danced by the National Ballet Company of Canada, and in May 1960 *The Barber of Seville* was produced as part of the same series. The production was by Franz Kraemer who also acted jointly with Eric Till as director. "Documentary '60" devoted itself to interviews by Herbert Whittaker with Oskar Peterson, Teresa Stratas, Lois Smith and David Adams, and "An Hour with the Stars" was also concerned with Canadian star performers.

The 1959–60 season of "L'Heure du Concert" was the most spectacular so far. It opened with *Le Roi David*, by Honegger, staged by Maurice Sarrazin and with sets by Robert Prévost. In November, the French Network was responsible for a remarkable presentation, consisting of the world television-premières of three ballets by Stravinsky. George Balanchine, together with the New York City Ballet, was again invited to the CBC Montreal studios, where they gave never-to-be-forgotten performances of *Apollon Musagète*, *Orpheus* and *Agon*. Later *La Voix Humaine* by Poulenc sung by Pierrette Alarie received its world television-première, and *L'Histoire de Daniel*, the anonymous thirteenth-century music-play, was staged by Jean Gascon and conducted by Noah Greenberg. The Peruvian soprano Juanita Porras was brought to Montreal to sing the title role in Massenet's *Manon*, and in March 1960 "L'Heure du Concert" came to a climax with another of Françoys Bernier's productions, *Dialogues des Carmélites* by Poulenc, an opera which proved to be ideally suited to television. Directed by Maurice Sarrazin, the cast (with the exception of Elena Nikolaidi) was all-Canadian. The programme organizer of the series, Gabriel Charpentier, recalls: "The intense spiritual value of that great work with its intimacy and secrecy was remarkably captured through the 'indiscretion' of the cameras."

In September 1960 CBC Vancouver presented a programme about Bruno Walter. The great conductor was making one of his infrequent public appearances at the Vancouver International Festival, when CBC cameras recorded him rehearsing Brahms' *Symphony No. 2*, and this film, together with an interview by Albert Goldberg, music critic of the *Los Angeles Times*, provided viewers with a remarkable insight into both the man and the musician.

During 1960 the Children's Department of the CBC, in collaboration with the Music Department in Toronto, started a series of outstanding concerts. They differed from Leonard Bernstein's children's concerts, which were being shown in Canada at that time, in that they were specially planned as studio productions, rather than as transmissions from a hall. This gave the producer, Paddy Sampson, scope to experiment with new ways and means of presenting music on television. The accent was on outstanding young artists who were drawn from Canada and elsewhere. Elmer Iseler recruited and trained a CBC Youth Choir and Mario Bernardi was engaged as conductor. Louis Applebaum acted as host. The first programme included the première of Godfrey Ridout's *The Dance* for choir and orchestra, which had been commissioned for the occasion. Amongst the soloists were Canadians such as Ronald Turini and Donald Bell, and overseas artists such as the Ceylonese cellist Rohan de Saram. In the final programme of the series, pianists Mario Bernardi and Ray Dudley played Roger Matton's *Concerto for Two Pianos and Percussion*.

A Public Affairs Department series playing an important part in the overall television schedule was "Music to See." These valuable telecasts were prepared and presented by Helmut Blume, who had established an enviable reputation as a broadcast commentator through countless radio broadcasts. "Music to See," of which there were several series, dealt with everything from Gregorian Chant to electronic music and did much to widen the potential audience for music on television. "Music in Miniature" was a Thursday afternoon series on the CBC English Network which started in October 1960 and originated in Toronto, Halifax, Winnipeg and Vancouver.

Again "L'Heure du Concert" presented a remarkable series of full-scale works in the 1961–62 season. It was organized by the poet and composer Gabriel Charpentier, who had been associated with "L'Heure du Concert" since its inception, and produced by Pierre Mercure. *La Bohème* with Claire Gagnier as Mimi once again, was heard in September, followed by Debussy's *Pelléas et Mélisande*. The world television-premiére of Gluck's *Orphée* took place at CBC Montreal in March 1961 and was staged by Powys Thomas and Jean Gascon. In the course of the season, extracts were presented from the very effective *musique concrète* ballet *Kaleidoscope* by Alwin Nikolais, performed by the Alwin Nikolais Dancers, as well as a production of the visiting Peking Opera and one of Stravinsky's *Pulcinella*, with choreography by Todd Bolender executed by Les Grands Ballets Canadiens.

In addition to "L'Heure du Concert," the French Network originated a long series of concerts on Sunday afternoons. Because each programme included at least one Canadian work, a great deal of Canadian music reached the national viewing audience for the first time. (There were seventy-three Canadian works presented in all.)

The Toronto series "Festival '61" replaced "Folio" and though not exclusively concerned with music, it became a vehicle for most of the English Network's major music telecasts. In January 1961 "Festival '61" presented the North American television-première of *Elektra* by Richard Strauss, produced by Franz Kraemer, who said: "*Elektra* is one of the hardest operas to perform in the whole literature because it has one big emotional thing to say after another, but it is ideally suited to the intimacy of television, because it has a smallish cast, a simple but powerful story and is in one act." Lister Sinclair introduced the opera and explained the plot with the help of figurines designed by Brian Jackson. Virginia Gordoni sang the demanding role of Elektra.

Glenn Gould, who was already very well known to television viewers, attracted a great deal of attention in February 1961, when he proved himself to be a commentator of great personal magnetism. In "The Subject is Beethoven" he not only performed the *Eroica Variations* and the *Sonata Opus 69* with the cellist Leonard Rose, but also discussed both works with a lucidity and enthusiasm which was infectious, judging by the many letters from all over the country which poured into Toronto afterwards.

Later in the season a series of five programmes from Vancouver called "Direction in Music" dealt with everything from music associated with the seasons of the year (filmed in and around Stanley Park) to Hans Werner Henze's *Apollo and Hyacinth*. But it was Verdi's and Boito's realization of Shakespeare's "fat knight," that brought the 1960–61 "Festival" season to a resounding close. The dimensions of Franz Kraemer's production matched the hero of *Falstaff* and could scarcely be contained within three studios. Louis Quilico, back at home after fresh triumphs in Europe, sang Falstaff and Donald Bell was a convincing Ford.

During the summer the Royal Winnipeg Ballet made its début on the full network and in the fall Norman Campbell transported Tyrone Guthrie's production of *The Pirates of Penzance* lock, stock and barrel from the Stratford Festival and adapted it for television. Also in the fall of 1961 "The Lively Arts," a series which was the brainchild of the producer Vincent Tovell, included music programmes on such artists as Zubin Mehta and Marek Jablonski.

Louis Applebaum, Television Consultant to the Corporation

for a time in Toronto, co-ordinated a Sunday afternoon series which began in January 1962 with "Portrait of an Orchestra," a programme about the CBC Symphony Orchestra with Geoffrey Waddington, Wilfrid Pelletier and Victor Feldbrill as the conductors. Glenn Gould, against a sumptuous backdrop which looked as though it came straight out of the Hermitage in Leningrad, discussed "Music in the U.S.S.R." and included the *Sonata No. 7* by Prokofieff on the programme. In March he was heard in an all-Bach programme.

Of the chamber operas seen, perhaps the most memorable was Eric Till's production of *Riders to the Sea* by Vaughan Williams. In addition, there was "An Evening with Gilbert and Sullivan," and from Vancouver came a rehearsal of Elliott Carter's *Quartet for Flute, Oboe, Cello and Harpsichord*, with a discussion of the work between the players and the composer, followed by a public performance at the University of British Columbia. The Winnipeg Symphony Orchestra contributed a programme conducted by Victor Feldbrill which included John Weinzweig's *Edge of the World* with a visual focus on Eskimo sculpture.

Much could be said of the Youth Concerts seen in the 1961–62 season. One of the most outstanding was a telecast which included the world première of Harry Somers' *Abstract for Television*, which had been commissioned for the programme. The work was "a dramatic experiment in relating musical sound to the visual without resorting to graphics—depending only on camera movements and lighting to underline, state, restate or complement visually what is being expressed at the same time in musical form." One of a number of letters commenting on the experiment said: "Mr. Somers' *Abstract* was a *coup* for the CBC—a fine work by a good composer and presented in a way which finally made an orchestra interesting to the viewer." In another inventive programme the producer of the series, Paddy Sampson, experimented with presenting chamber music on television with works as varied as a Haydn string quartet and a newly commissioned *Rondino for Nine Instruments* by Murray Adaskin of Saskatoon. "Music for a

New Set of Ears," produced by Franz Kraemer, dealt with some of the developments in musical language from Respighi's *The Pines of Rome* to Schoenberg's *Begleitmusik zu einer Lichtspielszene* Opus 34.

At Easter, Vancouver presented "The Third Day" with music by Robert Turner to a text by Peter Haworth from fragments of religious dramas of the sixteenth century, and also from Vancouver there came a programme which showed Benjamin Britten rehearsing and performing his *Nocturne* with Peter Pears, tenor, and the CBC Vancouver Chamber Orchestra.

The French Network again presented several major productions, including *Carmen* produced by Jean-Yves Landry, and *Bluebeard's Castle* by Bartok, produced by Pierre Mercure. *Bluebeard's Castle* was videotaped in two versions, one English and the other French, and the sets were by the famous French-Canadian artists Mousseau and Rinfret. Apart from these two operas, *L'Enfance du Christ* by Berlioz was produced by Jean-Yves Landry from the Basilica in Quebec City.

Of the ballets presented on "L'Heure du Concert" in the 1961–62 season, two of the most interesting were those choreographed by George Balanchine and danced by the New York City Ballet. They were *Divertimento No. 15* by Mozart and *Liebeslieder Walzer*, Opus 52 and 65 by Brahms. In 1962 a recital series which had been started by the French Network in 1959 came to an end. Included in the galaxy of "stars" presented in ninety telecasts were Maureen Forrester, Julian Bream, Glen Gould, Elisabeth Schwarzkopf, Léopold Simoneau, Marcel Grandjany, Zara Nelsova, Witold Malcuzynski, Betty Jean Hagen and Pierre Fournier—to mention but a few.

On June 11, 1962, "Festival" presented "Stravinsky at 80." Produced by Franz Kraemer, this programme was a view of the great composer seen through the eyes of his friends and colleagues, through photos of the past and, most important of all, through his music. There were comments by George Balanchine, Nadia Boulanger, and Robert Craft, and, of course, statements by the composer himself. In a fascinating rehearsal sequence of *L'Histoire du Soldat* Stravinsky was shown in conversation and gestures that revealed the kernel of the music. Following this and some ballet extracts, the programme came to a climax with a moving performance of the *Symphony of Psalms* sung by the Festival Singers of Toronto with the CBC Symphony Orchestra conducted by the composer.

In the course of the 1962–63 season "L'Heure du Concert" produced *Haensel und Gretel* by Humperdinck, presented by Jean-Yves Landry, with Claire and Eve Gagnier and conducted by Alexander Brott. This series also presented *La Vie Parisienne* by Offenbach and staged by Jean Gascon. Produced before an audience as a French extravaganza in a circus-like setting and with a French-Canadian cast, the programme was enthusiastically received by Canadian viewers. Later it met with equal success when shown in Europe.

In January 1963 the "L'Heure du Concert" production group began a series of production experiments in an effort to achieve increased dramatic tension through action-reaction camera counterpoints. The first example of this technique was Todd Bolender's ballet *The Still Point*, based on a poem by T. S. Eliot and with music by Debussy. "L'Heure du Concert" also presented a Mozart concert conducted by Josef Krips, a programme devoted to the Ballet Espagnol Ximenez-Vargas, and a concert of French music.

In December a documentary called "The Looking-Glass People," produced by Norman Campbell, was shown. It was filmed at the National Ballet School in Toronto and at the Company's home base above the St. Lawrence market, as well as on part of a tour made the previous winter. It showed the Company's artistic director, Celia Franca, and other members of the Company at work. Betty Oliphant, Principal of the National Ballet School, was also shown training youngsters to become Canada's ballerinas and *danseurs* of the future. In December, "Festival" presented Norman Campbell's *Giselle*, danced by the National Ballet Company of Canada. In February there was a Youth Concert which included "Improvisations for Jazz Band and Symphony Orchestra," by Matyas Seiber and Johnny

Dankworth, and the première of the CBC-commissioned *Piano Toccata* by Clermont Pépin.

The Anatomy of a Fugue was the subject of one of the most brilliant programmes to be presented on television by Glenn Gould. After performances of fugues of the past, Mr. Gould concluded with his own *So You Want to Write a Fugue*, performed by the Canadian String Quartet and a group of singers. The producer was Eric Till.

In April, Karl Boehm was seen in a rehearsal and performance of Beethoven's *Seventh Symphony* and another Youth Concert took place. The latter included a commissioned jazz ballet from Norman Symonds and *Studies*, choreographed by Grant Strate for fourteen students from the National Ballet School. An English-Language production of *Otello* by Verdi turned it into *Othello*—and a popular success. "Music in the Family" was the subject of the final Youth Concert of the series and included performances by the Armin String Quartet from Windsor and the Brassard Family Choir from Quebec, consisting of twelve girls and one small boy. Later, from Vancouver, Sir John Barbirolli was seen in a rehearsal and performance of the *Oboe Concerto in C* attributed to Haydn, with his wife Evelyn Rothwell as the soloist.

Following a telecast of *The Mikado* in October, the 1963-64 "Festival" season got under way with two outstanding French Network productions. Elisabeth Schwarzkopf and Willi Boskowsky were the stars of a "Viennese Night". In striking contrast, Pierre Boulez conducted the Montreal Symphony Orchestra masterfully in a programme consisting of his *Improvisations sur Mallarmé No. 2*, with Josèphe Colle, soprano, Stravinsky's *Le Sacre du Printemps*, and Debussy's *Danses Sacrées et Profanes*, with Marie Iosch, harpist. The set consisted of bare walls and the producer, Pierre Mercure, used "simple" production techniques, often concentrating only on one camera.

A spectacular "Festival" production was Franz Kraemer's *Primer on Prima Donnas*, with Joan Sutherland. Evoking memories of prima donnas of the past, the programme was a remarkable portrait of the great *diva* herself.

A study of the Canadian dancer Lynn Seymour, filmed in England, was shown on "Telescope" in January, and in February "Festival" presented the Royal Winnipeg Ballet in a programme that included *Bitter Weird*—a ballet commissioned from Agnes de Mille. An interesting "Festival" was the programme of March 4 called "Invitation to Place des Arts," produced by the French Network, which gave viewers the chance to see Montreal's magnificent new concert hall and to listen to a performance of Richard Strauss' *Ein Heldenleben*, conducted by Zubin Mehta.

One of the most outstanding documentaries ever to be seen on Canadian television was "The Short Sweet Summer," about the National Youth Orchestra of Canada. Produced by Norman Campbell for the "Camera Canada" series, it showed the Orchestra undergoing intensive training in Toronto with the conductor Walter Susskind and numerous instrumental teachers, and then setting out on the most extensive tour ever to have been made by a Canadian orchestra. A CBC crew followed the players to Winnipeg, Saskatoon, Edmonton, Calgary and Victoria, and made two players the principal binding elements. One was a boy French-horn player from the prairies, the other a girl violinist from Quebec, and with them viewers experienced the struggle to make a great orchestra out of inexperienced players and the triumph of seeing this dream come to fruition. Reaction from the press and public alike was enthusiastic and it was remarked in one letter: "It should do so much to offset the general consensus that the youth of the nation is delinquent, derelict and lazy."

In honour of the Richard Strauss Centenary in 1964, CBC Toronto produced "A Tribute to Strauss" on "Festival". The Toronto Symphony was conducted by Dr. Heinz Unger and Lois Marshall sang the *Four Last Songs*. Sir Ernest MacMillan introduced the programme.

One of the most interesting projects of the twenty-one "L'Heure du Concert" telecasts in the 1963–64 year was the famous Puccini triptych *Gianni Schicchi, Il Tabarro*, and *Suor Angelica*. The first was directed by Jean Gascon, the second by

Jacques Letourneau and the third by Roland Laroche. A programme called "Contemporary Music and Dance," which broke new ground, was presented by "L'Heure du Concert" in February 1964. It showed Les Ballets Modernes de Montréal in *Refrain* by Stockhausen, choreographed by Françoise Riopelle. The conductor was Pierre Hétu. Mozart's *Der Schauspieldirektor*, staged by Guy Hoffman with costumes by Solange Legendre, enhanced the series, and colour was added by the Ensemble Vocal Lamèque—a remarkable group of schoolgirls from an island in New Brunswick—which contributed an impressive Bach programme.

"Première" was the first music telecast on "Festival" in the 1964–65 year. In it the Russian pianist Sviatoslav Richter made his North American television début and the American mezzo-soprano Marilyn Horne made her first Canadian television appearance. Lynn Seymour and Christopher Gable from the Royal Ballet, London, danced a new setting of the balcony scene from *Romeo and Juliet* by Prokofieff, choreographed by Kenneth MacMillan. Further distinguished Russian celebrities were presented on "Masters from Soviet Russia" in December 1964. Videotaped before audiences in Massey Hall in two separate sessions, David and Igor Oistrakh, and Mstislav Rostropovich, played with the Toronto Symphony conducted by Walter Susskind, and the two Oistrakhs played Bach's Sonata in C with harpsichordist Greta Kraus.

"Festival" 's major event during February was Franz Kraemer's production of *Rigoletto*, sung in English with Louis Quilico in the title role. He also appeared in "Concert Italian Style" with Renata Tebaldi. Later in the season the viewing audience was invited to "Meet Seiji Ozawa." This was the first time the dynamic young Japanese conductor of the Toronto Symphony had been seen on Canadian television, and his rehearsal and performance of the *Symphonie Fantastique* by Berlioz made it a memorable meeting indeed.

A high point of the 1964–65 "L'Heure du Concert" season was reached with an elegant production of the opera-ballet *Les Fêtes d'Hébé*, which was presented to commemorate the bi-centenary of the death of Rameau. It was staged by Jean Babilée, and Jean Beaudet directed an all-French-Canadian cast. Ida Haendel was the soloist in a Brahms programme, and, in the ballet field, Balanchine returned with the New York City Ballet to present *The Four Temperaments* by Hindemith and *Ivesiana*, produced by Pierre Morin. Another production of exceptional interest was the world television première of *Le Jeune Homme et la Mort*. Originally devised by Jean Cocteau, it was choreographed by Roland Petit and danced by the great Jean Babilée. A production of a recital by Wilhelm Kempff strove to consolidate techniques used the previous season when televising a recital by Claudio Arrau. These were primarily concerned with sharpening the *rapport* between the solo-artists and the viewing audience.

From Quebec City came a telecast of Geza Anda conducting and playing with l'Orchestre Symphonique de Québec, and a special programme, produced in the new CBC Québec TV studios, which was devoted to works by the well-known French-Canadian composer Roger Matton.

The 1965–66 "Festival" season opened with the National Ballet of Canada's production of *Romeo and Juliet* by Prokofieff, produced by Norman Campbell, with Earl Kraul and Veronica Tennant in the title roles. It was repeated in March 1966 after it won the Prix René Barthelemy at the International Television Festival at Monte Carlo.

In November 1965 another prize-winning production was telecast on the English Television Network. It was Pierre Morin's production of *The Barber of Seville* from "L'Heure du Concert," which was first shown by the French Network during the previous March. Between the French and English Network showings, the programme won an Emmy award—the CBC's first. Considering the number of countries competing against Canada in both Monte Carlo and New York, this recognition did much to boost the morale of the performers and attract wider attention to the productions in Canada itself.

Other television music programmes in the 1965–66 season included a public concert in Massey Hall with the Toronto

Symphony, conducted by Karl Boehm and with Jon Vickers as soloist, the film *Stravinsky*, produced by the National Film Board for the CBC, *The Magic Flute*, conducted by Walter Susskind, "The Exquisite Twenties" with Seiji Ozawa directing the Toronto Symphony in works by Gershwin, Ravel and Stravinsky, and a recital by Glenn Gould and Yehudi Menuhin.

In May 1966 the *CBC Times* announced that "a television trail-blazer, an unusual creation which might be called an opera, but which resembles no established forms in structure, sight or sound, and which uses every contemporary technique of screen and electronics" was to be telecast on "Festival." This was not the première of the work, however. *Loving* or *Toi*—a bilingual opera with both libretto and music by the Canadian composer Murray Schaefer—had been written for the French Network and was first seen on February 3. Murray Schaefer had worked closely with Pierre Mercure, whose tragic death in a car accident just before the première prevented two sections of the work from being included, and also with Gabriel Charpentier.

In an article in the *CBC Times*, Mr. Schaefer said in part:

Loving is about love between the sexes. This is not accomplished by narrating a romance between lovers, as in *Tristian*, but rather by looking directly at the confrontation of male and female psyches. . . . There are no characters then, but there are what we might call "attitudes." In the game of love, the masculine or feminine psyche adopts certain poses or "attitudes" to confront the opposite sex. Certain of these "attitudes" may be emphasized. Three feminine "attitudes" in particular dominate *Loving*, and for purposes of distinction in the text they are given the rather picturesque names of Vanity, Ishtar and Modesty. In the final aria, entitled "The Geography of Eros," a fourth voice would seem to sum up and fuse many of the characteristics of these three "attitudes." The man has a second voice, designated as the Poet. . . . The drama unfolds on many different levels, both conscious and unconscious. The editing units (scenes) are arranged in such a way that they will sometimes seem discontinuous, sometimes continuous. The whole attempt is to produce a "presence" rather than a story. . . . In the present version the man speaks French (in an excellent translation by Gabriel Charpentier). The woman speaks English and most of the arias are in this language.

Serge Garant conducted a highly individual orchestra and cast, which included Benoit Girard as Lui; Marilyn Lightstone as She; Carolyn Brown as the dancing She; Evelyn Maxwell as the modest She; Huguette Tourangeau as the vain She; Margo MacKinnon as Ishtar; and Phyllis Mailing as the Voice of Eros. The choreography was by Françoise Riopelle.

Other French Network programmes included a repeat of "Hommage à Claude Champagne" as a tribute following the composer's death, and a recital by Gérard Souzay which could have been subtitled "Portrait of a Great Artist." *Le Pauvre Matelot*, by Milhaud, was staged by Jean-Louis Roux and produced by Pierre Morin.

The most important technical development in 1966 was the commencement of colour television. "Byron Janis Plays Prokofieff" was the first music programme to be videotaped in colour in Toronto.

Beethoven's *Symphony No. 9*, with the Toronto Symphony, four Canadian soloists, and a specially recorded choir conducted by Seiji Ozawa, got the Centennial year off to a good start in January. "Teresa Stratas 1967" was also seen early in the year. Other events were the colour transmission of Harry Freedman's ballet *Rose Latulippe*, choreographed by Brian Macdonald with the Royal Winnipeg Ballet, the much publicized "Stravinsky at 85," and three different programmes called "Centennial Performance," which were transmitted simultaneously on the English and French Networks. These centred on George London, Maureen Forrester and Glenn Gould, and in each programme two promising young Canadian artists (chosen by a jury) also appeared. Apart from the broadcast fees, the sponsor, International Nickel, awarded a scholarship of $2500 to each of the young people.

During the summer the French and English Networks collaborated to present "Le Monde du Spectacle," or, as it was called on the English Network, "The World on Stage." These telecasts introduced artists and groups appearing in The World Festival and the National Pavilions at Expo in Montreal. In this way, Canadians unable to get to Expo were able to glimpse everything from The Ceylon Dancers to the Royal Stockholm and Hamburg Opera Companies.

Towards the end of 1967 the French Network showed a documentary programme on the Canadian composer Calixa Lavallée and on December 27, the National Ballet of Canada was seen in *Swan Lake* with a new choreography by Erik Bruhn.

Music television has come a long way since the early days and, with the advent of colour and other technological changes around the corner, the public can look forward in the future to further large-scale special events and music schedules more international in scope.

MUSIC AND THE PRIVATE STATIONS

Radio

This is an elusive subject. The private stations, unlike the CBC Networks, developed no grand design for music because in Canada there are two hundred and ninety-seven transmitters belonging to private stations and each one is geared to a local situation.

Some stations understand serious music to mean everything from "music from the shows" and popular arrangements to the symphonies of Beethoven. Other stations clearly differentiate between light music and serious music in the same manner as the CBC. This is important, because when numerous stations register certain percentages of their time as serious music it is difficult, without detailed knowledge of the content of their programming, to be sure if the term "serious music" is being used in a broadly consistent fashion.

The amount of time private stations devote to serious music varies according to the policies of each individual station. (Private stations affiliated with the CBC are obliged to broadcast a certain amount of serious music. In some cases this is expanded, in others it is not.) There are a great many stations that broadcast no serious music at all and a few, such as CHUM FM in Toronto and CJMS FM Montreal, which provide a comprehensive "good music" service of a very high order. CKVL FM

Montreal plays popular music on weekdays from 6 a.m. to 7 p.m. and serious music all night.

Where a company or management owns both an AM and FM outlet in the same city, the FM station usually pays more attention to serious music than its sister station. The majority of private stations programme mostly with commercial recordings and do not have large budgets for spending on the employment of professional musicians. For example, CHQT Edmonton, which supports local groups, would like to broadcast the Edmonton Symphony Orchestra but finds the cost of professional musicians too high to do this as a single-station venture. This is not to say that some stations do not go out of their way to assist the development of music in their particular centres. CKLW FM Windsor, Ontario, broadcasts concerts of the Windsor Symphony Orchestra and these are made available to the Program Exchange Department of the Canadian Association of Broadcasters for use by member stations. In this way twenty-six cities were introduced to the Windsor Symphony Orchestra last season.

Other stations making contributions in various ways to music organizations include CKCK Regina, CJOB Winnipeg, CFNB Fredericton, CHQT and CJCA Edmonton, CFAM Altona (Manitoba) and CKKW Kitchener. To be more specific, CFPL London broadcasts the London Civic Symphony concerts, CHSC St. Catharines carries the subscription concerts of the St. Catharine's Symphony Orchestra, and CHRC FM Quebec presents the Quebec Symphony Orchestra as well as being involved with other music activities. CKWM FM Kentville, Nova Scotia, broadcasts local amateur groups, and CKPR Port Arthur records local artists including winners of a local amateur music festival. CHQM Vancouver has helped to present the Royal Winnipeg Ballet, the National Youth Orchestra, and the Los Angeles Philharmonic in Vancouver. CFRW Winnipeg supports the Winnipeg Symphony Orchestra through public service announcements and interviews with the Orchestra's soloists. CKDS FM has conducted promotional campaigns for the Hamilton Philharmonic and other groups. CFMQ Stereo

Regina broadcasts local artists and promotes local and visiting musicians. CJBQ Belleville presents a series called "Music Quinte" which features local artists. Because it actively supports music, the Belleville Musicians Association presented a scroll to the station in 1966.

But what of the actual music programming? This often depends on where stations are situated. In more populated areas, the programming includes music from all periods, while in some small cities and towns "good music" programming tends to be mainly concerned with baroque and romantic music. (Some stations also show a shyness of chamber music.) However, it is difficult to generalize because there are too many exceptions. In large cities where there are many private stations, some, with a middle-of-the-road programme policy, include a limited number of serious music programmes devoted usually to very familiar standard repertoire, while in small centres it is possible to find stations which provide more adventurous and comprehensive programming than certain stations in Toronto or Montreal. CFAM Altona, Manitoba, is such an example.

Numerous private stations add American series to their own schedules, such as the New York Philharmonic, the Boston Pops, the Cleveland Orchestra and programmes obtained through the Broadcast Foundation of America, Radio Nederland, the BBC and other broadcasting organizations. Canadian orchestras broadcast by the CBC are heard on private stations affiliated with the Corporation. In the field of music appreciation CKCY FM Sault Ste Marie, produced "A History of Music" for the CAB Programme Exchange Department. Some, but far from all, of the private stations use the relatively few Canadian recordings of serious music available and many draw upon the Canadian Talent Library. This admirable project was initiated by CFRB Toronto and CJAD Montreal as a way of exposing Canadian artists and composers. Although the Canadian Talent Library is primarily concerned with light music, it has made two discs of the Hart House Orchestra.

Naturally the standard of presentation of music programmes

varies a great deal, and in more than a few cases announcers have pronunciation problems when it comes to the titles of works and composers' names. Nevertheless, a few private stations go to the trouble of hiring professionals as commentators for major series. Before each concert of the Victoria Symphony, CFMS has a two-hour symphony programme during which the works of the concert are played from recordings, with commentary and interviews conducted by Robin Wood. CJMS FM in Montreal makes use of artists such as Jean-Paul Jeanotte, Yoland Guérard, and Lionel Daunais. CHQM AM and FM in Vancouver, which play a considerable amount of serious music, make use of John Avison regularly. In Kingston CKLC AM takes a different approach with "The Kingston Symphony Association Music Hour"—in which this local Symphony Association selects the recordings, writes the script and generally produces the programme.

Television

In Toronto CFTO entered the serious music field with "Inside the Toronto Symphony" in 1964. This was followed by "Inside the Canadian Opera" in 1965 and "Inside the National Ballet" in 1966. For the last three years CFTO has presented the Toronto Symphony in special Christmas programmes called "A Gift Of Music." All these projects were made available to the CTV Network. There has been a limited amount of other support for Canadian orchestras; CJAY Winnipeg, for example, has presented telecasts of the Winnipeg Symphony Orchestra from time to time.

Private television has also supported serious music to a certain extent in the field of talent development. In the series "Canadian Talent Showcase," out of thirty-nine programmes, nine were concerned with promising amateurs in the serious music field.

CBC International Service

Following its establishment by the Canadian government in 1944, the CBC's International Service was mostly concerned with beaming news and information via shortwave to Europe. However, as early as March 1945, just as the war was drawing to a close, International Service arranged for two Canadian works to be recorded in Montreal with a CBC orchestra conducted by Jean-Marie Beaudet. They were the *Concerto for Piano and Orchestra* by Healey Willan, played by Agnes Butcher, and *Suite Canadienne* by Claude Champagne, sung by the "La Cantoria" Choir. Commenting in the magazine *Saturday Night*, John Watson said, "We hope this will prove to be the first of many such recordings. What finer service could the CBC perform for Canadian music, and for the Canadian public, than to record all the best works of our best composers interpreted by our most accomplished performers?" This wish, of course, was to prove prophetic, and it was not long before a second album was recorded of Canadian works by John Weinzweig, Georges-Emile Tanguay and Jean Coulthard with the Toronto Symphony Orchestra conducted by Sir Ernest MacMillan. (Two musical sketches by Sir Ernest were also included.)

All this reflected International Service's policy of coming to grips with the universal ignorance overseas of Canadian musical life, and the need to make music by Canadian composers known around the world. Initially, attempts were made to beam Canadian music overseas, but shortwave transmissions, while satisfactory for spoken word broadcasts, were not adequate for special music programmes. It became obvious that a greater service could be done to Canadian music if Canadian works were recorded and then shipped to major broadcasting organizations abroad for use in their domestic services. This led directly to the formal establishment of the CBC Transcription Service in 1947. The first programmes were cut on large, sixteen-inch discs and included works by Clermont Pépin, Maurice Blackburn, J. J. Gagnier, Pierre Mercure and Jean Papineau-Couture, Jean Coulthard, Oskar Morawetz, Gerald Bales and John Weinzweig. As the number of transcriptions increased over the years, the accent remained on Canadians performing Canadian music although, of course, the great masters were also represented. Some of the artists recorded were Frances James, soprano, Albert Pratz, violinist, Rose Pratt, pianist, and Zara Nelsova, cellist. Groups such as the Parlow String Quartet and the Montreal Bach Choir were included as well as major chamber and symphony orchestras.

Over one hundred programmes had been recorded by 1955, of which approximately half were devoted to serious music, and thousands of discs had been distributed abroad. However, the large discs were unwieldy, and a leap forward was made with the adoption of twelve-inch, microgroove recordings. A further development was the introduction of relays to add to the library of recordings of Canadian music. (Relays differ from transcriptions in that they consist of programmes taken from the CBC's domestic networks and made available for limited use within a certain time period by overseas broadcasting organizations. In other words, relays are transitory and transcriptions are permanent.)

Relays are valuable in reflecting events of great importance to the rest of the world, and it was in this manner that in 1960 much of the International Conference of Composers in Stratford, Ontario, was heard elsewhere. Again, in 1962 and 1967, relays brought Stravinsky's visits to Canada to the notice of millions of people overseas. However, in the normal course of events and quite apart from major projects, many programmes of Canadian music are made available to other countries in relay form.

Looking through the catalogues of the Transcription Service is like surveying a *Who's Who* of Canadian music, and it is interesting to see that apart from some of those already mentioned, artists like Glenn Gould, Maureen Forrester, James Milligan, John Newmark, Lois Marshall, Pierrette Alarie and Léopold Simoneau made their first recordings for the CBC. In addition, all of Canada's major composers are represented, and it is no exaggeration to say that CBC International Service has played a major part in giving many of them an international reputation.

With Catalogue No. 12, issued in 1965, CBC International

Service moved into the field of stereo recording to keep abreast with sophisticated developments in the recording field. These twelve stereo discs brought the number of programmes recorded by CBC International Service to two hundred and thirteen and included the *Symphony No. 2* by Clermont Pépin and the Piano Concerto by Oskar Morawetz, together with recitals by such artists as the baritone Donald Bell, and the harpsichordist Greta Kraus.

A very important development in the field of Canadian music was the announcement by RCA Victor and CBC International Service on February 24, 1966, of a joint centennial project consisting of an anthology of thirty-two Canadian works composed during the last one hundred years. On the eve of the twenty-first anniversary of CBC International Service, there was a release of *O Canada* by Calixa Lavallée, and later a further seventeen discs were issued as the first series of a continuing anthology of Canadian music recorded by CBC International Service and released on the RCA "Canada-International" label. This, of course, was a major break-through in terms of projecting Canadian music to a mass audience. Although the CBC had made over two hundred recordings during the previous twenty years, these discs could not be distributed commercially. Some of the composers represented were Istvan Anhalt, Alexis Contant, Sonia Eckhardt-Gramatté, Udo Kasemets, François Morel, Murray Schaefer, Jean Vallerand, Serge Garant, John Beckwith, Robert Turner, Victor Bouchard and Norma Beecroft. In the fall of 1967, RCA Victor and CBC International Service released a further eleven discs, nine of Canadian folk songs and two concerned with music by Canadian composers. (See "Recordings," p. 237 ff.)

Apart from the Transcription Service, CBC International Service has played an important role in obtaining many thousands of hours of music programming from broadcasting organizations overseas, including highlights of many of the world's leading music festivals. During 1967 it brought to millions of people overseas many of the enormous number of musical events in Montreal connected with Expo as well as Centennial events. CBC International Service has played an increasingly important role over the years in the dual function of importing and exporting high-quality music broadcasts. The success of this development is due in large measure to staff members such as the initiators Gérard Arthur and Jean-Marie Beaudet, the first full-time producer, Patricia Fitzgerald, Roy Royal, who succeeded her, and the present staff under Gérard Poupart.

As well as supporting Canadian composers and artists, CBC International Service, through the co-operation of the English and French Radio Networks, has been able to give Canadians a recorded perspective of their own musical history, stretching from the composers of the past, to the *avant garde* of today. This perspective will be further enhanced when more of the music specially composed for Canada's Centennial is recorded. The release of these discs should do much to remind people at home and abroad that the Canadian musical scene is no less dynamic, diversified, and fascinating than other aspects of Canadian life.

Films

The National Film Board of Canada came into being in 1939 and, largely through the development of documentaries, has played a vital role in interpreting Canada to itself and the rest of the world.

One of Canada's most distinguished film music composers, Louis Applebaum, established the music department in 1940. He was succeeded by the well-known conductor and violinist, Eugene Kash. The present music director is the Saskatchewan composer, Robert Fleming, who joined the staff in 1946. Robert Fleming is assisted by Eldon Rathburn and Maurice Blackburn. This outstandingly gifted trio are called upon to provide music for a great variety of documentaries and other films, and to continually adapt their ingenuity to technical developments in the industry and new editing techniques. In fact, composers at the Board must be constantly able to satisfy the countless demands of emerging films by supplying new music ideas. This they do with a facility and speed which is the direct result of years of experience in welding such disparate elements as dialogue, commentary and sound effects with fragments or more continuous sections of atmospheric or drama-heightening music.

In "Thoughts on My Craft," for Document No. 1 of La Cinémathèque Canadienne—a most valuable catalogue—Eldon Rathburn said, "Film music differs from traditional concert music in that it is often constructed of short, telescoped phrases, climaxes reached with little preparation, violent colour and textural changes and the lack of long transitional passages. Oddly enough, some of the present-day modern concert music has many of the above characteristics." Apart from those already mentioned, numerous other composers have been associated with the National Film Board. Howard Cable, William McCauley, Clermont Pépin, Barbara Pentland, Godfrey Ridout, Harry Somers, Jean Vallerand, Stéphane Venne, John Weinzweig are some of them.

Norman McLaren, the internationally renowned film maker and animator, has developed special experimental techniques in producing cameraless films and has become a legend in his own time during the twenty-five years he has worked for the National Film Board. As part of his concept of films such as *Neighbours*, McLaren has experimented with remarkable success with the synthetic creation of sound, musical and otherwise, by artificial, photographic and hand-drawn means. In other films, such as *Blinkity Blank*, apart from synthetic sound, instruments have been employed, and Maurice Blackburn has collaborated with McLaren on a number of such composite scores.

There have been experiments in other directions as well. For example, the late Pierre Mercure composed two scores, one of which, *La Forme des Choses*, uses sounds produced by the Montreal Brass Quintet treated electronically at the McGill University studios, while the other, *l'Eau*, is an imaginative electronic development of a multitude of solo flute phrases mixed with ethnic music and sound-effects.

Of course, the National Film Board has made considerable

use of Canadian performers in the recording of countless film scores and, in addition, there have been numerous documentaries about Canadian celebrities such as the pianist Glenn Gould and the contralto Maureen Forrester. *Bonsoir Monsieur Champagne* is concerned with the late French-Canadian composer, Claude Champagne, while *Man of Music* is a film profile of the dean of English Canadian composers, the late Healey Willan. A few years ago the National Film Board, in co-operation with the CBC, made a most ambitious documentary on the composer Igor Stravinsky which created a great deal of interest around the world.

In the field of music films for young people, three—*Rhythm and Percussion, String Instruments*, and *Woodwinds and Brass* —were drawn from Eugene Kash's Saturday children's concerts in Ottawa. Another, called *Youth and Music*, is about Les Jeunesses Musicales, and was shot at Mount Orford in rural Quebec, the picturesque setting of the organization's summer camp.

The Province of Quebec has experienced great developments in the feature film industry in the past few years with scores by Pierre Brault, Stéphane Venne, Maurice Blackburn, Jean Cousineau and Serge Garant. François Morel, Léon Bernier, Morris Davis and Georges Savaria are among the composers who have written music for l'Office du Film de la Province de Québec. Jacques Hétu and Claude Léveillé have also provided music for films made in Quebec. Some Quebec films have experimented with the use of sound in an effort to find new ways to enrich both the video aspects and the narration. Two good examples of this are *Il ne faut pas mourir pour ça*, with music by Andrée Paul, and *Rouli Roulant*, with a score by Pierre Brault.

Elsewhere in Canada there is a considerable amount of film making going on with much of it employing the skills of film composers. For example, Larry Crosley has composed music for a great variety of films mostly for Crawley Films Ltd., and William McCauley has also worked for the same company.

Expo provided a unique opportunity to experiment. Several Canadian composers took part in this development, not the least of whom was Serge Garant, who provided the music for *Man and the Polar Regions*. Mention should also be made of Eldon Rathburn's score for one of Expo's most popular attractions, Labyrinth.

The CBC has produced a wide variety of films in its main production centres. Robert Turner in Vancouver, Robert McMullin in Winnipeg and other composers in Eastern Canada have contributed to this area of CBC programming. Many people will remember Harry Somers' score for *Picasso*, Harry Freedman's for *The Seven Hundred Million* and *Nouvelle Ecosse* with music by François Morel.

In dealing with the vast subject of the development of music in the communications media in Canada, I have used a *lignes et points* technique to create a picture which is at best only a survey. Space would not permit a comprehensive history and this is why many *lignes et points* have been left out. By now, I hope it will be clear that, in broadcasting, the difference between music on radio and music on television is that on radio music is essential standard fare, seven days a week, fifty-two weeks a year, whereas on television it appears infrequently enough for each telecast to be regarded as a major event.

CBC radio feels the pulse beat of musical Canada. It makes the major music festivals and symphony concerts in most of the principal cities available to everyone from coast to coast, and, in its own programming, reflects the full spectrum of music from the dawn of Christianity to the *avant-garde* composers of today. Radio and television have, of course, nurtured Canadian musical life and today are still the most important outlets for the Canadian composer and the Canadian artist because (apart from financial considerations) it is only through broadcasting that a national audience can be reached.

CBC International Service acts as a two-way mirror, allowing the rest of the world to discover Canadian musical life and permitting Canada to experience the musical life of other countries. CBC Television is concerned with special events, such as operas and ballets, and, in the field of music documentaries, it has also met with spectacular success. In addition, there are also what might be described as television "essays" dealing with everything from a rehearsal and performance of a single work under a great conductor to journeys into new worlds such as the improvisations of the Lukas Foss Ensemble. Christmas, Easter and other times of particular significance create another outlet for music on television and there have also been poems in the chamber music area. It should not be forgotten that both radio and television have played a major role in the areas of audience building and talent development.

The various communications media are shaping the public of today and through the public they react to each other. Radio, recordings, films and television are doing much to sharpen our ears and eyes, and these, together with the increasing number of excellent books available, are widening musical audiences in Canada to a degree undreamed of a few years ago. The recent announcement that Canadians can expect a CBC satellite to be in orbit in the not too distant future opens large vistas: the riches of Canadian musical life exchanged with the artistic riches of other countries could do much to overcome language barriers by strengthening the spiritual bonds between men.

Recordings

In *Music in Canada*, published in 1955, John Beckwith discussed the state of the recording industry in Canada up to that time, tracing the history of Canadian recording artists from the era of the great diva Emma Albani to the announcement of Glenn Gould's first recording for Columbia Records.

Although thirteen years ago there were hopeful signs of a greater development on home ground, the Canadian recording industry was dominated by international giants such as RCA Victor, Columbia, Capitol, Decca and London. Naturally, these and other major companies were playing an important part in creating a demand for music in Canada by distributing an ever increasing number of recordings covering a wider repertoire; but major aspects of Canadian musical life, particularly Canadian music, were not being reflected in recording catalogues.

Although the Canadian record industry is still in its adolescence, there have been some encouraging developments, particularly the joint release of discs by RCA Victor and the CBC's International Service. The first set of seventeen records in 1966 of forty-two works by thirty-two Canadian composers represented a real break-through. (See International Service, pp. 229–233.) Both in and outside Canada, major press reports praised the boldness of the project and the quality of the Canadian artists and composers involved.

In the fall of 1967, RCA Victor and CBC International Service released a further eleven recordings. There was an album of nine discs called "A Centennial Collection of Canadian Folk Songs," employing many of Canada's leading folk singers; a recording of excerpts from Calixa Lavallée's *The Widow*, with the CBC Winnipeg Chorus and Orchestra directed by Eric Wild, and a further disc consisting of Canadian works by Matton, Mercure, Prévost and Somers, commissioned and performed by the Montreal Symphony Orchestra with Pierre Hétu and Zubin Mehta as the conductors.

Another development of importance was the recording project of the Canadian Association of Broadcasters and the Composers' Authors' and Publishers' Association of Canada Ltd. (CAB-CAPAC). This project was set up in 1963 for a five-year period with a quarter of a million dollars to encourage the creation, development and use of Canadian light and serious music. So far several discs of serious music have been released. One is a concerto album consisting of the *Piano Concerto* by Oskar Morawetz, with Anton Kuerti as soloist, and the *Concerto for Two Pianos and Orchestra* by Roger Matton, played by the duo-pianists Bouchard and Morisset. In both works, the Toronto Symphony was conducted by Walter Susskind and the disc was released through Capitol Records. Another disc, *Scored for Ballet*, consists of five ballet compositions by the Canadian composers, Robert Fleming, Pierre Mercure, John Weinzweig, Morris Surdin and Louis Applebaum and appeared under the Columbia label. Other CAB-CAPAC recordings are *Music in the Round*, consisting of works by Canadian composers, and *Souvenir de Québec*, ten marches of French Canada played by the Cable Concert Band. Both were released by RCA Victor. *Labyrinth* (the music of Eldon Rathburn for the Expo Pavilion of that name) and *Anne of Green Gables Plus Six Other Canadian Musicales* are distributed by Canadian Music Sales and "3–12" (*chansonnier* songs arranged and conducted by Neil Chotem) is distributed by Select Records. A Canadian jazz disc will shortly be distributed by Decca and in the planning stages is an album of Canadian songs with Lois Marshall and a similar one with Maureen Forrester. The fact that the RCA Victor "Canada International" and CAB-CAPAC discs are aimed at the international market should do much to enhance the reputation of Canadian composers and performers overseas.

In Canada we sometimes forget that our "best" can be compared very favourably with the "best" of other countries. This was demonstrated a few years ago when, following the success of a recording made by Glenn Gould with the CBC Symphony Orchestra of the *Piano Concerto* by Schoenberg and the *Piano Concerto in C Minor* by Mozart, a major project was launched by Columbia Records which gained very substantial prestige for Canadian performers abroad. Starting in 1962 Igor Stravinsky made several visits to Toronto to conduct the CBC Symphony Orchestra and the Festival Singers of Toronto at the invitation of the CBC; and as a result, Columbia Records stepped in to record all the works prepared for broadcasting plus several others as well. As part of this project Stravinsky's assistant, Robert Craft, also made numerous recordings of works by Arnold Schoenberg. Some of the works recorded were the *Symphony of Psalms, A Sermon, A Narrative and a Prayer, Svezdiliki, Babel, Mavra* and the *Symphony in C* by Stravinsky and the *Violin Concerto, Kol Nidre, Pelleas und Melisande, Variations for Orchestra, Opus 31* and the *Choral Works, Opus 50* by Schoenberg. Many reviewers in different countries were lavish in their praise. The *New York Times* said that these projects "should put both chorus and orchestra on the world map. They richly deserve it." The CBC Symphony Orchestra is now defunct and the Festival Singers is still searching for a company with a lasting interest in its future. (In 1968, through a grant from the Centennial Commission, Capitol Records will release two discs of this choir singing works by Willan and other Canadian composers as well as Poulenc's *Mass*.)

Of course, all these recordings are being released in stereo. In fact, it is true to say that the advent of stereo has reshaped the recording industry to meet the demands of record buyers with "new sets of ears"; and in the not too distant future stereo recordings will have totally superseded mono discs. Major international companies are pressing a large quantity of stereo discs in Canada (most of which are recorded outside the country) and Canadian companies have now geared themselves to the stereo development.

In Canada the major recording centres are in Toronto and Montreal. Some discs recorded in Toronto have already been mentioned. Amongst others, reference should be made to one released as a joint project by Columbia Records and the Canadian Music Centre in 1961. Included on the recording were Harry Somers' *Suite for Harp and Strings*, with Judy Loman as the soloist, Murray Adaskin's *Serenade Concertante* and Jean Papineau-Couture's *Pièce Concertante No. 1*, with Mario Bernardi as soloist. Another Columbia disc of Canadian music recorded in Toronto was the one made by the now defunct Canadian String Quartet, consisting of string quartets by Barbara Pentland, John Weinzweig and Clermont Pépin. Columbia also issued "An Evening with the Hart House Glee Club" of the University of Toronto and a recording of the cellist Ernst Friedlander; Capitol produced discs by the pianist Margaret Ann Ireland and the saxophonist Paul Brodie.

A Toronto project which has attracted a great deal of attention is Columbia's album of the Toronto Symphony, conducted by Seiji Ozawa in works by Berlioz, Morel, MacMillan, Freedman and Mercure. It was sponsored by I.B.M. (With the help of the Centennial Commission an album of Olivier Messaien's *Turangalila Symphony* will be released by RCA Victor, played by the same orchestra and with the same conductor.) Another sponsor was the St. Laurent Shopping Centre of Ottawa which was responsible for "Heritage," seven works by Canadian composers based on folk sources played by the Toronto Philharmonia conducted by Victor Feldbrill and distributed by Canadian Record Sales. RCA Victor has also released recordings of Canadian artists including the well-known Montreal choir "Les Disciples de Massenet." Again in Montreal, Vox has recorded "Le Petit Ensemble Vocal de Montréal" (George Little, Director) and the Montreal Consort of Viols (Otto Joachim, Director) with Gian Lyman at the organ. Two additional discs, issued by the same company of "Le Petit Ensemble Vocal," were concerned with vocal works by such composers as Gesualdo and Monteverdi. Vox also recorded the Montreal Bach Choir (George Little, Director) in a number of discs of music ranging from choral works by Jannequin to French-Canadian folk songs.

But what of the Canadian labels? Beaver Records is a company situated in Toronto and mostly concerned with recording the Mendelssohn Choir. Following a "Tribute to Elizabeth II" and "Highlights of Messiah," there was a release of *The Children's Crusade* by Pierné conducted by Walter Susskind. Hallmark Recordings, also centred in Toronto, issued more than ten years ago an interesting "Musica Antica e Nuova" disc with distinguished Canadian singers and performers presenting a wide variety of music from *Der May* by Oswald von Wolkenstein to *Eclogues for Contralto, Flute and Piano* by Jean Papineau-Couture. However, in recent years there have been no further releases from Beaver. Hallmark, while still recording music projects for other companies and the CBC, has ceased to issue serious music records under its own label.

In Montreal, Les Jeunesses Musicales du Canada have released two discs by Marek Jablonski who was the Grand Prize-Winner of the 1961 Jeunesses Musicales National Music Competition; in addition, there is a disc of Dale Bartlett, the winner of the National Music Competition in 1964, and a recording of the three finalists of the Third National Music Competition in 1963, Gloria Richard and Sylvia Saurette, sopranos and Josephte Clément, mezzo-soprano. The duo-pianists Victor Bouchard and Renée Morisset have recorded for Jeunesses Musicales under a label called "Club Musical Canadien." Recently Jeunesses Musicales released a recording by Robert Silverman, the winner of the Jeunesses Musicales Piano Competition in 1967. Acadia has recorded the violinist Arthur Le Blanc in two discs and the Allied Record Corporation has released "Musique et Poésie du Canada," five song cycles of Canadian poetry set to music by the Canadian composers Jean Élie, Pierre Mercure, Jean Papineau-Couture, Jean Vallerand and André Prévost and sung by Louise Myette. William Stevens made several recordings of piano music for Laurentian Records and included in one of them is *Etude de Sonorité No. 2* by François Morel; for Jupiter Records John Newmark recorded two discs of music by Max Reger. Two Montreal companies, Baroque Records and Janus flourished for a time. Baroque Records' catalogue includes several recordings by the Montreal harpsichordist and organist Kenneth Gilbert, such as a disc of harpsichord music by Bach and another of music by baroque organ masters. Other recordings for the Baroque label have been made by Charles Houdret, cellist (*Six Sonatas for 'cello* by Boccherini), and Hyman Bress, violinist (music by Schumann and many other composers and with the Sinfonia of Montreal, Five Concertos for Violin and Orchestra by Vivaldi). Baroque Records has also issued a disc of the Canadian conductor Alexander Brott directing the Greater Orchestra of Soviet Radio and Television in his *Spheres in Orbit* and in *The Pines of Rome* by Respighi and Steven Staryk has recorded "Four Italian Baroque Concerti."

Baroque recorded the pianist Marie-Aimée Varro in a disc which includes *Two Etudes* by Jean Coulthard, as well as standard repertoire, and also violinist Steven Staryk in an album containing the *Sonata Opus 121* by Prokofieff and the *Aria for Violin Solo* by Jean Papineau-Couture. The McGill Chamber Orchestra, conducted by Alexander Brott, made several recordings for the same company with the flutist Jean-Pierre Rampal as the soloist. Other artists to have recorded for

Baroque or Janus are Kenneth Gilbert, harpsichordist; Lise Boucher, pianist; Jacques Verdon, violinist and Gilles Manny, pianist in a group of works that includes the *Sonata for Violin and Piano* by André Prévost; Jacques Simard, oboist; Hubert Bédard, harpsichordist; Bernard Lagacé, organist and harpsichordist; Jean Morin, flutist and André Savoie, pianist. (The latter two artists recorded the *Suite for Flute and Piano* by Jacques Hétu.) Janus' catalogue also includes chamber music groups such as the Duschenes Recorder Quartet, L'Ensemble Baroque de Montréal, L'Ensemble Instrumental Arts-Québec, directed by Mireille Lagacé and with Micheline Tessier, soprano, and Le Quatuor Double directed by Yves Courville. Baroque Records and Janus are now part of Everest's group of companies in the United States and can no longer be considered Canadian. (Most of the original Janus recordings now appear in the Schwann catalogue under the Pirouette label.)

Apex Records (Montreal) has recorded *The Seven Last Words of Christ* with Théodore Dubois and André Turp, tenors; Louis Quilico, baritone; Claire Duchesneau, soprano; Bernard Lagacé, organ and Les Chœurs de Montréal directed by Lionel Renaud. Select Records some time ago issued three discs by the tenor Jean-Paul Jeannotte.

A new Montreal company is Madrigal, which has issued two discs with Bernard Lagacé, organist and harpsichordist, performing works by composers such as Bach and Frescobaldi. Released in 1967 were "Soirée Chez Bach," with a group of Montreal artists, "Le Chœur Polyphonic de Montréal," "Verses for the Magnificat" (an organ disc), a recording by Robert Peters, tenor, and "Les Jeunes Violinistes"—a new violin method for children by Claude Létourneau. Future projects include works by François Morel, Bach's *Art of the Fugue* and *Messe des Paroisses* by Couperin.

Prior to 1955 Canadian celebrities made most of their recordings outside Canada and the situation is very little changed today. Canada's busiest recording artist in the serious music field is Glenn Gould, who has made all but two of his twenty-eight recordings for Columbia in New York. One of his most recent discs is devoted to music by Canadian composers. A further four discs were released early in 1968. Among Canadian celebrities to be recorded by the major international companies in the last thirteen or so years are Donald Bell, baritone (Columbia, Epic, Angel), Pierrette Alarie, soprano (Epic, Deutsche Grammophon, Westminster, Philips), Jon Vickers, tenor (RCA Victor, Angel), Maureen Forrester, contralto (RCA Victor, Vanguard, Deutsche Grammophon, Odéon Records), Lois Marshall, soprano (Columbia, Angel, Capitol), Léopold Simoneau, tenor (RCA Victor, His Master's Voice, London, Decca, Angel, Columbia, Deutsche Grammophon, Epic, Philips, Westminster), Raoul Jobin, tenor (RCA Victor, London, Columbia), Ronald Turini, pianist (RCA Victor), John Boyden, baritone (Columbia), Louis Quilico, baritone (Vanguard, London, Angel), Joseph Rouleau, bass (Angel, London), Don Garrard, baritone (Columbia), James Milligan, baritone (Columbia, Capitol), André Turp, tenor (Westminster, Columbia), Richard Verreau (Deutsche Grammophon, RCA Victor), Colette Boky, soprano (RCA Victor), Zara Nelsova, cellist (London), Wilfrid Pelletier (RCA Victor), Pierre Duval, tenor (RCA Victor, London), Raymond Dudley, pianist (Lyrichord), Boris Brott, conductor with the Northern Sinfonia (Mace), Steven Staryk, violinist (Virtuosi, RCA Victor, Capitol, Telefunken), Reginald Stewart, pianist (Educo), Hyman Bress, violinist (Lyrichord, Mace, Oiseau Lyre, RCA Victor, Folkways) and George Zukerman, bassoonist (Turnabout).

A number of Canadian artists have been involved in a variety of recording projects by different companies. The discs made by Stravinsky and Robert Craft in Toronto are part of a plan by Columbia to record the complete works of Stravinsky and Schoenberg. Glenn Gould has recorded the *Five Piano Concertos* of Beethoven and the complete piano works of Schoenberg and is in the midst of recording the complete clavier works of Bach and the complete sonatas of Beethoven and Mozart. The violinist Hyman Bress has recorded a series in four volumes called "The Violin" for Folkways which presents works from J. S. Bach to Schoenberg. Folkways has also made recordings of

John Newmark playing works by three of J. S. Bach's sons and sonatas by Clementi on his Clementi piano. Composers Recordings Incorporated engaged the Canadian soprano, Teresa Stratas to sing in the recording of Peggy Glanville Hicks' *Nausicaa*. Kenneth Gilbert has recorded all of Bach's "Sixteen Concerti after Vivaldi and other Masters" for Baroque while for the historic opening of Montreal's Place des Arts, RCA Victor pressed for that organization an album of highlights of the first concert to be held in La Grande Salle (now called Salle Wilfrid Pelletier). Apart from various works conducted by Zubin Mehta, this project captured the world première of *Pièce Concertante No. 5 Miroirs* by Jean Papineau-Couture conducted by Wilfrid Pelletier. Recently Folkways released a disc of electronic music works by composers associated with the Electronic Music Studio of the University of Toronto. Space does not permit a comprehensive list of Canadian recordings in all fields of music but it is interesting to note that apart from the plain-song recordings of the Choir of the Benedictine Monks of St. Benoît-du-Lac in Quebec, the Choir of the Benedictine Nuns of the Precious Blood, Mont-Laurier, has made a "Polyphonie Grégorienne" disc and St. Michael's Cathedral Choir of Toronto has made a recording of religious music for London. A Christmas recording by the Montreal Girls Choir has also been released by RCA Camden.

Two widely distributed discs of Canadian music are Columbia's releases of the String Quartet by Glenn Gould and a recording of the English organist Francis Jackson playing organ works by Healey Willan. Mercury has recorded *Five Miniatures for Flute and Strings* by William McCauley with the Eastman Rochester Symphony and in the near future Deutsche Grammophon will release a disc of the Amadeus Quartet playing works by Sir Ernest MacMillan. In western Canada, Lumby of Saskatoon has released *Prairie Sketches* by Robert McMullin and Vancouver has made a recording of the Royal Canadian Engineers Band playing works by Farnon and Cable.

Developments in the chansonnier and folk music areas fall largely outside the scope of this book. However some of the best known *chansonnier* recordings in French Canada today are by Felix Leclerc, Claude Leveillée, Gilles Vigneault, Pauline Julien, Pierre Létourneau and Monique Miville Deschênes. Canadian folk singers are also numerous and have achieved a great deal of popularity through their recordings. Some which spring quickly to mind are Jacques Labrecque, Raoul Roy, Hélène Baillargeon, Alan Mills, Sharon Trostin, Tom Kines, Diane Oxner, Omar Blondahl, Kenneth Peacock, Karen James, Michel Choquette and Ian and Sylvia.

Finally, in the field of music education, the Canadian Broadcasting Corporation issued an album called "Form in Music" which grew out of the CBC Public Affairs Department's "University of the Air" series. In it, Helmut Blume discussed and illustrated the major musical forms so successfully that it is evident a great deal can be achieved with recordings of this kind.

While much has happened to be proud of during the past thirteen years, there is enormous scope for development in the Canadian recording field and it will be interesting to see just how much this latent potential will be realized during the next decade.

A word should be said about the "behind-the-scenes" people without whom CBC broadcasting could not have developed and flourished. Unfortunately, space does not permit me to record them all, but apart from those already mentioned, the names of producers such as Ernest Morgan, Norman Lucas, Tom Taylor, Keith MacMillan, Irving Glick, James Kent, Digby Peers, Richard Coulter, Lawrence Taylor, Kit Kinnaird, Robert Chesterman, John Reeves, Gerald Newman, Norman Newton, Michael Cass-Beggs and Norma Beecroft should sound familiar to many listeners of the English Networks. Included in the French Network's team of producers are Pierre Beaudet, Marie Bourneau, André Clerk, Jean-Yves Contant, Denis Harbour, Marcel Henry, Gilles Poirier and Paul Roussel. Hugh Davidson, now Assistant Programme Director of the English Radio Networks, has, over a period of years, held music positions with the English and French Networks, as well as with CBC International Service. Recently, Carl Little, after a long career as a producer and programme organizer, was appointed Assistant Supervisor of Music (English Networks). Many television producers have been mentioned so far. To complete the behind-the-scenes picture, the names of John Barnes, Television Network Supervisor, Music and Special Programmes (English Networks) and Armand Landry, Supervisor of the Television Music Section (French Network) must be added.

The Growth of
Music Education

ARNOLD WALTER

IMAGINE LISTENING TO a performance of *Don Giovanni* in the Place des Arts: there are close to three thousand people in the hall; an orchestra is playing in the pit, the conductor is waving his arms; on the stage are soloists, choristers, dancers; you admire the voices, the costumes, the movement of groups in *ensemble*; you appreciate the work of the stage director, the scene designer, the chorus master, the ballet mistress, the lighting crew; engrossed in la Ponte's play, carried away by Mozart's melodies you have no time to reflect that such a performance is, among other things, a triumph of education and organization.

Yet it is. A few short years ago opera in Canada did not exist: there were no buildings where it could be housed, no musicians to perform it, there was no public to demand it. The singers, the players, the directors and technicians had to be schooled and a public had to be developed before such an evening was possible. Every concert, every performance, every aspect of our musical life depends on trained professionals and enlightened listeners.

Professionals are specialists—composers, conductors, pianists, singers or orchestral players. Competition is their daily bread. Technical proficiency is indispensable but by no means the whole story. To be successful, performers must be more than simple craftsmen. They must be well versed in theoretical and historical disciplines and acquainted with a repertoire extending from the Renaissance to modern days: a difficult prescription requiring long years of preparation. The ever-widening horizon of contemporary musical life underlines the importance of institutional training. It still may happen that a gifted tenor acquires his craft in a private studio and learns to produce ringing high "C's" with dazzling success; but the majority of aspirants depend on professional schools and their offerings.

The listener on the other hand, the music-consumer, needs a different kind of education. He is called an amateur, a dilettante —and rightly so. The words *amare, dilettare,* have no derogatory connotation, they mean to love music, to delight in it. It seems rather strange though, that we should not be able to enjoy it without specific training, without setting an educational apparatus in motion. Why must we teach what ought to be a spontaneous, an unconscious activity?

An exciting rhythm or a lilting tune are grasped instinctively, but symphonies or string quartets are in a different category. From madrigals to music dramas, from Josquin to Stravinsky, we perform a repetitive repertory that could be likened to a museum. Wandering through the halls of a museum you often feel the need for background information. Icons and mosaics, primitives and moderns, Raphaels and Rembrandts and Ronaults—they will all be there, will overwhelm and puzzle you in turn; you will soon be groping for guidelines. This need for study is the penalty we pay for being rich, for being heirs of a cumulative civilization. As with many of the pictures we look at, much of the music we listen to stem from the past. A veil of strangeness hangs over them. They carry a glorious message but it will not reach us if we do not make an effort to decipher the hieroglyphics.

We need, then, two distinct types of music education—one for the few, the gifted, the perseverant, our future professionals, another for the many, for amateurs, concert-goers, opera lovers, record fans: for all those to whom music will be a source of delight and an enrichment of life.

Following such lines of thought we shall first study the offerings, the organization, and the productive capacity of our professional schools; afterwards we shall turn to the broader topic of the formation of the listener.

Until the nineteen twenties, professional music education in North America had little of which to boast. Europe was the Mecca of all gifted musicians, a place of pilgrimage; but it was reached only by the few who were fortunate enough to overcome the considerable financial difficulties. Edward Johnson sang operetta in New York to earn enough money to study in Italy. Sir Ernest MacMillan reached Edinburgh by accident—his father had been ill and went there to recuperate. Wilfrid Pelletier won the Prix d'Europe, Claude Champagne was awarded a *bourse*; they both proceeded to Paris. What other talents there were we shall never know; they disappeared in the wide open spaces which were as yet without cultural aspirations.

After World War I, the United States came into prominence. It is true, American composers (Roger Sessions, Aaron Copland, Virgil Thomson) still went to Europe, mostly to sit at the feet of Nadia Boulanger; but schools were founded (or reorganized) and proved their worth in years to come: Juilliard in New York, Curtis in Philadelphia, Eastman in Rochester—particularly Eastman, that archetype of a university school of music. The National Association of Schools of Music (1924) came into being, teachers' organizations like the Music Teachers' National Association and the Music Educators' National

Conference grew in importance and helped to overcome provincialism and isolation. A foundation was laid on which a magnificent edifice was soon to be erected.

Canada had to wait until the forties before such stirrings were to be felt. The somnolence of the twenties gave way to the miseries of the Depression. All too soon it was wartime again; whatever plans had been considered were shelved or at least postponed. The demand for musicians was rather modest in those years. The advent of sound films spelled disaster for orchestral players and unemployment was the rule rather than the exception. (To create work, the musicians' union organized a summer symphony in Toronto whose rotating membership put an effective brake on any conductor's ambition. If it helped the musicians it certainly did not help music.) Concert life was in the hands of United States agencies. An obvious lack of opportunity and a natural resistance to change kept things as they were.

Emigration of talent continued. Healey Willan and Claude Champagne took care of young composers in their formative years, but most of their students felt the need to widen their horizons. Louis Applebaum and John Weinzweig went to the United States to study under Wagenaar, Roy Harris and Bernard Rogers. Pierre Mercure a pupil of Claude Champagne) proceeded to Paris—again to Nadia Boulanger who was also the mentor of Jean Papineau-Couture, Gabriel Charpentier, John Beckwith, and Kelsey Jones. Paris and the United States— these were the magnets that attracted talented young Canadians.

Before the forties, Canadian schools had no chance of competing with foreign ones. Potential performers studied in conservatories (such as they were). The universities offered three-year courses in musical academies which were meant to train composers: the writing of a string quartet (or parts thereof) was a prerequisite for graduation. Such courses were replicas of traditional courses in Britain, rather thoughtlessly transplanted. Graduate studies were again limited to composers. Candidates for the degree of Doctor of Music had to present a thesis in the form of an exercise, a large-scale composition involving soloists, chorus, and orchestra. There was no provision for graduate studies in musicology, applied music or music education.[1]

Conservatories did not follow European models as their name seemed to imply. They were typical "American" conservatories so caustically described by Lavignac.[2] European institutions bearing that name (sometimes they are called Academy or *Hochschule für Musik*) were professional schools providing orchestras and opera companies with much-needed personnel, training soloists of the virtuoso type increasingly in demand since the nineteenth century. They channelled a country's talent into a single institution (only in large countries into several), they were state-supported, had a salaried staff, demanded no fees or negligible ones. The Paris Conservatoire (1795), the Vienna Conservatory (1817), the Leipzig Conservatory (1843) served as examples for similar institutions throughout the Continent.

American and Canadian conservatories were similar to European ones in name only. They were anything but professional schools. They taught all comers, anyone who would pay a fee. Lacking state support, they had no salaried staff, no prescribed courses. Teachers were paid on a commission basis which had a disastrous influence on the teacher-to-student ratio: they were in fact conglomerations of private studios vaguely held together by a name which Lavignac thought they took in vain.

All this will underline the importance of an event that took place in 1942: the first and only genuine conservatory on the North American Continent came into being, the Conservatoire de Musique et de l'Art dramatique in Montreal. The Conservatoire has all the required characteristics. It is state-supported, has a salaried staff, exacts no fees from the students and is closely patterned after the French institution whose title it adopted. Wilfrid Pelletier, its founder, was fortunate enough

1. *The Humanities in Canada* (Humanities Research Council: Ottawa, 1947), p. 218.
2. Albert Lavignac, *L'Education musicale* (Paris: Delagrave, 1902).

to enlist the help of the Quebec government; Quebec in turn was lucky to find in Dr. Pelletier a man of vision and a musician of high calibre with a burning desire to hand on the torch.

It was also in the forties that the Toronto Conservatory (which in 1947 was to become the Royal Conservatory of Music) began to upgrade its offerings. As early as 1938 Mr. Ernest Hutcheson (then President of the Juilliard School of Music) had been asked to conduct an inquiry into its operations and to recommend appropriate changes. The war intervened and no action was taken until 1945, when the "Hutcheson report" became the basis of a gradual re-organization that reached its final stage in 1952. Since then, the Royal Conservatory houses three fairly independent institutions: the Faculty of Music (closely affiliated with the university); the Opera School (to which the Canadian Opera Company owes its existence) and the School of Music (continuing the work of the old Conservatory). The terminology is rather peculiar, especially so since the Faculty is essentially a University School of Music as the term is understood all over the continent.

University Schools of Music are America's contribution to professional music education—an important and highly original contribution. Necessity was the mother of invention. Professional schools were needed, the conservatories were found wanting, public funds were not available. Thus there were only the universities left to shoulder the burden (and cover the deficits).

Can the academy be brought into the university? Can humanistic studies and practical training be fruitfully combined? Howard Hanson argued that future professionals would be infinitely better musicians for deepening their comprehension and widening their horizon by adding arts subjects to the traditional music curriculum. Manfred Bukofzer,[3] on the other hand, felt rather skeptical about such a compromise solution (as he called it). He preferred the clean separation of vocational training and humanistic discipline. Cultural courses, he thought,

3. Manfred Bukofzer, *The Place of Musicology in American Institutions of Higher Learning* (New York: Liberal Arts Press, 1957).

were all too often mere window dressing, robbing the student of much needed time. Future professionals were in danger of ending up with neither a liberal education nor sufficient technical competence. With a fine disregard for North-American realities, he opted for the European solution which pre-supposes ministries of culture and state subsidies, both in short supply on this side of the Atlantic.

The lines so clearly drawn in theoretical arguments became somewhat blurred in actual practice. American conservatories sought affiliation with universities and tended to re-organize themselves after the pattern of the school of music; European educators grew pensive in pondering American successes. Hans Sittner, the President of Vienna's famed Akademie für Musik und darstellende Kunst, advised his countrymen to incorporate the essence of university studies into the academy "if we don't want to be left behind one day" as he put it.[4] The compromise so airily rejected by Bukofzer emerged as a possible, perhaps the only possible, solution to the conflict. One of Bukofzer's arguments, however—the contention that four years are simply not enough to reach the aims of a composite course—was undoubtedly valid.

If we now turn to our present offerings in professional instruction we discover to our amazement how much has been accomplished in recent years. In 1955 it seemed sufficient to comment on the activities of the Conservatoire in Montreal and the Faculty of Music in Toronto.[5] In 1958, Sir Ernest MacMillan could truthfully say that (outside of Quebec) only one institution (Toronto) was adequately providing for the training of professional musicians in the framework of the university;[6] could argue that every one of our main geographical areas (British Columbia, the prairies, Ontario, Quebec, the Atlantic provinces) ought to have a professional school of its own. Now, barely eight years later, the Canadian Association of University Schools of Music (CAUSM) reports on seventeen institutions

4. Hans Sittner, *Aus Schriften und Reden* (Mozartgemeinde Wien, 1963).
5. *Music in Canada* (Toronto: University of Toronto Press, 1955).
6. *Canadian Music Journal* II, 3.

offering undergraduate degree programmes in music, with seven of them offering graduate programmes as well. Montreal and Toronto may still be the leading centres, but it is gratifying to observe how speedily the eastern and western provinces are overcoming their inertia.

The rise of the Conservatoire (following a French model), the development of Schools of Music (patterned on their American namesakes) changed the scene beyond recognition. Twenty years ago it would have been difficult enough to find a common denominator between the diverse types of schools attempting to provide professional instruction; currently everything seems in flux, re-organization is the order of the day. The mosaic has changed into a kaleidoscope. It is not possible to comment on every facet of the complex picture. We must limit ourselves to distinguishing two layers, an older and a newer one co-existing side by side. The latter has just been described: it consists of the Conservatoire in Montreal and the university schools offering courses leading to graduate and undergraduate degrees. These are so far the only schools catering to the students' needs for institutional training, practice and rehearsal facilities, ensemble experience, libraries and financial assistance. The older level, however, is still with us; conservatories continue to award professional diplomas without offering supervised coursework.

It should perhaps be pointed out that most conservatories function in several capacities—as music schools straight and simple, teaching children and amateurs; as examination centres; and (hopefully) as professional schools flooding the country with associate diplomas, licentiate diplomas or fellowships whose value varies from school to school, from province to province, and from examination system to examination system. Earlier in the century the Americans found themselves in a similar situation, one which was vastly improved by the establishment, in 1924, of a National Association of Schools of Music (NASM) that looks after accreditation on a national level. No such association exists in this country. The Canadian Association of University Schools of Music CAUSM (founded in 1964) restricts its membership to music faculties and departments in universities. It has no powers of accreditation. In spite of its limited field of operation, CAUSM opens the door to an exchange of information and co-operative planning.

A considerable number of conservatories are affiliated with universities. That of course does not turn them into schools on the university level but leads, in some cases at least, to a mutually beneficial symbiosis. There are, however, no types of affiliation; every one is *sui generis*. The Faculté de Musique of the Université de Montréal, for instance, serves as a unifying centre for no less than ten Écoles de Musique (L'École Vincent d'Indy is the best known) whose students are eligible for the degree of Bachelor of Music. The faculty sees to it that the students' theoretical studies are of a sufficiently high calibre to be worthy of a university degree. In the Royal Conservatory it is the Faculty of Music that offers professional degrees and diplomas; the School of Music limits itself to awarding extramural associate diplomas and looking after preparatory courses with an enrolment of approximately 120. (The number of non-course students is seven thousand.)

The Faculty of Music of McGill University re-organized itself on very different lines. Until recently the University owned and operated the McGill Conservatorium (founded in 1904) which in the fifties boasted nearly 500 students. "Only a tiny percentage of these" says Dean Blume,[7] "were potential professionals. The overwhelming number consisted of school children as well as adults taking the proverbial 'piano lesson', or voice, or violin, or other orchestral instruments, as well as elementary theory. Thus, the Conservatorium was, in reality, an extension of the private studios of individual teachers paid by hourly rates—a valid institution at a time when there were not many good private teachers around—but lacking in a true university function." A licentiate and an associate diploma completed the picture which, as we have seen, fits the description of Canadian conservatories in general. The McGill faculty realized the insufficiency of such training as far as it was meant

7. Helmut Blume, personal communication.

to be professional instruction. It cut the Gordian knot by discontinuing the licentiate and associate diplomas; by changing the conservatory in such a way that it became in effect a preparatory department. "The level of attainment in the Associate" (Dean Blume deserves to be quoted once more) "was a very junior one and did not justify the conferring of a row of impressive letters after the name of the successful candidate. We . . . felt that the public may be misled into believing that the holder of such a diploma has, in fact, attained a professional standing when actually he has barely passed the preparatory stage. . . ." The former McGill Conservatorium has become the "McGill Preparatory School of Music," an annex of the faculty with an optimum registration of 150 to 200. The McGill story is very instructive and highly significant. Here is a clear indication of what is likely to happen in the next few years, in spite of the well-known inertia of the educational apparatus.

Nonetheless, the schools have been surprisingly successful. They have presented us with capable orchestral personnel and with Canadian-trained university teachers. The Canadian Opera Company grew out of the Torontonian opera school; young Canadians sing in the Metropolitan Opera, in Sadlers' Wells, in Covent Garden, in European opera houses; Lois Marshall, Jon Vickers, Teresa Stratas, Lilian Sukis, Louis Quilico, and Joseph Rouleau, have gained a world-wide reputation—it is quite a remarkable record.[8] The National Youth Orchestra is another feather in our cap. Over a hundred youngsters in their 'teens and early twenties are annually selected from all parts of the country. Coached by eminent teachers, conducted by men like Walter Susskind (the founder of the organization), Wilfrid Pelletier, Victor Feldbrill, John Avison and Franz-Paul Decker, they perform with a glowing enthusiasm, with an enviable self-assurance that puts many an adult orchestra to shame.

No doubt the gap between export and import is narrowing, though it is not quite closed yet. Not so long ago Canada exported talent as if it were a kind of raw-material importing the

8. See *supra* "Performers," p. 154 ff.

finished product in the form of performers, conductors, even school administrators (the finished product). Those who went abroad rarely returned; an expanding musical life made larger imports necessary. At last there is hope that the vicious circle will soon be broken. Strangely enough, the change already effected has not penetrated the consciousness of people throughout the Dominion. Students and teachers, all too many of them, behave as if nothing had happened during the last twenty years. They dream of New York, they long for Paris or Vienna or Milan, they are convinced that whatever is good at home must be better abroad. Their longings, their erroneous convictions are exploited; they do not realize that foreign schools—some at least—need them more than they need them. English adjudicators roaming the country offer scholarships to the Royal Schools; American talent-scouts lure students to the United States where they are likely to stay; traditional scholarships—Quebec's Prix d'Europe is not the only one—send our most gifted candidates overseas.

All these migrations, peregrinations and pilgrimages are based on the assumption that foreign schools are better than even the best Canadian ones. Are they really better? Not in Europe. Splendid opera houses, illustrious orchestras, the glorious fabric of musical life over there should not prevent us from taking a hard look at the schools themselves, their offerings and output. The Gulbenkian report on professional music study in Britain is quite revealing in that respect.[9] Or, to quote an example from Germany, the Prime Minister of Baden, Dr. Kiesinger,[10] while commenting on the deplorable results of an international competition organized by the West-German Radio, found to his amazement that foreign schools were doing a better job than German ones.[11] The President of the Austrian State Academy came to a similar conclusion: "The most important, the most significant awards go to young people of other

9. *Making Musicians* (London: The Calouste Gulbenkian Foundation, 1965).
10. Now Chancellor of the Federal Republic of Germany.
11. *Deutscher Musikrat* (Referate, Hamburg, 1965).

lands." Where then, are the best professional schools? Watching the Tchaikovsky Competition in Moscow,[12] one comes to the inescapable conclusion that three countries are leading all others in that respect: the Soviet Union, the United States and Japan.

Russia and Japan are mercifully far away; the United States is all too near. The Americans built splendid schools in the twenties; Canada realized its shortcomings in the forties. The Americans, of course, did not wait for us to catch up; once more they are ahead of us. Their magnificent buildings, their outstanding libraries, their graduate schools in performance and high schools for the performing arts are hard to match. Eminent teachers command forbiddingly high salaries; fellowships are available in profusion; a research programme for the arts is backed by the United States Office of Education.[13] A reorganized Juilliard School is destined to become a constituent part of the Lincoln Centre, that American Acropolis for the performing arts. How can Canada compete with all that? Certainly not in quantity. The United States, on the other hand, has no monopoly on quality. No doubt we could hold our own if we wanted it badly enough, if we worked as hard as the Japanese and organized ourselves as well as the Russians. Once more the choice lies between continentalism and the attainment of a Canadian identity.

One of the shortcomings that would have to be overcome concerns the duration of studies in performance. Composers, musicologists and music educators are not limited to four years in undergraduate courses; they have graduate studies at their disposal. Graduate studies in performance, however, are virtually unknown in Canada. In European academies and in the conservatories of the Soviet Union future performers study at least five years. In the United States they can, if they wish, continue their training in graduate schools offering the degree

12. The author was invited to attend the International Tchaikovsky Competition of 1966.
13. *International Society for Music Education, Tokyo Report 1963*, p. 105.

of Doctor of Musical Art obtainable in no less than fourteen universities.[14] The establishment of the degree led to much controversy: it does seem rather ridiculous for a performer to prove his ability not by playing or singing but by producing a scroll signed and sealed by university officials. Howard Hanson, however—once more defender of the faith—justifies it on the grounds that "the arts, particularly music, have found a place . . . in the academic family and must now subscribe to the house rules which obtain for other members of the club."[15] It is not so much the degree that matters but the provision for extended studies—and the fact that Canadian institutions are in danger of turning themselves into preparatory schools for Yale and Eastman, Michigan or Indiana.

The training offered in four-year courses might prove less inadequate if entering students were better prepared. But it happens all too often that the mounting pressure of high school matriculation prevents potential performers from acquiring proficiency during the years in which it must be acquired. The problem can be solved in different ways. In Germany there are "Musische Gymnasien," in Hungary "Musikgymnasien," in the United States high schools for music and art (in New York, Winston Salem, Interlochen)—all secondary schools whose *curricula* make allowance for intensive musical training. In the USSR there exist twenty-two so-called "eleven-year schools" for especially gifted children: 6,000 are enrolled at the present time. Classes follow a general programme, yet music studies continue unabated. Graduates will normally enrol in one of the state conservatories (but can, if they wish, proceed to the university instead), so that the entire training period for professional musicians lasts for sixteen years. The system works extremely well—the Oistrakhs, Gilels, Richters, Ashkenasis, Rostropovitchs bear witness to that. It introduces specialization at an early age without in the least neglecting a general education. So far, only the National Ballet of Canada has managed to

14. *National Association of Schools of Music, List of Members 1966.*
15. *The International Musician,* March, 1964.

create a special high school for young dancers. Metropolitan Toronto is still debating the question.

A word or two might be said about the need for international comparisons in a survey devoted to the national scene. Constant reference to the United States of course is unavoidable. Canadian educators cherishing the notion of a spiritually, politically and economically independent Canada must be wary of their gift-bearing neighbours. There is only one way of stopping the talent drain so widely and loudly lamented: by seeing to it that Canadian schools do not fall below the level of American ones.

Comparisons with other countries are valuable, too. Half a century ago there was little incentive for undertaking such studies. The world was neatly divided between Europe, functioning as a production centre for music and musicians, and the territories beyond the seas which were content with imports. This is no longer the case. Countries anxious to project a cultural image—there are few left that are not—are forced both to collaborate and to compete with one another. To encourage further collaboration, a number of international bodies have come into existence: the Consejo Interamericano de Musica (CIDEM), the International Music Council (IMC) and the International Society for Music Education (ISME) the last two affiliated with UNESCO. A growing number of international competitions for composers, conductors, pianists, violinists, cellists, even chamber music ensembles, embark on talent search on a global basis. The more important ones (Brussels, Moscow) are in fact Music Olympiads bestowing enormous prestige on the winner; one has only to remember the van Cliburn story. Professional training is directly affected: Canada is by no means the only country creating new schools, re-organizing established ones, groping for higher levels, studying new systems, methods or forms of organization—it is happening everywhere.

It is generally admitted that during the period of industrial expansion after World War II the Canadian educational system was quite incapable of meeting the requirements for skilled workers. This led to recruitment abroad. The performing arts were in a similar predicament. While we may not have reached the critical stage of a cultural explosion, expansion is nevertheless the order of the day. One has only to reflect how Centennial projects were hampered by the lack of "skilled workers on high occupational levels"—orchestral musicians for instance, or actors. "Recruitment abroad" is hardly a solution to be adopted by a country insisting on cultural independence.

We know that we are not producing what the country needs, know it vaguely only. The relationship between training facilities and actual employment has never been explored. Professional music schools are costly undertakings and one would have thought that their establishment would be preceded by a careful investigation of supply and demand. This, however, has never been the case. It is startling to discover that the Economic Council of Canada can only deplore the complete lack of information regarding the demand for, and supply of, professional, technical, managerial and other highly skilled workers, musicians among them. "Because of the long periods of formal training required to produce these workers, it is necessary to anticipate possible areas of shortage well in advance so that policies to overcome these deficiencies may be developed and take effect in time. The need for more information and more forward planning in this vital field is urgent."[16] Indeed it is. But how should such anticipation come about? The schools have never concerned themselves with problems of supply and demand or import and export. They insisted that their business was education, not economics. That is perhaps a commendable position but it leads to unfortunate results. A country—any country—can absorb only so many pianists or bassoon players or music teachers; once the saturation point is reached, unemployment will set in. The opposite is equally true: it is no use to build opera houses if there are not enough training facilities for singers, orchestral players or stage technicians.

In an expanding economy (our cultural level is certainly rising) the danger of overproduction and underemployment is

16. *Economic Council of Canada, First Annual Review*, December, 1964.

remote; but even there adjustments might be highly desirable. Everyone knows how few soloists, particularly pianists, have a chance to take their places beside Horowitz or Rubinstein or Serkin—a dozen perhaps in the entire western world. Yet there are multitudes of young pianists who are encouraged to study, to hope for a career—being nothing but grist for the mills of the schools.

The "forward planning in this vital field"—how is it to be done? In a planned economy it is easily dealt with. The Ministry of Culture in Moscow, well knowing that the officially prescribed five years are not long enough to make musicians, plans ten years ahead. In the western world such things are not done. As a rare exception we might mention a study report by the German Music Council[17] that set itself the task of investigating the problems of replacement in musical professions. The results astonished even the investigators. Who would have thought that German orchestras are unable to fill their vacancies? That 30 per cent of soloists in opera houses are foreigners? That well-trained music teachers in high schools are at a premium? The value of such surveys cannot be overrated. We might do a bit of planning in disguise, enlisting the help of the Dominion Bureau of Statistics, the Economic Council and the Canada Council, collecting data that might be very revealing. To give a concrete example: there are nine metropolitan orchestras in the country (in Halifax, Quebec, Montreal, Toronto, Winnipeg, Edmonton, Calgary, Vancouver, Victoria) employing 635 musicians, approximately 25 per cent of them imported. Let us assume that ten years from now we shall have twelve (a reasonable prediction) employing approximately 1,000 players. Allowing for the replacement of imported and retiring musicians —25 per cent and 20 per cent respectively—we shall need 650 additional players, i.e., we must more than double the existing orchestral personnel.

The figure does not look forbiddingly high—until we re-

17. *Musikberufe und ihr Nachwuchs—statistische Erhebungen 1960–61 des Deutschen Musikrates*. Herausgegeben von Herbert Sass und Walter Wiora (Mainz: B. Schott's Söhne). Edition 5307.

member that at present we have not enough unattached players in the country to form a single new orchestra; that we are suffering from a disastrous shortage of string players which cannot be corrected in less than ten years. At what rate are we producing? The only figures at our disposal are contained in the Dominion Bureau of Statistics' Survey of Higher Education[18] dealing with enrolment in Canadian colleges and universities. In 1964–65 the number of full-time undergraduate music students was 826, the number of graduate students 48 (65 per cent were women); 724 undergraduate students, or 85 per cent, were enrolled in Quebec, Ontario and British Columbia. Private studios, music schools, conservatories and the Conservatoire were not considered in the survey. The actual figures will, therefore, be considerably higher. We do not know how many of the students involved are potential orchestral players. It is, nevertheless, quite clear that the figures are low and would still be too low if they were doubled. Admittedly, it is a long way from such statistical meditations to administrative action, but they might be helpful.

Non-professional music education to which we now turn is mercifully exempt from the law of supply and demand. It does not help anyone to make a living; it simply helps to live. It addresses itself to the amateur, the music lover and that, it is often argued, includes everyone. With the entire population involved, the education of the layman is a large operation indeed.

The forces at our command are formidable. An army of private teachers gives instruction in individual lessons. Conservatories teach, examine, distribute certificates by the tens of thousands. The school system—from kindergarten to university—includes music in its offerings. School broadcasts are specifically designed to assist the classroom teacher; but broadcasts generally, telecasts and tapes, films and recordings, are educational agencies of continually growing importance. Festivals, children's concerts, high school concerts, camps and sum-

18. Dominion Bureau of Statistics, *Survey of Higher Education*, Part I.

mer schools must be added to the list; it is a vast panorama we are contemplating.

Looking closer into the matter, we shall find that the offerings (excepting broadcasting of course) are very unevenly distributed. They vary from province to province. Even school curricula differ to an astonishing degree; yet the educational authorities are all wrestling with identical problems: should music be a compulsory subject or an elective? If compulsory, in what grades? What place should it occupy in the curriculum, how much time should be given to it? Should the general classroom teacher be in charge? Should specialists be employed? How should the teachers be trained?

These are not specifically Canadian problems. They are endlessly debated in all countries of the west. Curricula are crowded everywhere. There are too many core subjects: language and literature, history and geography, foreign languages, physics, biology and mathematics leave little time for anything else. We have to go as far as Australia to discover that the Wyndham scheme in operation in New South Wales recognizes music as one of four core subjects (together with art-crafts, English and mathematics).

Equally universal is the shortage of competent school music teachers. Departments of Education can hardly be blamed for preferring capable pedagogues with a slight knowledge of music to capable musicians only slightly acquainted with pedagogy. This is an understandable preference, but it militates only too often against music.

In spite of all the difficulties, disputes, and perpetual discussions, there is a consensus of opinion—astonishing under the circumstances—that music ought to be taught to everyone; and that it be taught by the schools. It is generally agreed that music is a good thing; King David playing the harp and the man "who has no music in himself" prove its worth. Sterner arguments are also adduced: music develops character, we know it from Plato; it is a form of spiritual contemplation, Aristotle defined it so; it is anchored in Carl Jung's collective unconscious. An incredible number of great men, from Augustinus to Nietzsche, with Shakespeare, Luther and Goethe among them, thought that a life without music was simply a mistake. Such claims—so different from one another—could be understood as rationalizations of a powerful feeling that elemental forces are at work here, forces which education cannot neglect. We have only recently learned to define them. Nobody denies the central position of language in education, its paramount importance in the development of human beings. In expression, however, in accent, in *melos*, language owes much to music—which in turn derives its rhythmic potency from movement, from the archetype of all instruments, the human body. Movement, dance, music, language, poetry, all form a chain whose links are intimately connected and interdependent; with music in the central position.

So understood, music is indeed one of the foundation-stones of civilization and everybody's birthright; the pedagogues were charged with the responsibility of imparting it to the young. The pedagogues, however (rarely experts on non-verbal education), began to speculate on the "uses" of music to justify its inclusion in the curriculum; Plato was first to think along these lines. Alas, music as a life-force may be indispensable; music as a useful subject among other useful subjects turns out to be rather vulnerable. The history of school music bears that out. In the sixteenth century it could happen[19] that otherwise capable teachers regarded as "amousoi," or unmusical, were dismissed—had Luther not said he had no use for a schoolmaster who could not sing? In the eighteenth century, the stand was completely reversed. Protestant theologians found it impossible to believe in Luther's authorship of the chorales which go under his name: to be a musician was clearly incompatible with the dignity of the great reformer. Man was a rational creature; progress depended on the exercise of reason; music was a pleasant pastime but certainly not essential as an educational tool. In our own century, school music is once more in the ascendancy, favoured by progressive educators but confronted

19. Hans Joachim Moser, *Handbuch der Schulmusik* (Regensburg: Gustav Bosse Verlag, 1962).

by an overcrowded curriculum and largely unaided by its former allies—the family, the home and the church.

It is in the ascendancy, but how far it has progressed is difficult to ascertain—nowhere more difficult than in Canada with its provincial fragmentation of education. Information is hard to come by and will remain so until a federal ministry of culture appears on the horizon or a national office of education established and maintained by the provinces. How troublesome it is to collect data, to gather material on which conclusions can be based, is demonstrated by referring to a questionnaire which, for purposes of this essay, was sent to the departments of education of every province. It took well over a year before the questionnaires were returned, and many a question remained unanswered. "Information not available," "no way of knowing," or "varies from school to school" were remarks frequently encountered. Newfoundland (as yet without music supervisors) had no statistics at its disposal; the Ministère d'Education du Québec reported a similar lack of data. Seeing that the problems of that province are *sui generis* (education in Quebec is being completely re-planned), they will be dealt with separately. The data which were supplied are summarized as follows:

In elementary education music is part of the regular curriculum in approximately 40 per cent of the schools in Prince Edward Island; in approximately one-third of the schools in New Brunswick; in *all* schools of the remaining provinces reporting.

Weekly periods devoted to music vary in number: one hour (or two half hours) in Prince Edward Island; one hour if taught by the regular classroom teacher or three if taught by the music specialist in New Brunswick; "at varied times" in Nova Scotia —class teachers there do not adhere to regular periods. In Ontario we find three to five periods devoted to music; in Manitoba schools are free to make their own arrangements; in Saskatchewan the time allotment is two hours (on the average), in Alberta the average is one hour—the duration of classes is not officially prescribed. British Columbia provides instruction time for a group of cultural and recreational activities including opening exercises, physical education, art and music which remain part of a package.

It is important to know whether music in elementary schools is taught by the regular classroom teacher or a resident music specialist, a travelling supervisor, a professional musician from the community. Here again the approaches vary. All provinces make use of the regular classroom teacher (though Prince Edward Island only occasionally). Resident music specialists are found in the larger schools of Prince Edward Island, in Nova Scotia and in 20 per cent of the schools of New Brunswick; they also occur in Ontario, Manitoba and in Saskatchewan (a few only) but none in Alberta or British Columbia. Travelling Supervisors are employed in the Atlantic provinces (in small rural schools of Prince Edward Island, in 15 per cent of the schools of New Brunswick, in 10 per cent of the schools of Nova Scotia), in Ontario, in Saskatchewan and Alberta. Professional musicians are rarely engaged. They do appear in schools in Nova Scotia, Manitoba and in Alberta; it is stipulated however, that the regular classroom teacher must remain in charge.

The qualifications of elementary school music teachers could not possibly be uniform in such circumstances, and of course they are not. In New Brunswick, the matter of qualifications is under consideration. Nova Scotia awards a music teacher's licence; Ontario an elementary school teaching certificate. Manitoba looks for qualifications from a recognized school of music but might be satisfied with "established ability." Saskatchewan asks for a regular teacher's certificate plus specialized training in music. Alberta demands no special qualifications but draws attention to the elementary stream of its Bachelor of Education programme. The same is true of British Columbia—no special qualifications are required, the University of British Columbia makes provision for specialization in its Bachelor of Education programme.

How is the time available divided between singing, instrumental instruction, listening and elementary theory? In Prince

Edward Island there is "nothing hard and fast laid down" but 60 per cent for singing, 10 per cent for instrumental work and 30 per cent for listening seem a reasonable proportion. In Nova Scotia there is no instrumental instruction in elementary schools, 90 per cent of class time is devoted to singing, 10 per cent to music appreciation. In New Brunswick, the proportion is 70 per cent and 30 per cent respectively, in Ontario 80 per cent and 20 per cent—it looks as if the provinces had solemnly agreed to disagree on the matter. In Manitoba the percentage varies from school to school; in Saskatchewan it is not specified. Alberta accepts varied proportions as long as the emphasis is on singing; British Columbia is not specific on the question.

What instruments (if any) are taught in elementary schools? In Prince Edward Island, rhythm bands (in primary grades), recorders, tonettes, plus some woodwinds and strings —in a few schools only, taught on an extra-curricular basis. In New Brunswick, recorders, tonettes, Orff instruments, woodwinds, brasses and percussion. Nova Scotia, as we have seen, has no instrumental programme. Ontario offers instruction in all the standard orchestral instruments, so does Saskatchewan and British Columbia; Manitoba limits itself to recorders, tonettes, Orff instruments; Alberta uses guitars, zithers, flutophones and recorders. It must not be thought, however, that the instruments described are taught in all schools of the provinces; that is never the case.

New approaches (Orff, Ward, Martenot, Kodaly, Suzuki had been mentioned in the questionnaire) were used in New Brunswick (Orff, Ward, Martenot); in Ontario (Orff, Kodaly); in Manitoba and Alberta (Orff, Kodaly, both on an experimental basis) and in British Columbia (Suzuki, Orff, Kodaly, all in limited areas). Saskatchewan has developed its own approach to musical understanding and performance.

In secondary education the differences are still more pronounced. We learn that in Prince Edward Island 14 (or 74 per cent) high schools teach music; in New Brunswick 30 (or 10 per cent); in Ontario 350 (or 70 per cent). Manitoba has no information available on that point. In Saskatchewan 100 (or 23 per cent) high schools teach music for credit (many more have non-credit musical courses). In Alberta it is not known how many schools are in that category; it is stated, however, that approximately 5 per cent of all senior high school students are enrolled in music (with a larger percentage in junior high). British Columbia offers music in all secondary schools—"where facilities are available."

Time devoted to instruction comes to one hour in Prince Edward Island (sometimes more); one hour in Nova Scotia and New Brunswick; two to six periods in Ontario. It varies in Manitoba—12 per cent of teaching time in grades X–XI, 18 per cent in grade XII. Saskatchewan reports an average of two hours. In Alberta, students in junior high schools may take from 75 to 187 minutes of music study; students in senior high schools are permitted to take, in any one year, five credits in vocal and five credits in instrumental music amounting to four hundred minutes per week. In British Columbia, grade VIII to X students may elect to take four hours of music in a seven-day week. Needless to say, such time-allottments are not prescriptive.

How many music teachers are there in secondary schools? There are 14 in Prince Edward Island; 60 in Nova Scotia; 10 in New Brunswick; 550 in Ontario. In Manitoba the figure is not known. In Saskatchewan there are 96. (Alberta and British Columbia left the question unanswered.) How many of those just mentioned have regular teaching qualifications? In Prince Edward Island ten have such qualifications; none in Nova Scotia; all in New Brunswick; 400 in Ontario; all in Saskatchewan. (Alberta and British Columbia withheld comments.)

Teaching qualifications for secondary school music teachers are dissimilar both in name and in content. Prince Edward Island will in future require what is known as Certificate I (but teachers already employed will be allowed to continue though holding lower certificates). Nova Scotia asks for a music teacher's licence; Ontario for a specialist certificate. In New Brunswick the matter is under review. Manitoba asks for B.Mus.

qualifications for instructors in grade XII (for lower grades "recognized musical skill" is sufficient). Saskatchewan insists on a regular teacher's certificate plus special musical training (the latter being somewhat flexible because of shortness of personnel). In Alberta qualifications are not specified. British Columbia relies on graduates from the University of British Columbia holding the degree of B.Ed. with a major in music.

Teaching time available is again divided in various ways to accommodate singing, instrumental training, listening and theory. Prince Edward Island favours singing, as the instrumental programme is not yet implemented. In Nova Scotia, 60 per cent of the time allotted goes to singing, 30 per cent to listening, 10 per cent to theory. New Brunswick apportions 30 per cent to singing, 30 per cent to instrumental music and 40 per cent to appreciation, theory and history. Ontario assigns 80 per cent to vocal and instrumental instruction, 20 per cent to history, theory and listening. Manitoba divides the available time between singing, aural and instrumental training (42 per cent) music history (33 per cent) and theory (25 per cent) in the lower grades; the divisions differ in grade XII where 30 per cent is devoted to singing, aural and instrumental training, over 33 per cent to music appreciation and history and over 27 per cent to theory. In Saskatchewan the time allotment is 50 per cent for singing, 25 per cent for instrumental training and 25 per cent for music appreciation. (There were no comments from Alberta and British Columbia.)

Instrumental instruction varies from province to province. In Prince Edward Island it is an extra-curricular activity; in Nova Scotia it does not exist; in New Brunswick it is different in every district. In Manitoba it starts at grade VII level in some schools, at grade X level in others; in Metropolitan Winnipeg strings are taught from grades III–IV on and woodwinds from grades VII–VIII. In Saskatchewan band and orchestral instruments start on the average in grade V. Alberta, Ontario and British Columbia offer (in some schools at least) courses in band and orchestral instruments. British Columbia adds an instrumental survey course available to grade XI and XII students who are majoring in music.

Ontario leads all other provinces in school music. If we reflect that it was only thirty-one years ago, in 1935, that music became a compulsory subject in public schools, that instrumental music had to wait until 1947 before it could be timetabled in school hours, we cannot but admire this achievement. Yet, even in Ontario, 20 per cent of elementary schools lack music supervisors; in 30 per cent of the secondary schools music is not taught at all. Of the remaining 70 per cent, or roughly 350 high schools, 70 limit themselves to vocal, 150 to instrumental instruction. About one hundred—or 20 per cent of the total number of secondary schools—are able to offer a combined programme. Which means that in Canada's most highly developed province no more than one-fifth of the secondary schools teach music as it ought to be taught.

Music education in schools could not be more diversified, more fragmented, less uniform than it turns out to be—a state of affairs that created enough unhappiness to inspire associations, commissions and committees to consider the problems involved, to prepare reports, to draw up recommendations. Music conferences in the Atlantic provinces (especially a music seminar held in Charlottetown during the summer of 1966) laid the groundwork for the introduction of instrumental music "as a continual process from kindergarten to the completion of schooling." A music education panel of the Canadian Association of University Schools of Music labours in the field of teacher training. An Ontario Music conference (sponsored by the Province of Ontario Council for the Arts and the Community Services Branch of the Department of Education) met at Geneva Park in 1966 and agreed on a set of recommendations to be forwarded to the Minister of Education. The annual conferences of the Canadian Music Council, whatever their main topic—"Needs and Resources" in 1966, "Media" in 1967 —always revert to educational problems. During the fall of 1967 a Canadian Music Centre conference discussed the future of the "John Adaskin Project," while a Saskatchewan music conference addressed itself to all the groups concerned with the rise of music and the development of music education in that province.

Quebec's problems are different from those experienced by the rest of the country; its entire school system is in process of being transformed. The recommendations contained in the *Parent Report* define the transformation in general terms without being specific in every instance. Thus it became necessary to appoint special commissions to deal with circumscribed subjects—with architecture for example or agriculture or technical training; to appoint also a commission on art and music education. Until this commission presents its final recommendations, it will not be possible to speak with authority on the subject. We know, however, what reforms are likely to be adopted. An admirable report prepared by "un groupe des professeurs de l'Ecole de Musique de l'université Laval" was published under the title *L'Enseignement de la musique au Québec à l'heure du Rapport Parent*.[20] The over-all aim is to create a system in place of the present confusion. Private teaching, convent teaching and conservatory teaching compete with one another; the schools—whether primary or secondary—do not pull their weight, leaving the majority of children without adequate instruction. On the post-secondary level, the universities are competing with the Conservatoire. (Originally, it was the Conservatoire that had been given the right to supervise all music education in the province,[21] though it never exercised the right.) The fact that the Conservatoire does not report to the Ministère d'Education but to the Ministère des Affaires Culturelles is quite significant; when it comes to music, even government departments seem to compete with each other.

The recommendations of the *Parent Report* (awaiting the report of the Rioux commission on art and music education) are not yet carried out. There is no doubt, however, that they will be carried out, that they will do away with inherited con-

20. Les Presses de l'Université Laval, 1965.
21. Loi Conservatoire, 1942.

fusion, with lack of integration, with the lack also of space, teaching materials and personnel. The Music Division of the Ministère d'Education has it all well planned and is only waiting for the starting signal.[22]

Wherever we turn there is criticism of things as they are, pressure for reform, demand for change, admiration for the achievement of countries like Hungary, Russia and Japan. "Pourquoi ne pas profiter de leur expérience?" asks the Laval report. Indeed, why not profit by the experience of such countries? There is much to be said for it though we must not forget that schools function within a given social context; the administrative procedures used in Hungary or the USSR are beyond the reach of western societies; it is debatable whether democracy really depends on the more extravagant forms of decentralization in education. Tiny Switzerland boasts of no fewer than twenty-five independent school systems. In England "neither the initiation nor the implementation of educational reforms depend wholly or even primarily upon the actions of the central or local government. . . . In the schools, for example, the place occupied by music in the timetable will be decided by the head. . . ."[23] In Canada education is, of course, in the gift of the provinces; in the United States it is the prerogative of the states. The diversity of offerings, the disparity of standards, the over-all confusion caused by relentless de-centralization can only be lessened by voluntary efforts. The magnificent progress made by the Americans must, in a measure at least, be attributed to national organizations—the Music Teachers' National Association, the National Association of Schools of Music, the Music Educators' National Conference—which act as a unifying force. Recently established Canadian associations —the Canadian Music Educators' Association, the Canadian Association of University Schools of Music—are charged with similar responsibilities.

Administrative procedures are one thing, the quality of in-

22. George Little, *Education Musicale au Québec Congrès sur l'enseignement musical* (Besaucon, 1967).
23. Noel Long, *Music in English Education* (London: Faber & Faber, 1959).

struction is another. Novel approaches to elementary training, to reading, to string instruction promise to re-vitalize the teaching of children—Orff, Kodaly, Ward, Martenot, Suzuki are widely recognized as leaders in the field. We should profit by such splendid examples. But it might perhaps be wise to check the naïve impulse to take Orff's or Kodaly's books off the shelves and use them as they are, to start teaching without further ado: they should be adapted before they are adopted. The German and Hungarian folk songs on which they are based might well be replaced by Canadian material that could only enhance the effectiveness of either approach without detracting from the essentials—Orff's insistence on improvisation or Kodaly's methodical development of musical literacy.

Universities, as we have seen, play a significant role in the training of professional musicians. They also contribute to the formation of receptive audiences by offering music courses to non-music students; approximately 40 per cent of our universities (the percentage is steadily growing) are in favour of such policies. The programmes stemming from such policies are of the utmost importance: what better opportunity is there to preach the gospel to young audiences? But the work is rarely well done. Timetable difficulties are in the way. There is also a lack of instructors who are capable of arousing the interest of non-specialists, of teaching courses "without prerequisites," of doing away with the props of technical terms and intricate analysis. Extension departments deal mostly with students patiently assembling credits for degrees; regional responsibilities are rarely recognized, let alone discharged. The heroic example given by the University of Alberta during the time of Dr. Henry Marshall Tory's presidency found few followers. Some institutions—not too many—are graced and enlivened by the presence of composers, even performers, in residence; yet the majority of universities seem unaware of the cultural leadership they could give by developing the performing arts through the use of campus buildings, by accepting the role of impresario, by establishing art centres so prevalent in the United States—in Berkeley for instance, in Los Angeles, Dartmouth,

Illinois, Nebraska, Indiana, to name some of them. Toronto is an exception to the rule; the Edward Johnson Building—its halls are rarely dark—fulfils the function of a university music centre, although it is not known by that name.

Music libraries, research libraries in particular, are totally dependent on universities. There are some important reference materials in the National Library, some periodical sets, the Percy Scholes collection, but that is about all; public libraries deal with the standard repertoire; the CBC Music Library serves the needs of broadcasters; the Canadian Music Centre specializes in contemporary Canadian composition. University libraries are beginning to fill the gap but their holdings are far too modest to be even compared with the magnificent collections south of the border (in the Library of Congress, for instance, the New York Public Library or Harvard). Music departments across the country are in the process of assembling basic materials—complete editions, important periodicals, primary and secondary sources, microfilms and microcards, historical record collections. Only Toronto has sufficient library tools to support historical and ethnomusicological research; the contents of the Edward Johnson Memorial Library are complemented by those of the Pontifical Institute of Mediæval Studies. Laval seems to be next on the list. But taking the country as a whole, there is no doubt that music collections in university libraries are very weak and in urgent need of improvement.[24]

Professional and non-professional music education intersect at one point: the training of school music teachers is the responsibility of university schools of music, that is, a part of professional education, while music instruction in public and high schools aims at producing the enlightened listener, the amateur, the man who does have "music in himself." Teacher training is easily the most important element in our educational complex; it is here where most damage can be done or the greatest good accomplished. Again we are dealing with a subject that does not lend itself to generalizations. Teachers' qualifications,

24. Cf. Edwin E. Williams, *Report of a Survey for the National Conference of Canadian Universities and Colleges* (Ottawa, 1962).

we know already, vary from province to province; so does teachers' training. It is probably safe to say that high school music teachers are better prepared than their counterparts in public schools—a melancholy state of affairs since children need our attention the more the younger they are. In Ontario, for instance, there are three universities offering music education courses for prospective high school teachers; public school teachers depend on teachers' colleges for instruction. The concern of the colleges is pedagogy rather than subject matter. Their courses last but one academic session. They cannot restrict enrolment to students who are musically gifted or sufficiently prepared; those who are neither cannot possibly acquire the necessary skills in a few months; yet every one of them will be required to teach music: educational philosophy demands that all subjects, music among them, be taken care of by the general classroom teacher. Sad and serious as it is the situation does not lack a touch of comedy. Many a young teacher is understandably afraid of teaching music—who likes teaching what he never learned himself? He is told by way of consolation that "any competent classroom teacher can teach music,"[25] that "the very strangeness of the subject should make music more challenging." By defending the indefensible, Luther's "amou-soi" are deftly turned into competent music masters.

The problem can obviously be solved only by lengthening the training period, by greater selectivity—by instituting university study for elementary teachers. The western provinces have already progressed to that stage. Elsewhere, in Ontario for instance, the matter is under consideration.

Conservatories have repeatedly been mentioned in the course of our deliberations. Quite a number of them conduct examinations which deserve a word of explanation; there are few countries where the examination system is used with such abandon. It is British in origin. In 1889 the Royal Academy and the Royal College of Music joined forces to create the Associated Board of

25. Paul Wentworth Mathews, *You Can Teach Music* (New York: E. P. Dutton & Company Inc., 1953).

the Royal Schools to conduct examinations in various centres throughout the United Kingdom—a highly successful operation later extended to the Dominions. Trinity College (London) developed a similar system; it entered the Canadian market in the early thirties of this century. The Royal Schools withdrew in 1954; Trinity College is still with us. Its examiners come from England; grade certificates, associate, licentiate, even fellowship diplomas are offered, also scholarships, medals and other awards. The examinations are held in local centres throughout the Dominion; in Ontario alone over five hundred practical examinations were given in 1965 bearing witness to the fact that Canadian customers found the system attractive, the diplomas worth having.

The figure quoted is small in comparison to the ever-increasing volume of examinations conducted by Canadian schools. The Maritime Conservatory, Hamilton's Royal College of Music, the Mount Royal College Conservatory, the Western Ontario Conservatory, McGill (the list is not inclusive) all invite students to sit for examinations, to be awarded with a variety of certificates and diplomas. The Western Board of Music and the Royal Conservatory are the most prominent examining bodies. The former was constituted in 1934 replacing half a dozen competing systems that formerly claimed the participating provinces (Manitoba, Saskatchewan, Alberta) as their territory. The Royal Conservatory is the largest examining body in the country. In 1965–66 it dealt with 59,000 candidates; since 1952 the number of applicants has increased 100 per cent; nine-tenths of the examiners are Conservatory staff members. Grade certificates and associate diplomas are offered, also extra- and intramural scholarships (the latter tenable only in Toronto).

It is no secret that the conduct of examinations is a highly controversial subject. It has its admirers and detractors; it is praised and cursed in turn. Parents frame their offspring's certificates with understandable pride while many a musician expresses grave doubts as to the educational value of the whole operation. The system aims at unification and improvement of standards; it claims to be helpful in discovering talent, in developing good student material, in covering areas where there are no music schools (e.g., in the Northwest Territories), in providing the country with a serviceable grading system. The argument referring to the unification of standards might carry more weight if there were not so many examining bodies fiercely competing with each other for financial reasons: only the Western Board uses the profit from fees for the development of music in the provinces where it accrues; in all other cases profits are used to balance the budgets of the institutions concerned. It is not a pretty picture either to see the country blanketed by a paper storm of diplomas, all professing to be professional diplomas, all given extra-murally to candidates who need never darken the door of the institution that certifies their capacity to perform or to teach. As to grade examinations: if a youngster cannot be induced to study music without appeal to his competitive instincts it might perhaps be better to let him play baseball instead. It is sad enough that professional musicians cannot escape the curse of competition. It is hard to see why children should be taught to identify the gentle art of music with drill, exams, prizes, gradings and certificates on the wall.

Private teachers are often rated according to the ability of getting their pupils through examinations, which of course limits their freedom of action. There is no law prescribing certification; anyone can teach music to his heart's content. Music teachers' associations (banded together in the Canadian Federation of Music Teachers' Association) try to rectify the situation; their members must submit proof of adequate training. Provincial newsletters and a *CFMTA Bulletin* provide information, conventions facilitate the interchange of ideas. The majority of the teachers are rather badly paid, which is one reason why smaller communities must often do without them.

Music festivals worship at the shrine of competition; they also have their admirers and detractors. In 1965 the Canadian Music Council convened a conference on "The Pros and Cons of the Festival Movement in Canada" which ended as such conferences often do—unable to find common denominators, to reconcile the opposing arguments. The Saskatchewan Music Festival Association, Les Jeunesses Musicales du Canada as well as the Federation of Canadian Music Festivals were represented and defended their points of view. Festivals were praised as a grassroots activity, as an incentive to students and an inspiration to teachers, as a means to raise standards and to provide youngsters with a chance to perform in public; more important still, as a means to interest large audiences in musical events. Festival foes pointed out that public performances by amateurs were not necessarily a good thing; they tended to discourage the dilettante, to give potential professionals a false sense of achievement. With reference to audience building, it was pointedly reported that a Kiwanis festival recently held in Halifax had drawn an admission-paying audience of thirty thousand while a symphony concert held in the same hall during the same week was attended by three hundred. "After the reading of these statistics," observes the report, "there was no further discussion of the festival's role in the development of audiences."

The curious custom of inviting English adjudicators to judge competitive festivals (actually a quaint relic from the past) was attacked, defended and condemned in turn. The discussion finally dealt with the non-competitive festivals but "few, if any, of those present . . . were prepared to eliminate altogether the competitive element." Which is, of course, the crux of the matter. If it is not eliminated music becomes a matter of winning prizes, pennants and citations—it is used as a means to an end instead of being an end in itself. This is well understood by the few; the many, it seems, will continue to crowd into halls to be gloriously entertained by a festive mixture of music and sport.

Whether competitive festivals can or cannot help us to build the right kind of audiences—Les Jeunesses Musicales certainly do. Their work has been called "the most important thing that has happened in Canada (in the field of music) because it is aimed at the next generation of musicians and listeners. It is Canada's musical future. . . ."[26] These are strong words but the appraisal is quite accurate. Founded in Brussels by Marcel Cuvelier during World War II, Les Jeunesses Musicales grew into a world-wide movement that reached Canada in 1949. Their aim is a simple one: to build the audiences of tomorrow. But is it really so simple to develop taste and sensibility in young people all over the country (as Gilles Lefèbvre put it), to provide a milieu for artists to live in?

In 1949 the JMC counted 3,000 members; they have 80,000 now, hold forth in a hundred cities located in nine provinces. In each city, or "section," four concerts plus commentaries are presented during the season; the performers are young musicians from Canada or Jeunesses Musicales member countries. Taped commentaries are prepared in advance and sent to every section, to be listened to prior to the concert to which they refer. No means are spared to arouse an interest in music: competitions, exchange programmes, record-making, publications (particularly *Le Journal des Jeunesses Musicales*)—it is all in the day's work for Gilles Lefèbvre, the remarkable man responsible for the whole undertaking and its brilliant success. The JMC's summer camp at Mount Orford, with forty woodland studios, guest houses, an unusually attractive concert hall, is an amazing achievement in itself. A special pavilion, designed with taste and imagination, represented Les Jeunesses Musicales at Expo '67; its title, most appropriately, was "Man and His Music."

An equally fascinating story could be told about the Banff School of Fine Arts. The story has, in fact, been told. In *Campus in the Clouds*,[27] Donald Cameron describes the development of the enterprise: how it started, in 1933, as an experimental school in the arts related to the theatre, sponsored by the extension division of the University of Alberta and accom-

26. Eric McLean in the *Montreal Star*.
27. Donald Cameron, *Campus in the Clouds* (Toronto: McClelland & Stewart, 1956).

modating forty students; how it grew into a centre of fine arts and adult education attracting many thousands; how it acquired chalets, school buildings and, finally, an auditorium on Banff's choicest site overlooking the Bow Valley and a majestic mountain range of the Rockies. Senator Cameron did more than tell the tale. He was the man who built the School from the ground up. He had the perseverance, the administrative genius, to translate his vision into reality. The Banff School, as its name implies, caters to all the arts but music plays a prominent part in its programme.

In Mount Orford as well as in Banff the student population is mixed; amateurs mingle with future professionals who avail themselves of the splendid opportunities offered. It is different with CAMMAC (Canadian Amateur Musicians—Musiciens Amateurs du Canada), a venture entirely devoted to non-professional music-making. In 1953 George and Carl Little (assisted by their wives Madeleine and Frances) founded the Otter Lake Music Centre in the Laurentians which, six years later, developed into the association named. Close to two hundred people spend their summer holidays in the camp on the lake. They play recorders or guitars, practise string instruments, sing Bach cantatas—they experience the joy of making music for its own sake on whatever level within their reach. The impetus is not entirely lost during the winter. CAMMAC branch activities in various cities lead to a revival of "music in the home" so dangerously eroded in an electronic age, so indispensable for a healthy musical climate.

Whether a renaissance of "house music" can be attempted on a larger scale cannot be predicted, it can only be hoped for. As it is, children receive their first musical impressions from records, radio and television, depend on schools for instruction on levels which formerly were in the purview of the family: the importance of broadcasting devices can hardly be overrated. They are available in profusion; teachers have school broadcasts, documentary films, record libraries, even video-tapes at their disposal, together with books on programmed learning,

Gestalt psychology and operant behaviour. To what extent, we must ask, are all these aids incorporated into the learning process?

Whenever a new medium comes into being it is jubilantly announced that teaching will be completely revolutionized. Waves of hope and enthusiasm spread in all directions: here, at last, is the shape of things to come. Traditional classroom technique will become obsolete, the classrooms themselves will disappear to be replaced by information centres replete with every kind of apparatus; the onrushing future will be upon us in no time at all. But it does not work that way, not yet at any rate, for a variety of reasons: the machinery is not always available or properly cared for; school boards are not always willing to underwrite the expense for costly equipment; the teachers themselves—so prone to teach as they were taught—are not over-fond of change. Even now, after twenty-five years of school broadcasting, the question is solemnly debated whether "direct teaching" is permissible or whether radio and television should be restricted to "enrichment" programmes. One cannot help feeling that a good deal of inertia hides itself behind the ceaselessly repeated assertion that the sacred teacher-student relationship must in no way be disturbed.

So far only radio has had an impact on the schools. School broadcasting could not have been developed without being supported by the CBC. With the CBC being a federal agency and educational matters being under the jurisdiction of the provinces, it was necessary to establish a National Advisory Council on School Broadcasting to assure smooth collaboration between broadcasters and educators. "The CBC has provided the main impulse," said Alphonse Ouimet, "the technical backbone and the nation-wide scope for school broadcasting in Canada ... On the other hand, the actual framing of the educational service itself—which includes planning of the curriculum, responsibility for programme content, utilization and evaluation of the broadcasts—has lain wholly in the hands of the provincial departments of education, the local school-boards and the teachers. The CBC has limited its functions, as it should, to encouragement and promotion, and to ensuring that its facilities were well used in terms of broadcasting technique."[28] The formative period in provincial school broadcasting, the advent of national school broadcasts as well as further developments (experiments in school television for instance), are admirably described in R. S. Lambert's *School Broadcasting in Canada.*[29] We have his word for it that progress made has been remarkable when compared with parallel progress in the United Kingdom (with its denser population), the United States (with its much greater financial resources) and other countries of the Commonwealth.

One would think that music, an acoustical phenomenon, would lend itself better to school broadcasting than anything else. This turns out to be a gratuitous assumption. A non-verbal medium (i.e., music) is talked about and "explained"; music plus explanation is incorporated into a third medium, i.e., broadcasting—one sees at a glance that there are too many variables in the equation. Which may be the reason why so many school broadcasts limit themselves to "music appreciation": an attempt to arouse interest in music in a general way instead of concentrating on a lesson to be learned. "In music appreciation" (to quote Mr. Lambert once more) "The (National Advisory) Council made repeated experiments with symphonic and choral music, and with opera, to bring to the schools of Canada outstanding live musical experiences which they could not expect to get in any other way in school hours. They included half-hour concerts by the Toronto, Winnipeg and Vancouver symphony orchestras, performances of Gluck's 'Orpheus' (1949), Benjamin Britten's 'Let's Make an Opera' (1951 and 1961) and Gilbert and Sullivan's 'Pirates of Penzance' (1953) and 'H.M.S. Pinafore' (1956) and dramatized biographies of great musicians . . . incorporating typical works. These experiments met with varying success. In some cases they were too far in advance of the musical level reached by

28. R. S. Lambert, *School Broadcasting in Canada* (Toronto: University of Toronto Press, 1963).
29. *Ibid.*

senior elementary students or were outside the ordinary range of music teaching in public schools. On the other hand, they were rarely listened to in high schools which might have bene-fitted most from them, because of curriculum and timetable difficulties. The experiments are still being continued in the hope of finding a formula that will meet the varied needs and standards of students in all parts of the country."[30]

In all likelihood a just verdict though a somewhat melan-choly conclusion. National programmes like the ones referred to have always been supplemented by provincial ones; their titles ("Let's Sing Together," "Sing and Play," "Airway to Song," "Secondary School Choirs") seem to indicate that more varied approaches might have been desirable.

Whatever the merits or demerits of radio in the past, it is supposed to be in decline; television is commonly regarded as a mightier instrument to raise the levels of awareness and taste, to inform and to teach. Is that really true? Radio has been abandoned by sponsors looking for mass audiences (or *the* mass audience), which left it poorer no doubt, but more flexible, better suited to court specialized audiences, to cater to minority groups. Good music, opera, or drama are available in profu-sion, both on FM and AM; "radio, with its greater economy, flexibility and ease of production, together with its longer sche-dule, is better suited than television to satisfy a variety of specialized interests."[31]

The argument is hotly contested, however. It is often said that the stronger medium carries the stronger message; from which it would follow that radio could not possibly be better suited than television to serve music education. Never mind that the teacher has already a whole arsenal of teaching aids at his disposal—it is still television that has an emotional impact on children which cannot be equalled by any other means.

Perhaps so. But relatively little has been accomplished so far, in spite of the countless experiments that have been conducted

30. *Ibid.*
31. *Report of the Committee on Broadcasting* (Ottawa: Queen's Printer, 1965), p. 268.

(especially in the United States), in spite of the countless reports that have been written. It has been estimated that there exist more than one thousand books on the subject of educational television, but the pedagogical and political problems stemming from the new medium have yet to be solved. Teachers prefer to teach as they were taught. They are afraid of change, afraid of becoming obsolete; they feel strongly that only they themselves can tell the broadcasters what to do. The broadcasters find the educators incompetent as far as the medium is concerned; yet the very same broadcasters depend on the very same educators to determine content, to act as representatives of the school system. We have only to remember that in Canada educational broadcasters are under federal jurisdiction while teachers are under provincial control to see at a glance how difficult it must be to create a Federal Educational Television Agency like the one proposed by the Secretary of State (February 1968).

It is by no means clear how educational telecasts will be transmitted in the future. Should VHF be used, UHF, closed-circuit TV, open channel broadcasts to be videotaped in schools? How will network telecasting be influenced by satellite-to-home transmission?

But suppose our political difficulties were overcome, suppose our technical problems were all solved: what would educational music television consist of? Music is for the ear, television is for the eye; how can one translate the one into the other?

It can be done; it has been done in various ways. It is easiest in the case of opera and ballet where visual and aural components are in equilibrium. Telecasts dealing with non-dramatic music work on the assumption that listeners concentrate better if their eyes are as occupied as their ears. Performers who talk with ease and conviction (Leonard Bernstein, for instance, or Glenn Gould) hold their audiences spellbound. Documentaries like CBC's *Stravinsky* or BBC's *Casals at 88* make it possible to present profiles of important men. All the foregoing, however, are examples of ETV proper; they are telecasts that arouse interest and widen the listener's horizon but do not teach in the strict sense of the term. This is what instructional television or ITV is supposed to do. By and large, it has not done it yet. Here is a whole new territory awaiting to be explored.

The reader of this essay may have been left with a jumbled lot of impressions reminding him of a kaleidoscope forming different images at every turn. He may wonder whether any definite pattern can be discovered in the mass of data supplied. The spectrum seems impossibly wide, ranging from tranquil inertia to purposeful activity; every department of education seems a law unto itself, every university, every conservatory, every examination system; French, English and American influences criss-cross each other. Are there no unifying forces, no guidelines, is there no key to understanding?

The confusion will be lessened if we remember that education does not exist *in vacuo*: it is a social invention, it helps to shape society, is shaped by it in turn and changes with it. A frontier society enjoys liberty but it lacks time and leisure for the pursuit of happiness. In such a society the gentle art of music will be left to grow like the lilies in the field. There will be no demand for professional musicians, laymen will be left to their own devices, a colonial attitude will prevail: a few imported performers will entertain small groups of *cognoscenti*. Professional schools—should they come into being—will operate on a lower level than their counterparts abroad; the educational authorities will pay scant attention to music. Teachers will be badly paid, badly educated; they will defer to examiners and adjudicators from overseas. Music, in short, will be classified as "entertainment"—a toy for the rich, a conversation piece for intellectuals.

In the early nineteen hundreds the North American continent could have been described in these terms. The United States had the advantage of a denser population and greater wealth; it grew more quickly: yet Canada's musical development is no less admirable. It gathered speed after the war and increases its momentum day by day. The rise of art centres bears witness to the fact; also the eagerness of government on all levels to assist, to stimulate, to assume the role of patron. The national debate on education helped to re-discover many an old truth about the part the arts must play in education and in hastening the transformations and transvaluations which we have examined.

The change came almost overnight. The educational establishment—notoriously slow in adapting itself to new conditions —could not respond quickly enough. Which is the reason why we are confronted by two different systems (if anything so unsystematic can be called by that name): an older one geared to what once was, and a newer one anticipating what is bound to be. The former is characterized by extra-mural diplomas, examination systems, foreign adjudicators, bady trained teachers; the latter by university schools of music, graduate studies, reform of school music and an emphasis on teacher training.

The older system cannot be expected to disappear at once: long after Gutenberg, monks sat in scriptoria and copied manuscripts as they had done for centuries. It will take time before music education in Canada will lose this double-headed, Janus-like quality, before the kaleidoscopic impressions will give way to an easily comprehensible and unified pattern.

National Organizations

KEITH MACMILLAN

ONE MIGHT EXPECT that the vast reaches of Canada and the great distances separating centres of population would encourage the formation of any number of national organizations to help bind the country together. However, the present patch-work state of national organization in music is testimony to Canada's comparative youth as a nation. One finds, for example, that at no time have the symphony orchestras made an attempt to form a national association of any kind, nor have choral organizations or, until very recently, the schools of music. One cannot escape the impression that a national consciousness among Canadian musicians in general, as distinct from local or regional consciousness, is still comparatively new to this country. But during the past generation or so such a development has, in fact, been taking place, reflecting the quickening pulse of musical awareness in covering half a continent.

FEDERAL GOVERNMENT AND CROWN AGENCIES

For many years the federal government had shown a typical North American reluctance to become directly involved in the arts, even though the necessity for government participation in principle had long been recognized, particularly in matters of communication, and the musical arts have always been concerned with communication. The Canadian solution has been the formation of the crown corporation, a non-government type of body owned by the people of Canada but with an independent board of governors who report, not to the government of the day, but openly to Parliament itself. The Canadian Broadcasting Corporation, the National Film Board and the Canada Council are examples. Since these organizations have for the past few years reported to Parliament through the Secretary of State, the individual holding this position has been more and more inclined to admit to a certain direct responsibility in the fostering of the arts, although each Secretary of State has disclaimed any responsibility for direct involvement in support of the arts. In June of 1966 the federal government found it advisable to formalize the situation in the "Department of State Act," which specifies, in part, that "The duties, powers and functions of the Secretary of State of Canada extend to and include all matters over which the Parliament of Canada has jurisdiction, not by law assigned to any other department, branch or agency of the Government of Canada, relating to . . . the encouragement of the . . . performing arts . . . theatres, films and broadcasting." Thus the government's involvement in support of the arts has been specifically channelled and its necessity acknowledged.

Whereas the responsibility of the Secretary of State has been confined to matters inside Canada, in recent years the Department of External Affairs has been much more receptive to the idea of direct support for artistic ventures outside the country, most pointedly in assisting substantially with the touring expenses of Canadian musicians abroad and especially in countries of French expression. The visit of the Montreal Symphony Orchestra to the U.S.S.R. in 1962, of the Toronto Symphony in 1965 to the Commonwealth Arts Festival, the European tour in 1966 of the National Youth Orchestra and the McGill Chamber Orchestra represent something of a revolution in the thinking of the Department and of the government in general.

Of all the government departments, the oldest substantial patron of music is undoubtedly the Department of National Defence, principally through the training and maintenance of service bands. The bands of both the Regular and Reserve Forces have, over the years, made a solid contribution to the lives and morale of the forces and also to the cultural life of the civilian community.

In many centres, military musicians provide the backbone of local musical groups from symphony orchestras to dance bands. In smaller centres, very often a touring military band is the only professional musical organization available. Ex-service musicians may be found in many communities, contributing in a variety of ways. Probably the most noteworthy are those who have become involved with school boards and districts and are actively engaged in teaching and directing school bands and orchestras.

The Regular Force establishment provides for seventeen military bands with an authorized strength of approximately eight hundred officers and men. In 1967 three of these bands were Naval, twelve were Army and two were supported by the RCAF, although early in 1968 the integration of the Canadian armed forces made the service distinctions obsolete. The Reserves have a somewhat larger musical component, the difference being that they are dependent for their livelihood on the community but wish to retain their military affiliations. In all, there are one hundred and thirty-three authorized bands in the Reserves, involving close to seven thousand musicians. In addition there are sixty-seven bands active with various cadet corps across the country. Although the number of personnel involved with these corps bands varies, it is fair to assume that it would be close to two thousand. If the point could be stretched to include these enthusiastic youngsters, one might say that as a national organization, the Department is directly or indirectly contributing to the cultural life of the Canadian community through nearly ten thousand musicians.

An establishment such as this must have a source from which

to draw its professionals, and a method of training the potential musician. It also should be capable of up-grading the individual's professional qualifications. For these reasons, a Canadian Armed Forces School of Music operates at the Canadian Forces Base, Esquimalt, providing instruction at three levels. A potential musician can graduate from this school as an instrumentalist and, after a few years of experience, advance his professional qualification to that of an assistant director or director of music.

It is impossible to assess accurately the costs of these activities, partly because the Department provides many kinds of subsidy, from partial to complete, and partly because many of these costs are inseparable from those required for the maintenance of the armed forces generally. A commonly quoted estimate is five million dollars a year. It is obvious, however, that the maintenance of eight hundred officers and men full time, the equipping of these seventeen bands, the operation of a music school, transportation of bandsmen about the country and a host of other expenses must require an expenditure considerably above this estimate. Needless to say, the presence of these musicians, both in and out of uniform, has long been influential in musical development in most parts of the country. Even today it would be exceedingly difficult, if not impossible, for orchestras such as those of Victoria, Calgary, Edmonton, Kingston, New Brunswick and others to function without the active participation of service bandsmen. The Department's contribution then is a very real one which is often overlooked.

Without question the most influential single patron of music in Canada is the Canadian Broadcasting Corporation. Without the CBC, as without the railways and airlines, Canada would probably long since have ceased to have meaning as a nation; nowhere is this more apparent than in music. So important is the CBC that its activities transcend the limits of this chapter, and it must have a chapter of its own (see p. 167). During the years 1956–66 particularly, music in Canada has undergone a remarkable development. In 1955, although some twenty-five orchestras could be listed in Canada (most of them amateur), no more than three were able to present their concerts to audiences larger than 1500, and of these only one, the Toronto Symphony Orchestra, could be heard in a proper concert hall. Opera in Canada was still a hit-and-miss affair depending heavily on student participation; the audience for ballet was virtually non-existent and the livelihood of a large section of the musical fraternity was often an uncomfortably hand-to-mouth affair.

Compare the thriving situation a dozen years later, as outlined in other parts of this book. This is not to suggest that musical Canada has suddenly sprung from barren soil during the past ten years—far from it! The roots were solid in 1955, the growth healthy and talent abounded everywhere. But with the founding of the Canada Council in 1957 the musical arts in Canada found themselves with a rich and thoughtful patron, in a position to dispense in subsidies to the arts some one million dollars per year. The Canada Council was established by act of Parliament (The Canada Council Act, March 28, 1957) on a government grant of one hundred million dollars, half to be used in capital grants to Canadian universities (which were at that time undergoing an unprecedented expansion), the other half to be used as an Endowment Fund whose income was to be distributed in support of the arts, humanities, and social sciences. The members of the Council are appointed by the Prime Minister of the day and are required to meet at least four times a year to decide on the exact allotments of each grant. Although the Council makes a point of meeting in various parts of the country, its executive offices are in Ottawa.

The Council has always adhered to the principle that its grants must not be used to pay off deficits or to replace existing sources of support, but to enable organizations and individuals to expand their activities and to achieve the highest possible standards. This systematic and well-planned foray of government into sponsorship of the arts has had an electrifying effect, especially on that expensive child of the family—music. Since 1958 the musical pattern of the country has undergone a startling change (hence the need for this new book, for example) and of course a remarkable development in both quality and quantity.

By about 1964 however, the demands resulting from this evolution and growth had placed a new and constant strain on the fixed resources of the Council. As the quality of more and more artistic endeavours improved and an enthusiastic public was created, the need for further subsidy mounted to an alarming degree. Demands on the Council's funds increased at a much greater rate than its capital (and income) growth, demands which in many cases had perforce to be accepted as new and continuing responsibilities, thus restricting to a frightening extent the Council's freedom of choice and action. Early in 1965 a national conference on the performing arts was held at Ste-Adèle near Montreal, at which the Secretary of State, the Hon. Maurice Lamontagne, was present as an observer and active participant. Soon after this conference the federal government voted an additional ten million dollars to be administered by the Canada Council during the following three years. This was supplemented the following year by an appropriation to the Canada Council of seventeen million dollars, made with remarkably little fanfare and, apparently, no opposition. Much of these funds of course were needed in implementing Canada's Centennial observances during 1967, but it was obvious to all that Canada's artistic life had risen to a completely new and expensive plateau from which retreat was unthinkable. The pressure on the federal government was renewed in 1967–8 toward even more subsidy for the arts in Canada.

One interesting side-effect of the Canada Council's activities has been a definite trend towards the establishment by provincial governments of responsible support of the arts. It is outside the scope of this national chapter to detail these; suffice it to say that Quebec has its own provincial Ministry for Cultural Affairs, with an annual music budget of five hundred thousand dollars; Ontario annually spends on music some two hundred thousand dollars through the well-informed and active Province of Ontario Council for the Arts; Saskatchewan (with a population of less than one million) has its Arts Board with an annual music budget of about thirty-two thousand dollars; and the Provincial Secretary's department of the Alberta government has established a Cultural Developments Branch with an annual music budget of more than $120,000. In 1967 the government of British Columbia set up a five million dollar Cultural Development Fund, the anticipated annual income of $270,000 to be disbursed at the discretion of a committee initially under the chairmanship of W. H. Murray, Speaker of the British Columbia legislature. These disbursements are intended to supplement, not to replace, the already established annual appropriations of about eighty thousand dollars to various British Columbia musical organizations. The other provinces make some grants in support of the arts through their office of the provincial secretary or department of education.

Canada is known to many audiences abroad as the home of the National Film Board, a crown corporation whose films have consistently been winners in international film festivals. Although the National Film Board uses music extensively and maintains permanently a staff including several composers, it exercises comparatively little direct influence on the development of music in Canada, except in providing additional employment for Canadian composers and performers. Music usually plays a supporting role in films, and such scores can rarely be played out of context. Comparatively few film scores have been reworked for concert presentation. On the other hand, many of Canada's leading composers have been invited at one time or another to write music for Film Board productions, a useful experience in any composer's development. It can certainly be said that Norman McLaren's experiments in "sound-writing-on-film" techniques continue to be of great interest to many of Canada's composers writing electronic music.

One other national federal organization requires mention, although it was ephemeral since it ceased to exist after 1967: the Centennial Commission. This body was concerned with Canada's 1967 Centennial observances of various kinds, from buildings to ballet. The Commission was created by the government on an initial appropriation of twenty million dollars, with the mandate not only to supply a Centennial purse but also to encourage other government bodies, provincial, regional and local, to make their contribution to the celebrations of the one hundredth birthday of Canada's Confederation.

The arts programme of the Commission was carried out under the heading of Festival Canada. Basically the administration was divided into four fields of activity:

1 "Festival Canada At Home," representing pre-production grants in support of special artistic events given by organizations in their own communities.
2 "Festival Canada On Tour," representing payment of travelling costs for Canadian and international attractions on national and regional circuits during 1967.
3 "Commissions," representing grants for new works to be premièred during 1967.
4 "Ticket Assistance," representing grants to enable ticket prices to be kept to a minimum for Festival Canada On Tour attractions.

Altogether, under the auspices of Festival Canada and of its four million dollar budget, some eighty-four performing arts organizations were seen and heard in events which included one hundred and twenty-five national première performances. Festival Canada On Tour performances alone numbered some seven hundred in all parts of Canada. Perhaps more important in the long run was the creation of new works, which included at least one hundred and ten musical works (including three operas and three ballets) as well as twenty-one new plays and musicals.

Yet another extraordinary achievement for Canada during 1967 was the world-famous EXPO 67, the "Universal and International Exhibition of 1967," which took place in Montreal from April 28 till October 27. Many of the national and other pavilions presented special programmes from time to time throughout the duration of EXPO. The Canadian Pavilion alone, on a performing arts budget of $800,000 presented a continuing series in which the finest of Canadian singers, pianists, chamber groups, dancers, and organists were presented in performances throughout each day for the entire six months of EXPO. This was surely the greatest showcase of Canadian talent ever presented.

Superlatives come easily in describing EXPO activities, and it is no exaggeration to say that the most extraordinary international performing arts festival of all time took place as but a part of this amazing spectacle. This was the World Festival of EXPO, which during its six-month run, featured appearances from more than twenty orchestras, twelve of them from Europe including the Concertgebouw and the Vienna, Berlin, Czech and New York Philharmonic Orchestras, eight of the world's leading opera companies, including the Bolshoi, La Scala, the Vienna and the Hamburg State Opera Companies as well as the Royal Opera of Stockholm, more than ten ballet companies including the New York City Ballet, the Paris Opera Ballet and the Royal Ballet from Covent Garden. Add to this a number of world-ranking soloists, two major international music competitions (Jeunesses Musicales and the International Institute of Music of Canada), many choirs and eminent chamber groups, not to mention a theatre festival of the first magnitude, a film festival, and a constant parade of popular entertainers of the calibre of Maurice Chevalier, Marlene Dietrich, Jack Benny, Pearl Bailey and the entire Ringling Brothers Circus, and it will be seen that the World Festival represented an event of unparalleled importance to Canada. Not the least of the beneficial effects of the World Festival was the realization that the best of Canadian groups, major orchestras, opera and ballet companies and theatres, stood up well to direct international comparison.

Despite their short span of existence, these three Centennial bodies, the Centennial Commission, the Canadian Government Pavilion at EXPO and the World Festival of EXPO, as well as the whole of EXPO itself, have provided a stimulus to the arts in Canada on a scale scarcely dreamed of a scant five years previously. Their effect will likely be felt for years, if not generations, to come.

Of the non-government musical bodies it is fitting that we first describe the Canadian Music Council. Most of the other national musical organizations mentioned in this chapter hold membership in the Council, which functions as the voice, the consensus perhaps, of music and musicians in Canada. The Council began life toward the end of World War II as a rather informal committee of musicians called together at the suggestion of the federal government to consider the musical aspects of Canada's post-war reconstruction. Sir Ernest Mac-Millan was asked to gather together a group representing each of the more-or-less nationally active musical organizations then in existence, along with certain individual Canadian musicians of experience. Later, in 1945, this rather loose group formally constituted itself into the Canadian Music Council, thus antedating the International Music Council of UNESCO (of which the Canadian Council is a member) and indeed the United Nations itself.

Over the years, the Council, on a voluntary basis and largely under the chairmanship of Sir Ernest MacMillan, continued to meet at more or less regular intervals. The full membership gathered once per year and the six-man executive (now eight) about three times a year. Although the Council's chief function has always been primarily to provide a forum for widely scattered members of the profession, it has also from time to time undertaken various projects. In 1955, for example, the Council, with the collaboration of the University of Toronto Press, and with Sir Ernest as editor, published *Music in Canada*, predecessor to this present volume. Between the autumn of 1956 and the summer of 1962, *The Canadian Music Journal* was published quarterly under the Council's auspices, with Geoffrey Payzant as editor and with Dr. Arnold Walter as chairman of the Editorial Committee. The Council's largest continuing project to date is the Canadian Music Centre (of which more later in this chapter), formed in 1958 to provide a central library and information source on the music of Canadian composers.

The pattern of organization in the arts in Canada is, at the time of writing, undergoing rapid changes, particularly with the larger disbursements of the Canada Council, with the proliferation of provincial arts councils and other forms of government support. It would now appear that the Canadian Music Council is entering a new and more rigorous phase of activity and influence. In 1965 the Council, in conjunction with its annual meeting, held the first of what has become an annual series of conferences, serving to focus professional, public and government attention on matters of musical concern. The 1965 conference examined the "Pros and Cons of the Competitive Festival Movement in Canada." In 1966, when the Council met in Ottawa, the theme was "Music in Canada—its Needs and Resources" and the financing of musical activity across the country. In March-April of 1967 the Council, by then under the chairmanship of Dr. Arnold Walter, accomplished the organization of two conferences in one week in Toronto. The first was a six-day conference of the Inter-American Music Council (CIDEM) with which Dr. Walter has long been associated and which was meeting for the first time in Canada. This was immediately followed by the Canadian Music Council's Annual Meeting and Conference, which discussed "Music and Media." The subject of the 1968 conference was "Music Education in Canada." Detailed reports on these conferences are published. In this way the Council is maintaining and developing an important role, particularly in fostering useful relationships between government and the musical arts in Canada.

At its Annual Meeting in 1966 the Council adopted the principle of obligatory rotation of its executive and Sir Ernest retired as chairman, to be succeeded by Dr. Arnold Walter, whose successor in 1967 was Jean Papineau-Couture. At the time of writing the Council's membership included, as well as a number of leading individual musicians, the following major musical organizations: BMI Canada Limited, Canadian Amateur Musicians-Musiciens Amateurs du Canada (CAMMAC), Canadian Association of University Schools of Music, Canadian Bandmasters' Association, Canadian Broadcasting Corporation, Canadian Bureau for the Advancement of Music, Canadian Federation of Music Teachers' Associations, Canadian Folk Music Society, Canadian League of Composers, Canadian Music Centre, Canadian Music Library Association, Canadian Music Educators' Association, Canadian Music Publishers' Association, Composers Authors and Publishers Association of Canada Limited (CAPAC), Federation of Canadian Music Festivals, Les Jeunesses Musicales du Canada (JMC), National Youth Orchestra of Canada (NYO), and the Royal Canadian College of Organists.

The Canada Foundation is an organization little known even in Canada. For the most part its work is involved with the professions of "the fine and lively arts" rather than directly with the public. It was formed in 1943, principally through the support of private citizens, the so-called "one thousand associates" who recognized, even then, the need for a central source of encouragement for, and information on, the arts in Canada. Except for certain specific projects, it depends entirely on private donations for its activities. Before the formation of the Canada Council the purposes of the Canada Foundation were directed toward the centralization of information concerning the arts in Canada and the raising of money for specific projects of urgent importance. The Foundation acted as a service agency and fund-raiser, although no grants as such were given from its operating budget. With the establishment of the Canada Council in 1957, the Foundation's activities have shifted away from fund-raising toward the provision of various other services, particularly the compiling of information. In 1961 the Canadian Cultural Information Centre was established within the framework of the Foundation, as a joint project with the Canada Council. The Centre now prints several booklets, such as "Facilities for Study in the Fine Arts in Canada," "Some Summer Courses in the Arts in Canada," and "Some Canadian Cultural Organizations." At the same time the Foundation acts as a service counterpart to the Canada Council (which is not a service agency) for the benefit of any person, organization or government agency in need of information. The Foundation is located in Ottawa, and carries on its work with a staff of six, including its Director (and founder) Walter Herbert.

Somewhat in the position of grandfather to the Canada Council is the Canadian Conference of the Arts (formerly called the "Canadian Arts Council"), which brought itself into existence at about the same time and for much the same reasons as the Canadian Music Council, although it embraced in a loose way all the arts in Canada. It was this Canadian Arts Council which, after the war, actively pressed for a Royal Commission on the Arts, to which the government responded with the establishment of the Massey Commission (named after its Commissioner, the late Vincent Massey, afterwards a Governor-General of Canada). This commission specifically recommended the establishment of the Canada Council, which was founded six years later.

With the establishment of the Canada Council, the *raison d'être* for the original Canadian Arts Council seemed to diminish somewhat, but in recent years the necessity for a concerted voice of the arts has again become evident. The Conference has accordingly shown signs of renewing its activity and its representation of virtually all the arts in Canada. It has organized several large-scale conferences, such as the Arts Conference of 1961 (at the O'Keefe Centre in Toronto), "Seminar '65" at Ste-Adèle mentioned above, its successor, "Seminar '66" held outside Toronto and on the subject of the visual arts, another on the topic "A Dialogue between Cultures" at Montreal in December of 1966 and in late 1967 another at Ste-Adèle to plan for the aftermath of 1967.

ORGANIZATIONS SERVING CANADIAN MUSIC

It is a truism that the reputations of Canadian performing musicians are better established than those of Canada's creative musicians. Such names as Glenn Gould, Maureen Forrester, Jon Vickers, Louis Quilico and Teresa Stratas are household words to music-lovers in many countries abroad. The name of the late Healey Willan is known to church musicians and congregations throughout the English-speaking world, but the music of Harry Somers, John Weinzweig, the late Pierre Mercure and François Morel has yet to impinge significantly on the consciousness even of Canadian audiences, let alone those abroad. In the sense that few if any Canadian works are part of the normal Canadian repertoire, Canada's is still essentially an imported musical culture. Certainly the Canadian composer has not developed what may in any sense be considered a distinctive national idiom. The late 1800s and early 1900s found Canada unready to take full advantage of the heady inspiration provided to European cultures at that time by their nationalistic and folkloristic schools; indeed it was not until after 1945 that the number of Canadians seriously intent on being composers was sufficient to warrant wider public attention from Canadian music-lovers.

With the resumption of peaceful preoccupations after 1945 came a rush of young creative talent, for the most part impatient with the musical expression of the past and eager to embark on the exciting and uncharted seas of "the new music." Finding a massive public indifference to their new music, and indeed from much of the musical profession itself, a group of composers established in 1951 the Canadian League of Composers, to focus attention on their activity as a creative force. Five years later the League counted some forty members and now numbers about sixty. No member is admitted who has not had sound professional training in composition, and who has not had works performed or published. For practical reasons the government of the League since 1957 has alternated at two-year intervals between Toronto and Montreal; the first presidents until 1966 were John Weinzweig or Jean Papineau-Couture. The present president is Srul Irving Glick. In the beginning the League organized many concerts of Canadian music and in 1957 assembled and catalogued its important collection of orchestral scores. All in all, its activities succeeded in attracting the attention and understanding of many Canadian musicians and broadcasting executives, and the fruits of its labours have been more and more evident in recent years.

Composers, like all of us, like to be rewarded for their professional labours. In Canada as elsewhere, their income depends on royalties from the sale of scores and sheet music, and on the payment of fees in consideration of the right to perform works protected by copyright. An often overlooked factor in the development of Canadian music is the evolution of an important Canadian-owned and Canadian-governed performing right society, the Composers Authors and Publishers Association of Canada (CAPAC). This organization was established in 1925 as the Canadian Performing Right Society, to administer in Canada the world-wide repertoire assigned to the Performing Right Society (PRS) of Britain and its affiliated societies throughout the world. Within a very short time, the American Society of Composers, Authors and Publishers (ASCAP) arranged with the PRS for the new Canadian society to administer in Canada the performing rights of its repertoire, and ASCAP became a joint-owner of the Canadian Performing Right Society. However, with the passing of the years and with increased Canadian creative activity, the two founding societies acceded to a series of steps which, between 1947 and 1962, achieved the establishment and full Canadian ownership of CAPAC and control by its Canadian membership. Thus CAPAC was born in 1947 and, with its development as a Canadian body under the managerial guidance of William St. Clair Low, has come increased recognition and encouragement for the work of Canadian composers. Today CAPAC has over a thousand Canadian members and, through agreements with foreign performing right societies, represents foreign composers, authors and publishers in approximately one hundred independent nations who reciprocally represent the interests of Canadian composers in their countries.

Such an organization has every interest in fostering increased recognition of the work of its members; CAPAC has encouraged this in many ways. It has initiated an ambitious project carried out jointly in collaboration with the Canadian Association of Broadcasters principally through the subsidy of commercial recordings; it publishes a bilingual monthly magazine, *The Canadian Composer*, detailing news of the activities of its composer and publisher members; it makes substantial grants to assure the establishment and continuation of the Canadian Music Centre; it sponsors the distinguished MacMillan Lectures given every year at the Summer School of the Royal Conservatory of Music.

Likewise engaged in the fields of publication and the administration of performing rights, but rather differently constituted, is BMI Canada Limited (Broadcast Music Incorporated). This body was created in 1940 by its parent body, Broadcast Music Inc. of New York, to acquire and to license performing rights of Canadian composers. Of its governing Board of five Directors, three are Canadian. Unlike CAPAC, however, which is an association of composers and publishers, BMI Canada has established its own publication division, becoming the most active publisher of serious music in Canada, and as such directly promotes the works of its composer members both as publisher and as performing right agent. In recent years BMI Canada has also contributed to the operating budget of the Canadian Music Centre. It publishes its own magazine, *The Music Scene—La Scène musicale*.

The Canadian Music Centre provides a central reference and circulating library of, and a promotion centre for, the music of Canadian composers. The creative activity of the unexpectedly large post–World War II crop of Canadian composers, mostly writing in the new (and unpopular) contemporary idioms, prompted not only the formation of the Canadian League of Composers but also led the Canadian Music Council to press for a central library and promotion centre with a full-time paid staff. With the Canada Council and CAPAC each guaranteeing to supply grants of $20,000 and $10,000 respectively a year for a trial three-year period, the Centre was launched on January 1, 1959, with Jean-Marie Beaudet as Executive Secretary. Since that time its activities have expanded greatly and require a full-time staff of five, with several other members part-time and on special projects, as well as a group of copyists engaged on a free-lance basis to help lift the onerous burden of copying from the composer's back.

Currently, the Centre's library contains scores of some 3,500 Canadian works, both published and unpublished. Publishers normally contribute at least two copies of each published work. For unpublished works, which are greatly in the majority, the Centre has developed an efficient method (based on photostatic processes) of hand-making and binding a minimum two or three copies of each work, to enable these to be circulated without fear of losing an "only" original. Nevertheless, the Centre acquires no copyrights and hence is not a publisher. Scores from this library are circulated to musicians in all parts of Canada and in many other parts of the world currently at the rate of about 1,500 to 2,000 per year.

In addition, the Centre is involved in many projects for the creation, promotion, and recording of Canadian music and acts as well as a source of information on musical Canada. The Centre publishes, in English and French, a monthly bulletin of musical news, *Musicanada*. The Centre has also developed a collection of recordings of several hundreds of Canadian works on commercial discs, transcriptions for radio and educational use, and tape recordings mostly taken from radio broadcasts. Since these latter may not be circulated, a well-equipped listening-room is provided.

From time to time the Centre initiates various projects designed to stimulate professional and public interest in the works of Canadian composers. One of the first was a recording of three orchestral works, and a subsequent album of string quartets, produced in collaboration with Columbia Records of Canada; the Centre has since collaborated with other agencies in many other recordings. During 1966 and 1967 it developed a programme of commissions, numbering forty-four in all, most of which were premièred during 1967. In 1962 the then Executive Secretary, the late John Adaskin, initiated a "composer-in-the-classroom" project to bring Canadian composers in touch with classroom students and music teachers and to produce a new contemporary repertoire suitable for teaching purposes. Now called the John Adaskin Project, this work continues in schools (and with the collaboration of some private teachers) in various parts of Canada.

The Canadian Music Centre is currently located in downtown Toronto and is governed by a Board of fourteen Directors, both English- and French-speaking, at least some of whom are nominees of the Canadian Music Council. Since the Centre does not charge for its services and receives no fees of any kind, its income is derived from grants, currently from the Canada Council, CAPAC, the Province of Ontario Council for the Arts, BMI Canada Limited and the Ministry for Cultural Affairs of the Province of Quebec.

It is an active member of the International Working Committee of Music Information Centres (within the framework of the IAML, the International Association of Music Libraries); the current Executive Secretary of the Canadian Music Centre, Keith MacMillan and the author of this chapter, is also Secretary of the International Committee.

The Canadian public has never overwhelmed its own composers with attention and the publication of serious Canadian music is not as active as in many other countries. Nevertheless, there are some twelve Canadian music publishers involved in publishing serious Canadian music, and several others exclusively concerned with lighter music. Common interests led to the formation, early in 1950, of the Canadian Music Publishers Association, principally to act as a concerted body in matters having to do with copyright, tax laws and fair trade practices. As a matter of practical convenience the CMPA has, since its inception, relied upon the secretarial and administrative services of the Toronto Board of Trade. Over the years it has provided a common meeting ground for its thirteen members (all based in the Toronto area), supported various musical conventions and festival activities, organized displays of Canadian music and has been instrumental in some revision of tax laws as they apply to the publication of music. The CMPA maintains membership in the Music Section of the International

Publishers' Association and contact is maintained with the music publishers associations of the United Kingdom and the United States.

There are few music libraries in Canada, outside those of the university faculties and departments of music; however, the Canadian Music Library Association numbers sixty-nine individual and corporate members. The CMLA publishes several useful reference lists concerning Canadian music libraries and is the official Canadian representative in the International Association of Music Libraries.

ORGANIZATIONS CONCERNED WITH PERFORMANCE

Most Canadian organizations engaged in the performance of music are active on a local or, at best, a regional basis. The recent formation of the regional Ontario Federation of Symphony Orchestras may presage a similar development along national lines, although at the time of writing the only indication of this is the current genesis of a national association of symphony women's committees. Meanwhile most Canadian orchestras are members of the American Symphony Orchestra League.

Almost all professional musicians in Canada are members of the American Federation of Musicians of the United States and Canada, which, as its name implies, is an international musicians' union. Except for church organists, virtually every professional instrumentalist in North America must be a member of this union since there is practically no professional outlet otherwise open to him. Thus the union makes it almost impossible for the amateur musician seriously to undercut the professional, a factor which undoubtedly has contributed substantially to the security and attractiveness of the profession. On the whole, the lot of the Canadian musician is individually comparable to that of his American counterpart.

This development has mitigated seriously against one phase of Canadian musical growth, however, that of recordings. By union contract, the Canadian musician must charge as much for his services in recording sessions as his American counterpart, but the potential market for Canadian recordings is a mere one-tenth that of the United States. For this and other reasons having to do with the whole influx of the products of American culture, the development of a Canadian record industry has been sadly lagging. Virtually all Canadian recordings of serious music must be sponsored or subsidized.

Organizationally the A.F. of M. makes no distinction between its thirty-seven Canadian locals and the 660-odd in the United States. But in very recent years there has been a tendency for the Canadian locals to confer more often among themselves, their problems differing somewhat from those of the American locals by virtue of dissimilar labour laws, economic considerations and so on. In fact, in 1966 a Canadian Conference was formally set up and so named, with its own executive board which meets twice per year. In 1967 the A.F. of M. formally adopted the principle of a Canadian vice-president, appointing to that office Allan Wood, head of the Toronto local. It is interesting to note that twenty-four of the Canadian locals are in Ontario (about one-fifth of the entire Canadian membership being in Toronto), three are in Quebec, with the remainder in the maritime and western provinces.

As has been mentioned before, symphonic and concert organizations have generally progressed on a local basis, apparently without feeling the need to form any national association. However, between the years 1952 and 1964 the CBC maintained in Toronto the CBC Symphony Orchestra as a national professional orchestra, for a time a unique concept in North America. It is perhaps worth mentioning that this orchestra in 1961 appeared in Washington, D.C., under the CBC's musical director Dr. Geoffrey Waddington and under Sir Ernest MacMillan at the United Nations on that organization's tenth anniversary. It is also noteworthy that this orchestra, in its later years, caught the ear of Igor Stravinsky who employed it for a few recordings on the Columbia label.

With the disbanding of the CBC Symphony Orchestra, the only symphonic aggregation in Canada with a strong claim to national status remains the National Youth Orchestra. First formed in 1960 under Walter Susskind (at that time conductor of the Toronto Symphony Orchestra but more particularly the former conductor of Britain's National Youth Orchestra), the NYO from the beginning was conceived as a training orchestra for talented youngsters aged 14–24 from all parts of Canada. Distance is always Canada's most formidable problem, making itself felt particularly in selecting and convening such a group from an area more than four thousand miles wide. The NYO has been so organized that the student-member is asked to contribute, for his four weeks of expert professional tuition and living and travelling expenses, no more than a fifty-dollar registration fee, all other expenses being borne by the Orchestra Association. By its nature, the Orchestra is able to convene only during the summer holiday months (although its first sessions were crammed into the brief Christmas vacation period). In its few years of existence the NYO has toured more widely than any other Canadian symphony orchestra, throughout eastern Canada (1964), and in the west to Victoria (1963 and 1965), in 1966 to Britain (including the Edinburgh Festival), France and West Berlin, and in 1967 across Canada again. The full training impact of this Orchestra has probably yet to be felt, but already about forty NYO alumni have taken positions with professional Canadian orchestras.

Concert touring in Canada has never been easy, again for the obvious reasons of distance. There is no single commercial agency organizing concerts or recitals on a truly national scale, although Overture Concerts, based in Vancouver, and Community Concerts, based in Ottawa (integrated suppliers of talent for more-or-less independent local pre-subscription concert organizations), between them cover most of the country— Overture Concerts from the west coast to the Great Lakes region and Community Concerts throughout eastern Canada.

There is, however, one agency which organizes young audiences and provides a truly nation-wide series of concert circuits for many exceptionally talented Canadian artists, the active (and partially subsidized) Jeunesses Musicales du Canada. This remarkable organization is described under various headings in this book, most notably under Music Education, because of its activities not only in the development of young audiences but also because of its competitions, its music camp and other forms of talent search and development. It is of interest here for having organized, during the eighteen years of its existence, some 175 concert groups of young people in almost one hundred population centres across Canada. Almost seven hundred concerts and recitals were given during the 1966–67 season to young audiences totalling close to 90,000 in cities across the country from St. John's, Newfoundland, to Vancouver, British Columbia. A special feature of the JMC presentation pattern is that before each concert its young members are given a short talk on the works to be heard, these talks being distributed on tape-recordings especially prepared with young people in mind. Although admittedly Les Jeunesses Musicales du Canada originates in the Province of Quebec and is most active in French Canada, a healthy percentage of its membership is English-speaking. The organization has apparently never felt the necessity of adopting an English title.

The Royal Canadian College of Organists can boast a history longer than almost any other national musical institution in Canada. It was in 1909 that a group of organists met in Brantford, Ontario, to form the Canadian Guild of Organists, "a College of organists in Canada, similar to that existing in England." In 1920 the name was changed to "The Canadian College of Organists" and the prefix "Royal" was permitted by Her Majesty in 1959, the College's fiftieth anniversary. Like its British model, the Canadian College has been in no sense a teaching institution—its first aim was, and is, to "hold examinations in organ playing, the theory and general knowledge of music, and to grant diplomas." Communication between the Centres in various parts of Canada was established in 1921, at first through the existing magazine *Musical Canada* established in 1921, also through a college bulletin begun in the 1920s and now published regularly; and since 1939 by the *College Year Book*. Since 1933 the College has also adopted the international organists' magazine, *The Diapason*, as an official communication link. Many of the individual Centres (of which there are now thirty-three) send periodic newsletters to their memberships.

Until 1965 the College held annual national conventions, but has recently adopted the principle of holding national conventions biennially (from 1967), and biennial regional conventions (from 1966). The College administers two scholarship funds, the Healey Willan Scholarship and the Eric Rollinson Scholarship, for students who have performed outstandingly in the College's examinations. One of the most ambitious single money projects to date has been the raising of $35,000 for Coventry Cathedral in England to pay for an organ in the new Cathedral after World War II. Currently the College is accumulating a building fund toward a permanent home for its headquarters.

Although the growth of opera in Canada has been remarkable during the years since World War II, only one company, the Canadian Opera Company, can lay claim to being a national institution. Its roots go back to the foundation by Dr. Arnold Walter in 1946 of the Royal Conservatory's Opera School. The Company did not achieve its professional status until about 1954, under the name of the "Opera Festival Company of Toronto" with Dr. Ettore Mazzoleni as director and Herman Geiger-Torel as stage director and producer. Within three or four years a drastic re-organization had become necessary and by 1959 the group had adopted its present name, the Canadian Opera Company, supported by its invaluable offshoot, the Canadian Opera Guild (publisher of the national magazine, *Opera Canada*). Throughout most of this period the Company's development was materially assisted by the activities of the CBC Opera Company in Toronto.

From the beginning, a fundamental problem has been that of full seasonal, or, better still, year-round employment for the artists. Even its nineteenth season in Toronto, in the fall of 1967, presented six productions covering no more than five weeks. The most practical solution has always been the development of a touring schedule. In Canada, even on a regional basis, this is a difficult undertaking, although many regional tours of the company as a whole were accomplished up till 1957. Since 1958, however, the emphasis has shifted toward the development each year of a much more widely-ranging company presenting chamber opera with a small cast and piano accompaniment. The success of these tours is verified by the repeat engagements year after year in centres large and small. Thus, the fall season is now taken up with preparations and presentation of the major Toronto-based productions while during the winter months a substantial percentage of the Company is busy preparing for the exhausting cross-Canada tour which usually lasts well into the spring. In this way the nucleus of the Company is held together, a rigorous professional training-ground is provided for budding professionals, and well-produced live opera productions are seen in as many as ninety centres from one end of the country to the other.

Meanwhile at "home" in Toronto, the audiences and the opera habit grow each year, to the point at which considerable box-office risks may be taken. In 1966, for example, the company, still under the directorship of Herman Geiger-Torel, presented, very successfully, its first production of a Canadian opera, *Deirdre*, by the late Healey Willan to a text by John Coulter. The 1967 season presented two full-scale Canadian operas especially commissioned for the Centennial year, *The Luck of Ginger Coffey* by Raymond Pannell and Ronald Hambleton, and *Louis Riel* by Harry Somers and Mavor Moore, the latter being the hit of the season. With opera companies in Vancouver (actually older than the Canadian Opera Company), Edmonton, and Quebec City, not to mention the many lavish and excellent productions given under the sponsorship of the Montreal Symphony Orchestra, opera in Canada is obviously very much on the way up. Especially of interest at this time of writing is the serious study headed by Léopold Simoneau toward the establishment of a Quebec opera company.

It is not quite so easy to decide which, if any, of Canada's ballet companies should be considered a national organization within the scope of this chapter. The National Ballet of Canada is the largest and most opulent of the Canadian companies, but their touring schedule has seldom paralleled that of the Canadian Opera Company: a compact road company of sixteen dancers and twelve musicians was developed for extensive cross-country touring in 1967. The Royal Winnipeg Ballet, on the other hand, has toured much more extensively during the past not only in Canada but throughout many parts of the United States as well, on the Sol Hurok circuit. And, for the first time in its history, the company of Les Grands Ballets Canadiens of Montreal, early in 1966, ventured beyond the boundaries of its native Quebec across Ontario and into the United States.

MUSIC EDUCATION ORGANIZATIONS

Notwithstanding the fact that educational matters in Canada fall within provincial jurisdiction, the need for inter-communication in this field also has resulted in the formation of several useful bodies. One of the most recent of these, but potentially the most influential, is the Canadian Association of University Schools of Music, organized in 1964 under the chairmanship of Dr. Arnold Walter, Director of the Faculty of Music, University of Toronto. This Association, by 1967 under the presidency of Father Clément Morin, Dean of the Faculty of Music, University of Montreal, numbered some seventeen full members: university schools and faculties of music (and the Conservatoire de musique du Québec in Montreal) which offer degree courses in music.

At the secondary-school level, teachers in each province (except Newfoundland which has special sectarian problems) have organized their provincial Music Educators Associations, whose membership is made up of secondary school and some elementary school music teachers. In 1959 the national Canadian Music Educators Association was formed, which includes representatives on its national council from each of the provincial Associations. To date, the CMEA has been comparatively ineffective, largely because of the provincial orientation of education in Canada and the usual reasons of distance and difficulties of communication. The CMEA has been able in the past to hold its national conventions only every two years. A centralized store of information on music education in Canada is being developed. The Association's most useful project is its quarterly magazine, *The Canadian Music Educator*, which does provide a specialized national forum and communication link.

The private music teachers have long since organized their provincial Registered Music Teachers Associations which together have formed the Canadian Federation of Music Teachers Associations. Here again, the orientation is strongly provincial and regional for the usual reasons, national conventions being held every two years. The national body publishes a periodic CFMTA Bulletin. It may be noted in passing that neither the CMEA nor the CFMTA can claim a membership from French Canada proportional to the French-speaking population of Canada as a whole. In fact both *The Canadian Music Educator* and the *CFMTA Bulletin* are published exclusively in English.

The impact on the public consciousness of the National Youth Orchestra has been mentioned before in this chapter. It is worth emphasizing again, however, that the NYO has always been conceived primarily as a training orchestra, providing a measure of practical experience for the budding professional, a factor of no slight significance in this account of national organizations involved in music education.

FOLK MUSIC SOCIETIES

With her mixed background of Indian, Eskimo, French, British and other peoples, Canada has a varied folk culture—or perhaps it would be more correct to say folk cultures, since there has been comparatively little intermingling of these. This aspect of our national heritage is covered more fully in another chapter of this book. It is sufficient to mention here that, contrary to general belief, comparatively little of this music had been "collected," to use the folklorist's pleasantly acquisitive term, until this century. The great figure in Canadian folk music is of course Dr. Marius Barbeau, and it was Dr. Barbeau whom the International Folk Music Council asked to form a Canadian branch of the IFMC. This he did in 1957. Since that time the Canadian branch, which is called the Canadian Folk Music Society, has grown in size and independence, so that in 1963, under its new president, Dr. Graham George of Queen's University, it began drafting its own constitution, although still affiliated with the IFMC. Entirely a volunteer body, the Society in 1961 organized an international conference of the IFMC in Quebec City, and has since undertaken several other projects. Distribution to its membership of a more-or-less quarterly *Bulletin* began in the summer of 1965, and several large-scale research and publication projects are already under way with the help of some provincial and Canada Council grants. The interim *Reference List on Canadian Folk Music* is one of the first fruits of this new activity, with work continuing on a comprehensive volume dealing with the subject.

Whereas the CFMS concerns itself almost exclusively with research and documentation, the newly formed Canadian Folk Arts Council is dedicated almost entirely to performance, the presentation to the public of the broad spectrum of our national ethnic background. Unlike our American neighbours to the south, Canadians seem to have preferred the "mosaic" to the "melting-pot." Consequently the many and varied ethnic groups have often, even for generations, preserved many manifestations of their past; folk-art festivals still abound across the country.

During recent years one of the most impressive of these has been the annual "National Builders" show at the Canadian National Exhibition, organized and produced by Leon Kossar on behalf of the Toronto Community Folk Arts Council, warmly supported by the Toronto metropolitan government. In their planning for 1967, the Centennial Commission became very interested in the possibilities of rather large-scale folk-arts exchanges between different parts of the country, and late in 1964 sponsored a Folk Arts Conference in Ottawa, from which grew the present Canadian Folk Arts Council. It was natural that Mr. Kossar was asked to head the Council as executive director, in which he was joined by an associate executive director in Quebec City, Maurice De Celles. Although such an arrangement obviously contains the seeds of a dangerous dichotomy, in practice it has worked extremely well; provincial folk-arts councils have now been organized in more than half the provinces. These, together with the national body, have organized many exchange programmes, mostly of choirs and dance groups between such widely separated centres as Toronto and Quebec City, Winnipeg and Granby, Quebec, Hamilton, Ontario and Regina, and Quebec and British Columbia.

Although the folk-arts movement has been greatly accelerated by the coming of the Centennial, there seems little doubt that it will continue to thrive after 1967 to provide a growing number of colourful links between different parts of Canada. Obviously, then, as the Canadian Folk Music Society concerns itself with the more scholarly aspects of folk-lore, the Canadian Folk Arts Council is essentially an amateur "show-business" enterprise. It comes as no surprise to hear that no rivalry exists between the two societies which are in constant touch with each other, doubtless to the mutual advantage of both.

AMATEUR SOCIETIES

The competitive festival movement in Canada is now at least sixty years old and some two hundred festivals are held every year, usually in the spring. Although for the most part these are organized independently of each other (with the notable exception of those in Saskatchewan which are all organized centrally from Regina) some seventy or more now hold membership in the Federation of Canadian Music Festivals, including most of the larger festivals of the metropolitan centres and the Saskatchewan organization as well. The interchange of views and information is growing every year and the FCMF publishes a substantial annual *Report*. In 1967, for the first time, provincial competitive festivals were organized in each province, and the winners competed in a national festival in

Saint John, New Brunswick. Plans are being laid to ensure that these provincial and national festivals will continue beyond 1967 and, if they do, it will doubtless be upon the FCMF that the burden of organization will fall.

Canadian Amateur Musicians—Musiciens Amateurs du Canada, more briefly and commonly known as CAMMAC, is another amateur musical organization, originating from Montreal but with some sixteen chapters and representatives in most provinces from British Columbia to New Brunswick (and with two in the United States). Basically, the aim of CAMMAC is to provide interested amateur singers and players with opportunities for "ensemble" music-making, often under the direction of a professional conductor. At its most ambitious, this often enables choral, solo and instrumental groups to spend time reading through some of the Bach cantatas. The movement was originally organized by George and Madeleine Little of Montreal and was officially inaugurated in 1959. CAMMAC now operates for all its members a central lending library in Montreal, publishes a quarterly bilingual magazine, *The Amateur Musician*, and each summer organizes a summer camp in the Laurentian lake region north of Montreal (the summer Music Centre has actually been operating since 1953). Obviously, the enthusiasm of these players and singers accounts in large measure for the vitality of the CAMMAC organization which has grown handsomely in the past few years.

NATIONAL ARTS CENTRE

For years many Canadians have deplored the status of the nation's capital, Ottawa, as a culturally under-developed area. It would certainly be an injustice to several excellent and hardworking Ottawa musicians to suggest that there is no musical activity of any consequence, but the fact remains that for its available population (500,000) the Ottawa area is certainly not as active musically as many another Canadian city of like size. The city has the dubious distinction of being one of the very few to have actually *lost* a thriving symphony orchestra—the Ottawa Symphony Orchestra discontinued its concerts in 1960.

One giant project currently under development bids fair to change drastically this situation. In July of 1966 Parliament passed the bill which brought into existence the National Arts Centre, with an appropriation of $36,000,000 (later raised to $46,000,000) for the construction of the building complex itself, fronting on Confederation Square in the heart of the city, and with legislation for the establishment of an administrative corporation. However, even before that date, the site had been acquired and much of the foundation work actually accomplished.

When complete in 1969 the complex will consist of three units: the 2,300-seat hall (Grande Salle) for major opera and concert presentations; a 900-seat theatre equipped for apron as well as proscenium staging; and a 300-seat studio theatre for intimate and experimental productions. This much essentially is merely a matter of money and willingness. Rather more difficult is the development of the artistic community itself, both lay and professional, to take the fullest advantages of the Centre and to provide a local substratum of stimulating interest upon which any nationally significant activity must be based. It is expected for example that not only will the major performing companies of Toronto and Montreal appear often, but that leading performing groups from all over the country will participate, immediately posing the inevitable problem of travelling costs. More difficult still is the question of the development of major musical companies for the national capital, a first-class orchestra at the very least and opera and theatre companies as well.

At the time of writing, with the actual building yet to be completed, any peep into the future must be speculative indeed. Suffice it to say perhaps that the formation of a first-class forty-five-piece orchestra has been decided upon and is under way; also the renowned theatre company of the Stratford Shakespearean (summer) Festival will make the National Arts

Centre its winter home, thus providing year-round employment for the Company and its administration. It is hoped that the presence of the orchestra will stimulate local universities to expand their teaching of music, both theoretical and practical, although so far no definite progress in this direction has been announced. It is certain, however, that by the creation of the National Arts Centre the federal government has committed itself more deeply than ever before to the direct support of the performing arts. For Canada this is still a new thing and the promise is an exciting one.

INDEX

Canadian Folk Arts Council, 314, 315
Canadian Folk Music Society (CFMS), 87, 89, 299, 314, 315
Canadian Grenadier Guards Band, 170
Canadian League of Composers, 181, 299, 301, 303
Canadian Music Educators' Association, 22, 273, 312, 313
Canadian Music Centre, 18, 21, 240, 271, 275, 297, 299, 303, 305
Canadian Music Council, 22, 23, 271, 278, 297–9, 303, 305
Canadian Music Educators' Association (CMEA), 299, 312, 313
Canadian Music Journal, 22, 54, 297
Canadian Music Library Association, 299, 306
Canadian Music publishers, 22, 23; Canadian Music Publishers Association (CMPA), 299, 305
Canadian Music Trades Journal, 54
Canadian National Film Board, 139
Canadian Opera Company, 4, 18, 19, 150, 165, 201, 252, 256, 310, 311
Canadian Opera Guild, 310
Canadian Performing Rights Society, 173, 302
Canadian pianists, 156
Canadian Piano Quartet, Montreal, 159
Canadian String Quartet, 191, 220, 240
Canadian Talent Library, 228
Cantoria Choir, 175, 230
Caron, Gerard, 157
Carson, Clarice, 155
Carter, Elliott, *Quartet for Flute, Oboe, Cello and Harpsichord*, 217
Cass-Beggs, Barbara, 79
Cass-Beggs, Michael, 246
Cassenti Players of Vancouver, 159, 188
Cassily, Richard, 212
Cathedral Singers, 170
Celles, Maurice De, 315
Celibidache, Sergin, 147
"Centennial Collection of Canadian Folk Songs," 238
Champagne, Claude, 58, 60, 102, 104, 111, 127, 140, 171, 196, 235, 249, 250; *Altitude*, 108; *Danse villageoise*, 106; *Evocation*, 174; *Hercule et Omphale*, 104–5; *Images du Canada français*, 106, 107; *Marines*, 107;

Piano Concerto, 108; *Suite Canadienne*, 92, 106, 230; *String Quartet*, 108; *Symphonie Gaspésienne*, 107
Chance music, 134, 135, 136
Chantal Masson Vocal Ensemble of Quebec, 161
Charpentier, Gabriel, 133, 182, 214, 215, 224
Chausson, Ernest, *Poème*, 207
Chicago Symphonic Orchestra, 156, 168
Child ballads, 78, 79
Chiocchio, Fernande, 155, 166
Chiriaeff, Ludmilla, 205, 207
Le Choeur Polyphonic de Montréal, 243
Les Choeurs de Montréal, 243
Choir of the Benedictine Monks of St. Benoit-du-Lac, Quebec, 245
Choir of the Benedictine Nuns of the Precious Blood, Mont-Laurier, 245
Choquette, Michel, 246
Choral music, 43, 54, 55, 83; The Choristers (Winnipeg), 175, 177
Chotem, Neil, 182, 239
Chotzinoff, Samuel, 204
Chuhaldin, Alexander, 169
Ciamaga, Gustav, 24
Cimarosa, Domenico, *The Secret Marriage*, 210
La Cinémathèque Canadienne, 234
Clarke, Douglas, 58, 170
Clarke, Herbert Lincoln, 39; *The Lays of the Maple Leaf, or Songs of Canada*, 48
Clarke, James, 52
Clément, Josephte, 242
Clementi, Muzio, 245
Clerk, André, 246
Clerk-Jeannotte, Albert, 55
Cleve, George, 148
Cliburn, Van, 260
Clouzot, Olivier, 139
Codman, Stephen, 48
Colle, Josephe, 220
Collections of hymns, 53; of national songs, 53; of parlour ballads, 53; of sacred songs, 53; of tape recordings of Canadian works, 304; of transcriptions of Canadian works, 304
Collegium Musicum, Toronto, 159
Commonwealth Arts Festival, London, 145, 289

Doat, Jan, 211
Donalda, Pauline, 57, 157
Donizetti, Gaetano, *Don Pasquale*, 151
Dorian, Frederick, *Commitment to Culture*, 17
Doukhobor music, 81–3
Dounais, Lionel, 175
Doyle, Gerard S., *The Old-Time Songs and Poetry of Newfoundland*, 77
Dubois, Jean-Baptiste, 58
Dubois, Théodore, 95–7, 243
Duchesneau, Claire, 243
Duchov, Marvin, 22
Dudley, Ray, 18, 156, 214, 244
Dufourq, Norbert, 140
Dukas, Paul, 105
Dulongpré, Louis, 36, 37
Dumont, Henri, 92
Duncan, Chester, 22
Duschenes Recorder Quartet, 243
Dussault, Michel, 191
Duval, Pierre, 155, 244
Dvorak, Anton, 189

Eastman School of Music, 249, 259
Eckhardt-Gramatté, Sonia, 232
Ecole de Musique de l'Université Laval, 272
Ecuyer, Charles, Abbé, *Sanctus*, 37; *Ode*, 37
Edmonton; Chamber Orchestra, 149; Opera Association, 18, 153, 154; Opera Company, 311; Rolston Quartet, 159; Symphony Orchestra, 148–9, 158, 227
Eimert, Herbert, 24
Einarsson, Magnus, 86
Eisler, Hans, 11
Electronic music, 15, 24, 125, 133, 136, 137, 138, 189, 190, 199, 215, 234, 245, 294; Division of the National Research Council, 24; quasi-electronic music, 124, 127; laboratories, 60, 132, 135; studio, Faculty of Music, University of Toronto, 125, 245; studio of McGill University, 136, 234
Elgar, Sir Edward, 101, 121; *Dream of Gerontius*, 99
Elgar Choir, Montreal, 161
Elie, Jean, 242
Enjalran, Jean, Father, 31

English Opera Group, London, 165
Ermatinger, Edward, 72
Eskimo music, 27, 63, 69, 70, 71, 87, 111

Faculty of Music, McGill University, Montreal, 255
Faculty of Music, University of Montreal, 255, 312, 102
Faculty of Music, University of Toronto, 58, 150, 155, 252, 253, 255, 312
Farnam, Lynnwood, 157
Farnham, Robert, 172
Farnon, Robert, 174, 245
Fauré, Gabriel, 92, 97, 105, 106, 110, 140; *Requiem*, 169
Federation of Canadian Music Festivals (FCMF), 279, 299, 315
Feldbrill, Victor, 148, 165, 181, 190, 196, 200, 217, 241, 256
Fenwick, John, 148
Ferras, Christian, 199
Ferrier, Kathleen, 186
Ferrier, Winifred, 186
Festival Canada, (Festival Canada at Home, Festival Canada on Tour), 19, 295
Festival Singers, Toronto, 161, 164, 192, 194, 195, 209, 212, 219, 239, 240
Festival Society, Montreal, 159
Festival Theatre, Stratford, 160
Fiore, Nicholas, 176
Fischer-Dieskau, Dietrich, 188, 189
Fitzgerald, Patricia, 233
Five Years of Achievement, 168
Fleming, Robert, 139, 141, 174, 233, 238
Fletcher, Herbert, 55
Flibotte, Simone, 175
Florence, 93, 183
Foli, Lea, 156
Folio, 207–15 *passim*
Folk dance groups, 57
Folk instruments, 87
Folk music, 7, 20, 33, 34, 51, 59, 62, 63, 71–7, 80, 81, 83, 85, 86, 92, 100–6 *passim*, 111, 114, 241; performance, 314; research, 23, 63, 78–79, 314
Folk singers, 62, 238
Folk song, traditional recordings, 63
Forrester, Maureen, 155, 160, 164, 188,

Grieg, Eduard, 189
Guerard, Yoland, 204, 229
Guerrero, Alberto, 58, 176
Guthrie, Sir Tyrone, 160, 216
Guttman, Irving, 153, 154, 166, 204

Haendel, Ida, 156, 223
Hagen, Betty Jean, 156, 164, 218
Halifax; Concert Orchestra, 169;
    Philharmonic Society, 44; Symphon-
    ette, 180; Symphonic Orchestra,
    148, 184; Trio, 159, 165, 188, 200
Halpern, Ida and Marguerite Sargent
    McTaggart, *Indian Music of the
    Pacific Northwest Coast*, 67
Ham, Albert, 50, 55
Hambleton, Ronald, 165, 311; and
    Raymond Pannell, *The Luck of
    Ginger Coffey*, 311
Hamilton; Philharmonic Orchestra,
    227; Philharmonic Society, 44
Handel, George Frederick, 37, 45, 96,
    172; *Messiah*, 172; oratorios, 173;
    Solomon, 197
Hanslick, Eduard, 120
Hanson, Howard, 252, 259
Harbour, Denis, 177, 246
Harcourt, Marguerite Béclard d', 66
Harper, Norman, 155
Harris, Charles, 99
Harris, Loren, *Blue Mountain*, 123
Harris, Roy, 250
Harriss, Charles A. E., 50; *Torquil*, 50
Hart, Harvey, 210
Hart House Orchestra, Toronto, 158,
    164, 182, 191, 198, 228; Hart House
    String Quartet, 56, 170
Hassall, Christopher, 213
Haworth, Peter, 218
Haydn, Joseph, 37, 45, 195; *Creation*,
    44; *Lord Nelson Mass*, 184; *Oboe
    Concerto in C*, 220; *Seven Last
    Words*, 182, 200, 243
Heinze, Sir Bernard, 175
Henry, Marcel, 246
Henze, Hans Werner, 191, 192; *Apollo
    and Hyacinth*, 216
Herbert, Walter, 300
Hersenhoren, Samuel, 172
Hétu, Jacques, 235; *Suite for Flute and
    Piano*, 243
Hétu, Pierre, 157, 199, 222, 238
Hewlett, William, 50

Hidy, Martha, 156
Hidy Trio, Winnipeg, 159, 164
Hindemith, Paul, 116, 140, 194; *The
    Four Temperaments*, 223
Hockridge, Edmund, 178
Hoffman, Guy, 222
Holst, Gustav, 102; *The Planets*, 120
Homburger, Walter, 163
Honegger, Arthur, 105, 110, 127;
    Jeanne d'Arc au Bucher, 213; *King
    David*, 169, 213
Horne, Marilyn, 222
Horowitz, Vladimir, 262
Houdret, Charles, 242
Hoyte, William Stevenson, 100
Hulme, Doreen, 178
Hurteau, Jean-Pierre, 155
Hutcheson, Ernest, 252
Hutcheson Report, 252
Huxley, Thomas, 14
Hyrst, Eric, 205, 213

Ibert, Jacques; *Angélique*, 206
Institut de Folklore de l'Université de
    Sudbury, 73
Institut International de Musique du
    Canada, 201
International Association of Music
    Libraries (IAML), 305, 306
International Conference of Com-
    posers, Stratford, 190, 231
International Folk Music Council
    (IFMC), 314
International Institute of Music of
    Canada, 296
International Music Council (IMC),
    260, 297
International Society for Contem-
    porary Music, 116
International Society for Music
    Education (ISME), 260
International Television Festival,
    Monte Carlo, 223
Iosch, Marie, 209, 220
Ireland, Margaret Ann, 240
Iseler, Elmer, 160, 192, 209, 214
Iturbi, José, 149, 160

Jablonski, Marek, 156, 216, 241
Jackson, Brian, 216
Jackson, Francis, 245
James, Frances, 174, 175, 178, 231

177, 198, 200, 212, 221, 231, 239,
244, 256
Martin, Charles-Amador, Abbé, 32
Mascagni, Pietro, *Cavalleria
Rusticana*, 152
Massenet, Jules, 97, 99, 105; *Manon*,
153, 214
Massey Commission, 17, 300
Massey Hall, 7, 43, 183, 184, 192, 201,
222, 223
Massicotte, Eduard Zotique, 34
Mather, Bruce, 196
Mather, Christine, 159
Mathieu, Rodolphe, 104
Matton, Roger, 130–1, 182, 183, 210,
223, 238; *Concerto for Two Pianos
and Orchestra*, 238; *Concerto for
Two Pianos and Percussion*, 214;
*Deux Mouvements Symphoniques
I and II*, 131; *The Forge*, 131; *Horo-
scope*, 131, 187, 213; *Te Deum*, 142
Maxwell, Evelyn, 225
Maxwell, Joan, 200
Mayer, Thomas, 148, 184, 186
Mazzoleni, Ettore, 121, 172, 174, 177,
181, 209, 310
McCauley, William, 234, 235; *Five
Miniatures for Flute and Strings*,
245
McGill Chamber Orchestra of
Montreal, 158, 164, 191, 198, 200,
209, 242, 289
McGill Conservatory, Montreal, 53,
99, 255, 277
McGill Preparatory School of Music,
256
McGill Quartet, 170
McIntyre, Paul, *Judith*, 188
McLagan, P. R., 45
McLaren, Norman, 25, 139, 234, 294
McLuhan, Marshall, 167
McMullin, Robert, 236; *Prairie
Sketches*, 245
McPhee, Colin, 50
McTaggart, Margaret, 67, 77, 87;
Seven Songs from Lorette, 66
Mehta, Zubin, 146, 166, 187, 216, 221,
238, 245
Mendelssohn Choir, Toronto, 55, 58,
161, 169, 176, 182, 241
Menotti, Gian Carlo, *The Consul*, 204;
The Old Maid and the Thief, 208;
The Telephone, 206

Menuhin, Yehudi, 160, 224
Mercer, Ruby, *Opera in Canada*, 22;
Opera Time, 197
Mercure, Pierre, 25, 132–3, 196, 204,
205, 206, 209, 213, 215, 218, 220, 224,
230, 238, 240, 242, 250, 301; *Cantate
pour une joie*, 132; *Divertissement
pour Quatuor à cordes et orchestre
a cordes*, 133; *Eléments*, 3, 133;
Formes, 64, 133; *Incandescence*, 133;
Kaleidoscope, 132, 205; *Pantomime*,
132; *Psaume pour abri*, 133, 193;
L'Eau, 234; *La Forme des Choses*,
234
Merineau, André, 157
Mess, Suzanne, 211
Messiaen, Olivier, 92, 103, 122, 128,
132, 135; *Turangalila Symphony*,
196, 240
Milhaud, Darius, 105, 100, 124, 179;
Le Pauvre Matelot, 206, 225;
Poèmes Juifs, 110
Mille, Agnes de, *Bitter Weird*, 221
Milligan, James, 177, 182, 188, 210,
231, 244
Mills, Alan, 246
Miramichi Folk Festival, 78
Mittelmann, Norman, 155
Miyoshi, Akira, *Ondine*, 191
Mizerit, Klaro, 148
Modalisme, 140; modal writing, 92, 93
Moiseivitch, Benno, 188
Molt, Theodore, 30, 52, 95
Monteux, Pierre, 110, 146, 190
Monteverdi, Claudio, 195, 241
Montreal; Bach Choir, 188, 241;
Brass Quintet, 234; Consort of
Viols, 194, 241; Festivals, 133, 175,
183, 188; Girls Choir, 245; Opera
Company, 55; Philharmonic Society,
45; Sinfonia, 242; String Quartet,
186, 189; Symphony Orchestra, 18,
145, 146, 152, 165, 166, 170, 184,
220, 238, 289, 311
Mossfield, Harry, 184
Moore, Mavor, 165, 311
Moore, Thomas, *Canadian Boat Song*,
29
Morawetz, Oskar, 141, 178, 230;
Piano Concerto, 232, 238;
Symphony No. 2
Morel, François, 128–30, 136, 142, 146,
182, 185, 235, 236, 240, 243, 301,

Rousselière, Father, 71
Roux, Jean-Louis, 225
Roy, Carmen, 72, 86; *Littérature orale en Gaspé*, 72; *Saint Pierre et Miquelon: une mission folklorique aux îles*, 72
Roy, Leo, 60
Roy, Raoul, 246
Royal Canadian College of Organists, 299, 309
Royal Canadian Engineers Band, 245
Royal College of Music, Hamilton, 277
Royal Conservatory of Music, Toronto, 52, 58, 102, 115, 122, 252, 255, 277, 303
Royal Conservatory Orchestra, 121
Royal Winnipeg Ballet, 216, 221, 225, 227, 312
Royal, Roy, 199, 233
Rubes, Jan, 178
Rubinstein, Arthur, 262
Rudnyckyj, Jaroslav, 83

Saint-Saëns, Camille, 95, 97
Salemka, Irene, 204
Salo, Matti, 86
Sampson, Paddy, 214, 217
Sanders, Herbert, 50
Sandwell, Bernard Keble, 56
Sangster, Allan, 186; *Music of Handel*, 197
Sapir, Edward, 64
Sargent, Sir Malcolm, 186
Sarrazin, Maurice, 213, 214
Saskatchewan Arts Board, 293
Saskatchewan Music Conference, 272
Saskatchewan Music Festival Association, 278
Sauguet, Henri, 139
Saurette, Sylvia, 241
Sauvageau, Charles, 38
Savard, Claude, 156
Savaria, Georges, 235
Savoie, André, 243
Savoie, Robert, 155, 166, 184
Schabas, Ezra, 24
Schaefer, Murray, 22, 24, 137–8, 194, 196, 232; *Canzoni for Prisoners*, 137; *Dithyramb*, 137; *Five Studies on texts by Prudentius*, 138; *Harpsichord Concerto*, 137; *The Judgement of Joel*, 137; *Loving (Toi)*, 138, 224; *In Memoriam: Alberto Guer-* rero, 137; *Protest and Incarceration*, 137
Schaeffer, Myron, 24, 125
Schaeffer, Pierre, 24, 133
Scherchen, Hermann, 196, 200
Schmitz, Robert, 124
Schoenberg, Arnold, 110, 116, 137, 140, 195, 239, 244; *Begleitmusik zu einer Lichtspielszene, Opus 34*, 218; *Choral Works, Opus 50*, 239; *Kol Nidre*, 239; *Pelleas und Melisande*, 239; *Piano Concerto*, 191, 239; piano works, 244; *Prelude to a Genesis Suite*, 192; *Six Songs, Opus 8*, 196; *A Survivor from Warsaw*, 192; *Variations for Orchestra, Opus 31*, 239; *Violin Concerto*, 239
Schools of Music, 254; Canadian, 250; Curtis, Philadelphia, 249; Eastman, Rochester, 249; Juilliard, New York, 249; Toronto, 252, 255
Schubert Choir, Toronto, 55
Schuller, Gunther, *Five Shakespeare Songs*, 196
Schumann, Clara, 189
Schumann, Robert, 242
Schwarzkopf, Elizabeth, 218, 220
Scott, Cyril, 50
Searle, Humphrey, *Diary of a Madman*, 189
Segovia, Andres, 198, 205
Seiber, Matyas, *Improvisations for Jazz Band and Symphony Orch.*, 219
Serialism, 110, 111, 113, 115, 118, 123, 127, 129, 134, 136, 137, 140
Sessions, Roger, 249
Semour, Lynn, 194, 221, 222
Shields, James, 177
Shostakovich, Dmitrij, 191
Shumsky, Oskar, 160, 190
Sieb, Calvin, 156
Sibelius, Jan, 99, 181, 183, 196, 198
Silverman, Robert, 242
Simard, Jacques, 199, 243
Simmonds, Mary, 184
Simmons, Mary, 190, 196
Simoneau, Léopold, 152, 155, 164, 188, 209, 218, 231, 244, 311
Sittner, Hans, 253
Skibine, George, 209
Smith, Gustave, 42, 43, 50
Smith, Leo, 58
Smith, Lois, 207, 209, 213

Smith, Nellie, 177
Soloviov, Nikolai, 211
Somers, Harry, 25, 122, 124–6, 136,
193, 195, 196, 234, 236, 238, 301;
Abstract, 124; *Abstract for Tele-
vision*, 217; *Evocations*, 200;
Fantasy for Orchestra, 124; *Five
Concepts for Orchestra*, 124; *Five
Songs for Dark Voice*, 184; *The
Fool*, 126, 198; *Louis Riel*, 142, 165,
201, 311; *Passacaglia and Fugue for
Orchestra*, 126; *Picasso*, 236;
Quartets, 126; *Stereophony*, 125–6;
*Suite for Harp and Chambre
Orchestra*, 124; *Suite for Harp and
Strings*, 240; *Symphony*, 126
Souverain, Pierre, 183
Souzay, Gerard, 225
Spivak, Elie, 178
St. Clair Low, William, 302
St. Michael's Cathedral Choir,
Toronto, 245
St. Saviour's Choir School, 100
Staryk, Steven, 156, 242, 244
Sternberg, Jonathan, 148
Stevens, William, 187, 242
Stewart, Reginald, 58, 169, 244
Stockhausen, Karlheinz, 24, 131, 132,
133, 134; *Refrain*, 222
Stokowski, Leopold, 121, 128, 181
Stratas, Theresa, 155, 166, 190, 213,
245, 256, 300
Strate, Grant, 220
Stratford; Festival, 160, 183, 184, 185,
197, 216; Festival Orchestra, 160,
190; Shakespearean Festival Com-
pany, 317
Strauss, Johann, *Die Fledermaus*, 206
Strauss, Richard, 99, 221; *Elektra*, 215;
Four Last Songs, 221; *Heldenleben*,
221
Stravinsky, Igor, 115, 116, 118, 119,
132, 140, 179, 192, 195, 201, 213, 231,
235, 239, 244, 248, 307; *Abraham
and Isaac*, 196; *Agon*, 213; *Apollon
Musagète*, 213; *Babel*, 239; *Canon
on an Old Russian Folk Song*, 200;
Eight Instrumental Miniatures, 192;
Mass, 186; *l'Histoire du Soldat*, 206,
219; *Mavra*, 195, 239; *Les Noces*,
207; *Oedipus Rex*, 184, 209;
Orpheus, 213; *Petrouchka*, 211;
Pulcinella, 215; *The Rake's Pro-
gress*, 181; *Le Sacre du Printemps*,
220; *A Sermon, a Narrative and a
Prayer*, 192, 239; *Svezdiliki*, 239;
Symphony in C, 239; *Symphony
Opus 1*, 200; *Symphony of Psalms*,
219, 239
String ensembles, 57; String Ensemble,
Vancouver, 170
Stumpf, Carl, *Bella Coola Melodies*, 66
Sukis, Lilian, 155
Sullivan, John, 110
Sumberg Trio, 174
Surdin, Morris, 238
Susskind, Walter, 186, 190, 200, 221,
222, 224, 238, 241, 256, 308
Sutherland, Joan, 152, 188, 191, 220
Swarowsky, Hans, 199
Symonds, Norman, 220; *Concerto
Grosso for Jazz Quintet and
Symphony Orchestra*, 184
Szeryng, Henryck, 207

Takata, Martha, 86
Taktakishvili, Shalva, *Mtsyri*, 190
Tallchief, Marjorie, 209
Tanguay, George-Emile, 230
Taylor, Kendall, 193
Taylor, Lawrence, 246
Taylor, Tom, 246
Tschaikovsky, Piotr Ilyich, 195;
Eugene Onegin, 182, 211; *The
Nutcracker*, 205, 212; *The Sleeping
Beauty*, 207; *Swan Lake*, 209, 226;
Symphony in E Minor, 101
Tebaldi, Renata, 222
Teit, James, 65
Tennant, Veronica, 223
Tessier, Micheline, 155, 243
Thalberg, Sigismund, 46
Théâtre Lyrique du Québec (Théâtre
Lyrique de Nouvelle France) 4, 153
Thomas, Philip, 79
Thomson, Heather, 155, 166, 191
Thomson, Virgil, 249
Till, Eric, 212, 213, 217, 220
Tilney, Philip, 86
Tippett, Michael, 195; *Concerto for
Orchestra*, 199
Toronto; Community Folk Arts
Council, 314; Philharmonic Society,
46; Philharmonic Orchestra, 169,
241; Symphony Orchestra, 18, 56,
58, 145–6, 166, 169, 176, 179, 182,